GRACE
REVOLUTION

ALSO BY JOSEPH PRINCE

Reign in Life
The Power of Right Believing
100 Days of Right Believing
Destined To Reign
Destined To Reign Devotional
Unmerited Favor
100 Days of Favor
Healing Promises
Provision Promises
Health And Wholeness Through The Holy Communion
A Life Worth Living
The Benjamin Generation
Your Miracle Is In Your Mouth
Right Place Right Time
Spiritual Warfare

For more information on these books and other inspiring resources,
visit JosephPrince.com.

GRACE
REVOLUTION

Experience the Power to
Live Above Defeat

JOSEPH PRINCE

Faith
Words

New York   Boston   Nashville

All Scripture quotations, unless otherwise indicated, are taken from the New King James Version. Copyright © 1982 by Thomas Nelson, Inc. Used by permission. All rights reserved.

Scripture quotations marked AMP are taken from the Amplified Bible. Copyright © 1954, 1958, 1962, 1964, 1965, 1987 by the Lockman Foundation. Used by permission.

Scripture quotations marked KJV are from the King James Version of the Bible.

Scripture quotations marked NASB are from the New American Standard Bible. Copyright © 1960, 1962, 1963, 1968, 1971, 1972, 1973, 1975, 1977, 1995 by the Lockman Foundation. Used by permission. (www.lockman.org)

Scripture quotations marked NIV are taken from the Holy Bible, New International Version, NIV. Copyright © 1973, 1978, 1984, 2011 by Biblica, Inc. Used by permission of Zondervan. All rights reserved worldwide. (www.zondervan.com)

Scripture quotations marked NLT are taken from the Holy Bible, New Living Translation. Copyright © 1996, 2004, 2007. Used by permission of Tyndale House Publishers, Inc, Carol Stream, Illinois 60188. All rights reserved.

Scripture quotations marked YLT are taken from the Young's Literal Translation of the Bible.

FaithWords
Hachette Book Group
1290 Avenue of the Americas
New York, NY 10104

faithwords.com

Printed in the United States of America

RRD-C

First Edition: October 2015
10 9 8 7 6 5 4 3 2 1

FaithWords is a division of Hachette Book Group, Inc.
The FaithWords name and logo are trademarks of Hachette Book Group, Inc.

The Hachette Speakers Bureau provides a wide range of authors for speaking events. To find out more, go to www.hachettespeakersbureau.com or call (866) 376-6591.

The publisher is not responsible for websites (or their content) that are not owned by the publisher.

Library of Congress Cataloging-in-Publication Data

Prince, Joseph.
   Grace revolution : experience the power to live above defeat / Joseph Prince. — 1st ed.
      pages cm
   Includes bibliographical references.
   ISBN 978-1-4555-6129-2 (hardcover) — ISBN 978-1-4555-3622-1 (hardcover large print) —
   ISBN 978-1-4555-6388-3 (international trade paperback) — ISBN 978-1-4789-5991-5 (audio cd)
   — ISBN 978-1-4789-5992-2 (audio download) — ISBN 978-1-4555-6131-5 (ebook)   1. Grace
   (Theology)   2. Christian life.   I. Title.
   BT761.3.P76 2015
   248.4—dc23
                                    2015025419

CONTENTS

PART 4

Speak the Language of Faith

PART 5

Receive His Abundant Restoration

INTRODUCTION

A grace revolution is sweeping across the world today. It is a revolution that is tearing down the walls of legalistic Christian religion and bringing a brand-new generation of believers into a deep and intimate relationship with the person of Jesus. As a result, precious lives are being transformed, marriages are being restored, the sick are being healed, and many are being freed from the bondage of legalism. This liberty has in turn given them the strength and power to rise above their challenges.

In this book you will hear their stories and find out just how a genuine encounter with their beautiful Savior changed everything in their lives. If you are facing some challenges in your own life, you don't have to get to the end of this book to find the answer. I want you to know from the outset that Jesus is your solution. He is your answer, your hope, your joy, your peace, and your security. When you have Him, you have everything.

The grace revolution is all about bringing Jesus back to the forefront. For too long the Christian faith has been reduced to a list of dos and don'ts. That's not why Jesus came. That's not what Christianity is all about. Jesus did not come to point out our faults. Truthfully, many of us know what our faults are, and if not, our spouses do a pretty good job of highlighting them to us!

Jesus came that we might have life and have it more abundantly. He came to save, to redeem, and to reconcile us to God so that "whoever believes in Him [Jesus] should not perish but have everlasting life" (John 3:16). That's the gospel right there, wrapped up in the beautiful simplicity called "grace"—eternal life for us paid for by the blood-stained sacrifice at Calvary. The cross is God's masterpiece. It is also His master plan to save humanity from itself. It is a foolproof plan without pages of complicated caveats that only a trained lawyer can decode. The truth is that uneducated fishermen, hapless harlots, and the poor could all understand Him.

A rising tide of grace preachers all around the world are preaching the unadulterated gospel of Jesus. A pastor who listens to my messages regularly took over a church as its senior pastor when it had an average attendance of about a thousand members. He and his wife started preaching strongly on the gospel of grace and unveiling the love of God. He shared with me that in under six months, his congregation doubled in size—they now have more than two thousand people coming every weekend and they are rapidly expanding to new campuses. Why? Because the gospel works! Why should we be surprised that when Jesus is preached and lifted high, lives are touched, changed, and transformed? Come on, this is the grace revolution!

Grace is not a subject and the grace revolution is not a movement. Grace is a person and His name is Jesus. The grace revolution is an explosive revelation that occurs in the innermost sanctum of your heart when you meet Jesus. It is not an outward revolution but something that is incepted from the inside out.

Even when you fail, you are failing forward. And when you fall, you don't crash out. Grace imparts hope to those who are hopeless and help to those who are helpless. When you are worn out, torn down, crushed, depleted, and on the brink of giving up, grace is the hand that pulls you out of the miry pit of defeat. Grace is the supply that floods every crevice of need. Grace is the person Who was nailed to the cross for your redemption.

My dear reader, I want to thank you for picking up this book. Thousands of new books are published every year and the reality that you and I are having this conversation is not a coincidence. This is a divine appointment. I prayed that this book would find its way to the right person at the right time. You may be going through a severe challenge in your life right now. Things may seem bleak and dismal. The report you just received may be discouraging and disappointing. It may seem as if there is no way out of the quagmire you're in.

The truth is that you are not at the end of your rope. Now is the time to lean your full weight on Jesus. Now is the time to stop trying to save yourself and let the Savior save you. Now is the time to step into His love and allow Him to transform you from the inside out.

Would you give these pages a chance? I believe the truths here will give you new perspectives that will challenge you to live above defeat and experience lasting breakthroughs. To help you on this journey, I have identified five practical and powerful keys:

- Grow in Boldness and Confidence
- Build a Foundation for Lasting Breakthroughs
- Value the Person of Jesus
- Speak the Language of Faith
- Receive His Abundant Restoration

As you take time to understand and internalize these five simple but highly effective biblical principles, I have no doubt that you will be greatly encouraged and strengthened. The scriptural truths shared in this book will not only inspire you to live above defeat, they will also serve as a powerful step-by-step guide to piling deep into your heart an unshakable, rock-solid, and immovable foundation for last-ing breakthroughs.

This is what the grace revolution is all about. It is about your life touched, changed, and transformed from the inside out. It is about living a victorious life. A life that wins. A life that reigns triumphant over failure and frustration. When you encounter the person of grace and when the veil of Christian religion is removed, there is no turning back. You'll begin to step away from defeat and take a massive leap toward your victory!

PART ONE

GROW IN BOLDNESS
AND CONFIDENCE

CHAPTER 1

LET THE REVOLUTION BEGIN

The grace revolution begins with Jesus. It is not a movement, teaching, or subject to be studied. It is all about a person. What you believe about this person makes all the difference. I am sure you have heard about Jesus and are familiar with His name. You may even have attended Sunday school as a child and heard all the Bible stories about Him. The question is, do you know Jesus personally? Is He a historical figure, a prominent Jewish rabbi, or simply the son of a Galilean carpenter? Who is He to you? Is He just another teacher? Or is He your Savior?

Whatever adversity, challenge, or circumstance you may be faced with today, your answer is found in the person of *Jesus*. Today a grace revolution is sweeping across the globe, because the person of Jesus is boldly preached, proclaimed, and lifted high.

Whatever adversity you may be faced with today, your answer is found in the person of Jesus.

We are receiving testimony after testimony about how people's lives have been touched and transformed by the grace of God. Many are finding freedom from their long-term conditions, addictions, and bondages. They share joyfully with us how the Lord supernaturally delivered them from panic attacks, substance abuse, and decades of depression. Others write in, brimming with thanksgiving, because God has restored their marriages and their relationships with their estranged children, and healed their bodies when doctors had given them no hope.

I wish I could read all of them to you, because you will notice that one common thread is woven through all these letters. One common denominator took these people from defeat into victory, from breakdowns into breakthroughs: they all had *an encounter with Jesus*. They all caught a revelation of His grace.

The Power of an Encounter with Jesus

Dean from Maryland wrote to me to share how his life was transformed by the goodness of God. He said, "Dear Pastor Prince, it brings me so much excitement to share with you the radical change in my life in the last year. I have been watching your television program for a solid year now and read *Destined To Reign*, *Unmerited Favor*, and just finished *The Power of Right Believing*. It's a thousand pages of one message—grace. I don't know how I ever missed it all these years. Your teaching on grace and truth has been so revolutionary to me and I want to thank you personally."

In the twelve pages that followed, Dean shared with me the story of his life and how the Lord had transformed him. When he found out at age twelve that he had been adopted, he began a lifelong battle with feelings of rejection, abandonment, inadequacy, and fear. He even contemplated suicide and started to believe that life was not worth living. In his teen years he started mixing with all the wrong people and developed several addictions: "At fourteen, I began drinking on weekends, at fifteen I was smoking weed, and I was taking cocaine when I was about sixteen. By seventeen, I was without doubt bound with addictions and in flat-out rebellion against God and man."

The older he got, the more Dean intensified his drinking and drug use to numb his pain and confusion. He spiraled out of control and lost all respect for authority figures in his life. Just before his eighteenth birthday, he was arrested for driving while intoxicated.

To make matters worse, he discovered meth (methamphetamine) after he got married. Recounting that part of his life, he shared with me, "Up to that time, I had no idea of its destructive and demonic power. At first, it was great as it seemed to take away all my pain—the depression, oppression, rejection, inadequacies, loneliness, and fear. It even curbed my drunkenness. I developed confidence and a feeling of being in complete control. I thought I had found the cure and I never wanted to be without it. So I continued taking meth for the next nine years and started dealing small amounts to feed my habit. I got caught, had my first felony drug conviction, and had my first trip to prison rehabilitation for 120 days." Following his first imprisonment, Dean continued to struggle to find peace and answers, and went through many ups and downs while heading in and out of prison.

Dean's turnaround happened only when he began to hear about God's grace. He realized that "grace was not about what I deserved, but all about the Lord's love and the unearned, unmerited favor that He gives freely without demanding anything." This revelation simply blew his mind, especially since he was full of guilt over the damage he had done to everyone in his life. It was the light that shone into his darkness and the start of his liberation. Simply put, the revolution in his life began with a revelation of God's amazing grace.

Your turnaround happens when you begin to hear
about God's grace.

What Simply Believing in God's Grace Can Do

Dean continued to share with me:

Within days of this revelation, another turning point hap-
pened. I had kept my television turned on to a Christian
channel. Your program was on and you started talking about
"rest." When I heard that word rest, *it got my attention. You*
were speaking from Hebrews 4 and as you spoke about rest,
I got up and went to my Bible on my computer and began to
study the passage intently. I quickly found that the word rest
used in Hebrews 4 was a noun and that upon entering this
place of rest, I never ever have to leave. Without doubt, I saw
the only way into this place was to simply believe what God
was saying about grace.

My problem was, I could not simply believe, or really take
God at His word. I believed that I was His child and had for-
giveness of sins, but I had also come to believe that I had to
carry my own punishment for the repeated failures in my life.

I dove into the Word and in the days and months ahead,
my life began to change. I began seeing in the Scriptures the
simplicity of the gospel of Christ and the revelation of God's
grace began to transform me from the inside out. I repented
by changing my thinking and that began to change what I had
been believing. My emotions and behavior began to change

effortlessly. I didn't have to try to feel right, or act right; I just did, and still do. And while I still have my moments, they are getting fewer and further apart.

I realized that all I had to do was to focus on Jesus' finished work on the cross and keep my eyes and ears open to His gospel, the good news of grace. I was seeing things I'd never seen before in the Word and understanding what grace means and how this truth sets one free. I began to realize that grace is undeserved favor and there was nothing I could ever do to earn or re-earn this unmerited favor in my life, regardless of my sins or efforts to make things right. I began to realize that I am highly favored and accepted in the beloved family of my Lord.

To sum it all up, I will say this: As a young boy, I believed in Jesus as my Savior. I knew many of the stories in the Bible. I went to church. But I lived life with a slave and orphan mentality for over thirty years because I could not understand or believe the whole truth of God's grace—this grace, which is the power of God unto salvation, this grace, which is the light that shines into the darkness.

I could accept that I was His child forever and would go to heaven, but because of my repeated failures, I believed that I would never have love, favor, and acceptance in this life. I believed that I had to suffer for my mistakes. Finally, I believed that I had to carry my failures all the way to heaven, resulting in much pain and damage that almost crushed me to death.

As I write this, I have been freed of alcohol and drug abuse for over two years and freed of dependence on medication for well over a year. Most of my life, I hated going to bed because I would toss and turn in torment thinking about all my failures and weaknesses. I hated waking up because I knew it would start all over again. In the last year, all that has changed. I go to bed without thoughts of my past. I can't wait to wake up each morning to expect more of His grace. The guilt, shame, bone-crushing weight of condemnation, and ever-looming depression because of fear, failure, and punishment have all disappeared like the darkness in the light of the rising sun.

What a revolutionary story of transformation and breakthrough! Thank you, Dean, for having the courage to share your story. I am truly humbled and honored to have been a part of your journey to recovery by pointing you to the person of Jesus.

My dear reader, I want to encourage you to believe that you too can experience the freedom that Jesus brings. Dean experienced victory over defeat in his life and so can *you*. Whatever is keeping you down, be it frequent bouts of depression, self-doubt, or fear, there is a person Who has the power to turn everything around for your good. His name is Jesus.

See Breakthroughs Because of What Jesus Did

In taking this journey to understand the grace of God, it is essential you understand the difference between the old covenant of law and the new covenant of grace. To help you accelerate your understanding of law and grace, I want to share with you one of my favorite Scriptures. I have preached this verse around the world, from Hillsong Conference in Sydney, Australia, to Lakewood Church in Houston, Texas.

For the law was given through Moses, but grace and truth came through Jesus Christ.

—John 1:17

The law was given through a servant. Grace and truth came through the Son. The law talks about what man ought to be. Grace reveals Who God is. In the first miracle of Moses, he turned water into blood, resulting in death. In the first miracle of grace, Jesus turned water into wine, resulting in life and celebration. The letter kills, but the Spirit gives life (see 2 Cor. 3:6).

Under the law, God demands righteousness from sinfully bankrupt man. But under grace, God provides righteousness as a gift. Now, which covenant would you like to be under? The answer is obvious!

Under grace, God provides righteousness as a gift.

The truth is, through the cross at Calvary, all who believe in Jesus and acknowledge Him as their Lord and Savior are under the new covenant of grace. Yet today many believers are still living in confusion, and get law and grace all mixed up by holding on to some aspects of the law and some aspects of grace in their Christian walk. Jesus said you cannot put new wine into old wineskins. The new wine will ferment and break the wineskins, and you will lose both (see Matt. 9:17). In the same way, you cannot put the new wine of grace into the old wineskin of the law. One will cancel out the other (see Rom. 11:6).

Under the law, God said, "I will by no means clear the guilty, but

I will visit their sins to the third and fourth generations" (see Exod. 34:7). But under grace, God says, "I will be merciful to their unrighteousness, and their sins and lawless deeds I will remember no more" (see Heb. 8:12).

There has been a change! Can you see with absolute high-definition clarity that *there has been a radical change* and it is all because of Jesus?

Yet there are many still preaching the law. They are still preaching that if you obey God, God will bless you; if you disobey God, He will curse you.

Now, that sounds right, but it's a dangerous teaching because it nullifies the finished work of Jesus. The law is man-oriented and says, "*You shall* have no other gods before Me. *You shall* not make for yourself a carved image.... *You shall* not take the name of the LORD your God in vain" (Exod. 20:3–4, 7, emphasis mine). Grace is God-oriented and says, "'*I will* put My laws in their mind and write them on their hearts; and *I will* be their God, and they shall be My people.... *I will* be merciful to their unrighteousness, and their sins and their lawless deeds *I will* remember no more'" (Heb. 8:10, 12, emphasis mine).

The law is man-centered whereas grace is Jesus-centered. The law focuses on what you must accomplish; grace focuses entirely on what Jesus has accomplished. Under the law, you are disqualified by your disobedience; under grace, you are qualified by Jesus' obedience. Under the law you are made righteous when you do right; under grace you are made righteous when you believe right. Take a look at the following table, which lists the key differences between law and grace.

Under the law you are made righteous when you do right; under grace you are made righteous when you believe right.

LAW	GRACE
Given impersonally through Moses, a servant of God	Came personally through Jesus, the Son of God
Reveals what man ought to be	Reveals Who God is
Results in miracles of death	Results in miracles of life
The letter of the law kills	The Spirit of grace gives life
Demands righteousness from sinfully bankrupt man	Provides righteousness as a gift to man
Old, inflexible wineskin	New, intoxicating wine
Sins remembered and punished by God	Sins forgiven and remembered no more by God
Dispenses blessings and curses	Dispenses only blessings
Man-centered—what you must do for God	God/Jesus-centered—what God will do for you/what Jesus has done for you
You are disqualified by your disobedience	You are qualified by Jesus' obedience
You are justified by your works	You are justified by faith

The key differences between law and grace

Beloved, aren't you glad the Lord Jesus came and died for your sins on the cross so that you can now come under God's grace and experience the breakthroughs you need?

The King Came Down

When Jesus preached the Sermon on the Mount, He said, "Love your enemies" (see Matt. 5:44). Today we have problems loving our neighbors, let alone our enemies. Jesus also said, "If your right eye offends you, pluck it out, throw it away from you. If your hand offends you, cut it off" (see Matt. 5:29–30). Have you seen anyone who's fighting for the law do that? Have you seen any church practice that? Come on, that church would look like a huge amputation ward! So what was Jesus doing when He said those things?

Jesus was bringing the law back to its pristine standard, as the Pharisees had brought it down to where it was humanly possible to keep. For example, Jesus said that if you look at a woman to lust, you have already committed adultery with her (see Matt. 5:28). The Pharisees thought that unless you physically commit adultery, you have not sinned. You see, Jesus is an expert at using God's law to bring man to the end of himself so that he will see his need for the Savior. My friend, He didn't mean for you to pluck out your eye or cut off your hand. (I hope you are not yelling out, "Pastor Prince, why didn't you write this book earlier?")

The Pharisees boasted of their law-keeping; hence Jesus demonstrated to them what it truly takes to be justified by the law. He showed them that it was impossible for man to be justified by the law. For instance, the moment you are angry with a brother in your heart, you have committed murder (see Matt. 5:22)! Now, by a quick show of hands, based on Jesus' definitive and impeccable interpretation of God's holy laws, who can stand? No one! Yet many are still preaching the law and wanting people to be under the old covenant of law.

Follow me now, I want you to catch a beautiful picture of God's grace. The good news is that Jesus didn't stop there. He preached the Sermon on the Mount and then He came down. Spiritually speaking, if the King had stayed on the mountain, there would have been no redemption for us.

Are you getting this? If Jesus had stayed high up in heaven and decreed God's holy standards from there, there would have been no hope and no redemption for us. But all praise and glory to the King Who chose to come down from heaven to this earth! He came down the mountain. He came down into suffering, crying, and dying humanity. At the foot of the mountain we see how He met a man with leprosy, a picture of you and me before we were washed clean by His precious blood. Imagine: an unclean sinner, standing before the King of kings. There was no way the standards of the Sermon on the Mount could have saved him. There was no way the pristine and perfect standards of God's holy commandments could have saved us. The King knew that and that's why He came down to where we were.

The King chose to come down from heaven into
suffering, crying, and dying humanity.

In those days people with leprosy were considered unclean, and wherever they went they had to shout, "Unclean! Unclean!" (see Lev. 13:45) so people would know to run the other way lest they became defiled by the disease. Needless to say, those with leprosy were not welcomed in public places. Yet here the man was before the King, saying, "Lord, if You are willing, You can make me clean" (Matt. 8:2). Notice he didn't doubt that Jesus *could*; he doubted that Jesus *would*.

Without a moment's hesitation, our Lord Jesus reached out and *touched* the afflicted man, saying, "I am willing; be cleansed." And immediately his leprosy was cleansed (see Matt. 8:3). Now watch this: under the law those with leprosy—the unclean—make the clean unclean. But under grace Jesus makes the unclean clean. Under the law, sin is contagious. Under grace, righteousness and God's goodness are contagious!

Under the law, sin is contagious. Under grace, righteousness and God's goodness are contagious!

Grace Brings Victory

We need not fear that being under grace will cause licentiousness, because the Word of God clearly states,

> *For sin shall not have dominion over you, for you are not under law but under grace.*
>
> —Romans 6:14

Unfortunately, there are people twisting God's Word today. They preach that when you are under grace, sin will have dominion over you. This cannot be further from the truth! Many have been hoodwinked by this false teaching that makes people fearful of God's grace. God's Word is so clear: when you are under grace and not under the law, sin shall NOT have dominion over you. The word "sin" here is a noun. It is the Greek word *hamartia*, meaning "a failing to hit the mark."[1] So you can say it this way: sicknesses, diseases, eating disorders, addictions, and any form of oppression or bondage (all examples of our missing God's mark or standard for a glorious life) shall not have dominion over you. When? When you are not under the law but under grace!

This idea that grace will cause people to sin without restraint is from the pit of hell. You cannot be under grace and not be holy any more than you can be underwater and not be wet! It is being under grace that gives you the power to live a victorious life.

You cannot be under grace and not be holy any more than you can be underwater and not be wet!

Only Grace Brings Lasting Freedom

Let me show you how being under grace enables you to overcome your challenges and live victoriously, with an amazing testimony from Anna of Iowa. Anna recounts how the Lord in His grace set her free from many painful years of addiction to cigarettes and marijuana:

> *For the better part of sixteen years, I have been addicted to cigarettes and marijuana, but because of the grace of my Father, I am now free!*
>
> *Although I grew up in a godly environment, attended a charismatic church, spent daily time with God, and even taught in a Sunday school, I was an addict who knew how to hide my addictions well! While I have always been known to love people and be kind, I felt as if I was not being kind to God or myself—I was hurting the temple of God and being a hypocrite. I felt absolutely worthless and thoughts of suicide often raced through my mind.*

Throughout the sixteen years of bondage, I attempted so many times to quit my addictions, including the time I was pregnant with my two beautiful boys! I did quit for a while but as soon as I gave birth, I quickly picked up the habits again because the desires had never left my heart.

While my prayers for others have always been powerful and effective, I was very mad at God because my prayers for my own freedom seemed to go unheard, or at least unanswered.

Then, about a year and a half ago, I began to watch Joseph Prince's television program daily. Sometimes, I would watch a certain program multiple times. At one point in time, Joseph Prince almost completely filled the space available in my digital video recorder.

I also began ordering materials that the Holy Spirit led me to get, and I was in the word of grace for hours daily, even while under the influence of cigarettes and marijuana. Hope began to fill my heart—not hope that I would soon be free, but hope that no matter what my state was, my Father would NEVER be mad at me! His grace was enough for the apostle Paul, and His grace is enough for me!

For so long, I tried to earn the blessings of God. But after allowing the water of the Word to cleanse me daily, I was able to receive His love, grace, shalom, and all of His blessings, regardless of behavior. Every time I used cigarettes or marijuana, I would say, "Thank You, Father, that I am the righteousness of God in Christ Jesus!" I quit trying to quit and decided that His grace was enough for me!

One day, several months ago, I was set free from both addictions! I didn't try to quit; it just happened. My heavenly Father has completely taken the desires away from me. Even when I am in public and exposed to others who are smoking, I still have no desire to do the same! Even right now, thinking about this great freedom, I have to cry, and cry out, "My Father is SO faithful!"

Thank you so much for daring to speak the truth. I'm sure it's not easy sometimes, but I am so grateful that Christ, through your ministry, has set me free! I now have my family, who are involved in prison ministry, listening to and reading your materials. I myself am now part of this prison ministry and write letters containing the truth to those behind bars. It's time for the captives to be set free in the name of Jesus!

Wow, that is truly the grace revolution in action! I rejoice and celebrate with you, Anna, for being completely free from two sixteen-year addictions! Thank you for taking the time to write and testify about what Jesus has done in your life. I believe that many will be touched and inspired by your testimony.

What willpower and self-effort couldn't do, God did by the power of His amazing grace. His living and eternal Word proclaims, "For sin shall not have dominion over you, for you are not under law but under grace" (Rom. 6:14). Grace is the power over every addiction that is destroying you. Only grace can give you lasting freedom.

What willpower and self-effort cannot do, God will do by the power of His amazing grace.

Let the revolution begin!

CHAPTER 2

INSIDE-OUT TRANSFORMATION

It had been one of those nights they dreaded. Famished and fatigued from working all night at sea and catching nothing, the fishermen carried their fishing nets to shore as the golden sun rose over the Galilean horizon. That morning the shoreline of the Sea of Galilee was bustling with unusual activity. Children fresh from a good night's rest ran gleefully along the water's edge in front of their parents. Large numbers of people began to throng the waterfront. The entire stretch was brimming with a festival-like atmosphere.

What are all these people doing here? wondered Simon Peter, perplexed and mildly annoyed at the festivities and the din from the crowds of people pouring onto his beach. Sleep-deprived and frustrated that they had no catch to show for their arduous fishing expedition, he shook his head and began washing his fishing nets.

Then he saw the man everyone was crowding to see.

Before he knew it, this man headed in his direction and got into his boat! He then gestured to Peter, and Peter and his crew instinctively grabbed their nets and went back into the boat. The man smiled warmly at Peter, as if he knew Peter was the proprietor of the boat, and asked if Peter could push the boat out some distance from the shore.

By this time the waterfront was blanketed with people eager to hear this man speak.

Without a moment's hesitation, Peter turned to his seasoned crew and instructed them to push the boat out. The crew responded swiftly to their captain and watched the stranger in their boat attentively. The man nodded in appreciation to the crew, sat down by the edge of the boat, and began teaching the multitudes gathered on the shore.

When he was done speaking, he turned to Peter and requested that Peter and his men launch out into the deep and let down their nets for a catch. The request stung Peter's heart and he explained to the man that they had been fishing all night and had caught nothing. Nevertheless, he was willing to comply with the man's request.

As they sailed out into deep waters, Peter was certain that they would catch nothing. After all, they had already tried all night. He had been fishing in these waters since he was a youth and knew the most opportune time to fish—definitely not this late in the morning!

The Man You Want in Your Boat

Peter found himself wondering, *What would a carpenter from Nazareth know about fishing?* As the boat reached the deep waters, Peter just went through the motions and cast one net into the water. One net, he thought, was enough to prove his point that there simply weren't any fish to be caught! Had it been anyone else—anyone but this man who carried himself with quiet authority and a warm friendliness—he would have scoffed at the request. But this man...something in his voice and carriage just made Peter acquiesce, despite every instinct telling him *nothing* was going to happen.

What happened next stunned Peter.

It was as if the net suddenly became a fish magnet! Massive schools of large tilapia began rushing into the net from every direction. Fish after fish that had eluded them all night started swimming into their net, straining its capacity until it began to tear as Peter and his men began to haul up this unprecedented load of fish. The amazed and frantic fishermen quickly hollered to their friends in another boat to come and help them. Now two boats were side by side, with both crews hauling fish into their boats. The men worked furiously, loading onto the boats the thrashing fish with their silver scales glistening in the sun...until *both* boats were so full of fish that they began to sink!

Blown away by what he was witnessing, Simon Peter knelt before Jesus and proclaimed, "Depart from me, for I am a sinful man, O Lord!" (Luke 5:8).

Been Toiling All Night? Let Jesus Save You

Now, which came first: Peter's repentance or God's blessing? Under the new covenant of grace, God blesses you first, and His blessings, favor, and overflowing love lead you to repentance! Peter and his crew of mariners had toiled painstakingly all night and caught nothing. Then, when Jesus stepped for the first time into his boat, Peter's business suddenly began to flourish and thrive beyond his wildest imagination.

God's blessings, favor, and overflowing love will lead
you to repentance!

Do you feel as if you have toiled all night and caught nothing? Perhaps you feel as though you are in a dead-end situation in your career. Or perhaps whatever you have been trying to do to save your marriage just isn't working. Maybe your toil is in the area of your parenting— no matter how much effort you put into reaching out to your child, the relationship just seems to grow colder and more distant by the day.

Now is not the time to give up, but to listen to your wonderful Lord and Savior, Jesus. Hear Him. Rather than depend on your experience and expertise, lean in to Him. You are not alone in your boat. Listen to Him and do exactly what He tells you to do. Our Lord Jesus told Peter to let down "your *nets*"—plural. Peter said, "At your word I will let down the *net*"—singular (see Luke 5:4–5). It is no wonder the net began to break and Peter had to call for his friends to come and help him.

Jesus is your very present help in time of need. Whatever your struggle is today, you can know beyond the shadow of a doubt that He is with you and knows exactly how to help you.

Whatever your struggle is today, God is with you and knows exactly how to help you.

There are also people who have been toiling relentlessly, trying everything they know to get their lives right and win God's approval. The more they try, the more distant they feel from Him. The harder they push, the more they feel that they consistently fail and disappoint Him. They are just as exasperated, fatigued, and frustrated as the fishermen who had labored all night and caught nothing.

My dear reader, if this describes you, I want you to know that God loves you even with all your imperfections. Yes, in all your failings, in all your mistakes, God still loves you! Come to Him just as you are.

God loves you, even with all your imperfections.
Come to Him just as you are.

But Pastor Prince, you don't understand. I have this horrible addiction.

Whatever that addiction is, my friend, come to Jesus. Let Jesus embrace you, hug you, and hold you. Don't worry or be consumed by your weakness. Instead allow Him to love you into wholeness. Jesus will transform you with His perfect love.

Let me sort out my life first, then I will come.

No one tries to clean himself before he takes a bath. Jesus *is* the bath! Come to Him with all your inadequacies, all your addictions, all your habits, and all your hang-ups, and let Him do what He does best. Let Him save you and restore you to wholeness!

When you think of Joe Montana, what do you think of? Possibly one of the best quarterbacks to ever play football. When you think of Michael Jordan, you think, *One of the best basketball players ever.* Now, what do you think of when you think of our Lord Jesus? While it is great that you know what all these sports superstars do, the reality is that what they do on the fields and courts won't change your life. It is much more important that you know our Lord Jesus as your *Savior.* Saving is His job description. Saving you is what He does best!

Return to Grace

At this point you may be thinking, *Pastor Prince, I want to believe you and just come to Jesus as you say, but isn't there a place for repentance when you have fallen short? I've been cautioned that grace preachers like you don't teach repentance.*

My dear friend, let me say this right from the start. I believe whole-heartedly in preaching repentance. Let me show you something beautiful about the word for repentance in the Hebrew language. The Hebrew alphabet is made up of twenty-two letters, from *aleph* to *tav*. And each Hebrew letter has a picture, numerical value, and meaning.

The Hebrew word for repentance is *teshuvah*,[1] which is made up of five Hebrew letters—*tav, shin, vav, bet,* and *hei*. The first letter, *tav,* has as its pictogram a cross.[2] The last letter, *hei,* is the fifth letter in the Hebrew alphabet,[3] and the number five in Bible numerics represents grace. Sandwiched between *tav* (cross) and *hei* (grace) are the letters *shin, vav,* and *bet.* These three letters form the word *shuv,* which means "to return."[4] Putting it all together, *teshuvah* or repentance means this: "Because of the cross of Jesus, return to grace"!

Hei	Bet	Vav	Shin	Tav
(grace)	(to return)			(cross)

Taking note that Hebrew reads from right to left, we see that teshuvah *(repentance) means this: "Because of the cross of Jesus, return to grace."*

Isn't it amazing that hidden in the Hebrew letters we just saw are God's heart and explanation of what true repentance is? Repentance is all about returning to God's grace because of His goodness demonstrated at the cross of Jesus. It is not about returning to the law of Moses. It is about turning to the cross and returning to His grace. His grace is your source of power and strength over every sin.

Repentance is all about returning to God's grace because of His goodness demonstrated at the cross of Jesus.

So if you have made a mistake, or you are struggling with a sinful habit today, repent by turning to the cross—seeing that mistake punished in the body of Jesus—and receiving God's unmerited favor to overcome this area of weakness. This is how you practice true repentance when you have failed. Don't run away from Him. Run *to* Him! He is your solution. He is your answer. He loves you and longs for you to return to His loving embrace!

Test What You Hear about Grace

If repentance is returning to God's grace, how can grace be a license or excuse to sin, as some claim? Grace is the power of God to overcome every sin. But if anyone who is living in sin claims that he is under grace, let me be the first to tell you that this person is not living under grace. The authority of God's Word proclaims that "sin shall not have dominion over you, for you are not under law but under grace" (Rom. 6:14). No one can use God's grace to justify his or her sin! It is contrary to God's Word and contrary to the gospel of grace. True grace swallows up the destructive power of sin.

Some people have been using the word *grace* freely. They call themselves grace preachers, grace ministries, or grace churches. But I encourage you to be discerning and to test everything you hear. Just because they use the word *grace* in their teachings doesn't mean they are accurately or truly representing the gospel of grace. Test everything! Be sure that their position against sin is clear.

Sin is destructive and brings with it a whole host of damaging consequences. The consequence of committing a sin is not God's judgment or punishment, any more than placing your hand in the fire and getting burned is a punishment from God. The destructive and painful effects of your hand being burned aren't from God. They are a consequence you face for using your free choice destructively. In the same way, if someone is deliberately dabbling in sin and living a sinful lifestyle, they will be burned by the destructive consequences that come with sin.

Don't Add More Fuel to the Fire

The only way to help precious people overcome the power of sin is to preach them into God's amazing grace. Some ministers think that when there is sin, they need to preach stronger, harder, and harsher sermons on the law of Moses. I believe with all my heart that they are sincere. But the Word of God tells us that "the strength of sin is the law" (1 Cor. 15:56). Preaching more of the law is like adding more fuel to the fire. People don't get liberated and transformed when we beat them down with the law of Moses. They get liberated and transformed when they encounter the love of their Savior!

People get liberated and transformed when they encounter the Savior's love!

I believe that truly born-again believers are not looking for an excuse to sin. How can they, if they have been impacted by Jesus' love and sacrifice? I believe that they are looking for a way out of sin and out of the prison of fear, guilt, and condemnation. And the more strongly I preach God's amazing grace and unconditional love, the more my ministry office receives testimony after testimony from people who have been set free from all kinds of sins and addictions.

These accounts tell us that God's people don't want to sin and are overcoming sin by turning to the cross and returning to grace. We receive testimonies from people who have been liberated from pornography, alcoholism, drugs, and sexual immorality. Now *that's* the power of our Lord and Savior, Jesus Christ. Sin no longer dominates people and true repentance occurs when the gospel of grace is preached!

Change Your Mind to Believe Right

We have looked at the Hebrew word for repentance. Now let's look at the Greek word for repentance—*metanoia*. *Meta* means "change," while *noia* is from the word *nous*, which means "mind." So *metanoia* or repentance means "a change of mind."[5] Why is changing your mind important? Simply because right believing always leads to right living.

When you believe right about God's grace, about your righteousness in Christ, and how you are called to be set apart for holiness, everything changes! His love touches you in the deepest recesses of your heart and you begin to experience transformation from the inside out. That's the grace revolution in action. You begin to live above defeat and experience lasting breakthroughs because the power to fight off any temptation is not from without, but from within. It is not contingent upon your willpower; it is contingent upon the power of the Holy Spirit living mightily and actively in you, bearing witness to the gospel truths you believe.

When God's love touches you in the deepest recesses of your heart, you begin to experience inside-out transformation.

Let me share with you a precious testimony I received from Robert, which bears out this point poignantly:

I am a pastor in North Carolina who works full-time outside of ministry. I also attend a theological seminary. I was preaching right living and was trying to live right and do increasingly more to serve Jesus. Life was very demanding and I felt myself being burned out. I had considered stepping out from ministry for a short while to finish school. It was all just too much for me.

I also had a fifteen-year struggle with addiction to spit tobacco. I even stood on the pulpit one Sunday and confessed my addiction. I held up a can of tobacco and said that I, as David did to Goliath, would cut off its head and feed its carcass to the birds.

Full of remorse, I told the people I had resolved to put the addiction away, and many came to the altar that day to cast off their addictions too. However, I was back at mine within a week and feeling great condemnation. I am positive that many others who came down that day also did not have lasting victory. I fought and fought, quit and quit, over and over again.

I eventually found Joseph Prince Ministries and a friend gave me some of Pastor Prince's teaching materials. I was amazed at what I was hearing and reading, because I had never heard the gospel preached in this manner. I knew it was truth and it began to set me free. I heard Pastor Prince preach a sermon where he said that the solution was to quit trying to win on my own and to confess to the Lord, "Lord, I cannot, but You can."

This became my motto and I quit trying to quit using tobacco. I no longer stayed buried under guilt and condemnation. I believed and confessed that even though I was struggling with this tobacco habit, God still loves me no less and that Jesus' finished work still avails for me. I can now testify that I have been tobacco-free for more than a year. Every time an urge pops up, I say to the Lord that I know His grace and what He has for me are much better than tobacco, and the urge leaves.

Praise God! This message of unmerited favor has changed my life and ministry. I am now preaching and teaching grace every time I step onto the pulpit!

Thanks be to God and thank you, Pastor Prince.

Robert, thank you for sharing your story and encouraging so many who are searching for the key to lasting victory!

Embark on an Upward Cycle of Lasting Victory

My dear reader, no matter how long you may have struggled with a bad habit, I want you to know it is never too late to invite our Lord Jesus and His grace into your situation. It is never too late to return to His grace, the only power that can give you permanent inside-out transformation.

Perhaps you too have been trying to quit whatever has you in bondage but still find yourself unable to truly break free. I want you to pay attention to how Robert found freedom and the power to stay on an *upward cycle of victory.* Notice how Robert said that in his desire to quit his addiction, he had "fought and fought" only to have to "quit and quit, over and over again." Despite publicly committing to "cast off" his addiction before his congregation, he was back at it within a week. Robert, like many sincere believers, had gone down the "feel remorse and repent" route numerous times and still not found the victory he needed.

But real change for Robert happened when he discovered the truth of God's grace, what the Lord Jesus has done for him on the cross, and how God still loves him and would help him despite his failings. And as he began to *focus* on these truths and *return* to these truths of God's grace every time he felt an urge to return to his habit, he began to experience victory over his addiction.

This is what believing right—true repentance—did for Robert. It didn't give him an excuse to continue in his sin or take sin lightly. No, it made him an overcomer. It made him a testimony of God's amazing grace at work in the life of someone who chose to depend on that grace. Notice that the right living Robert wanted to experience became a reality not when he was trying to make it happen on his own, but when he discovered and then kept returning to grace whenever he was weak. This, dear reader, is the key to overcoming sin and every bondage in your life.

Today, if you've been trying to quit a habit, I encourage you to return to the truth of God's grace—that what our Lord Jesus has done for you at the cross is so much greater than all your failings. That because of His perfect, finished work, you are still deeply loved, highly favored, and greatly blessed. When you let such a revelation of God's grace wash over your heart again and again, you can't help but deeply appreciate what the Lord has done for you and how His grace has set you apart to shine for His glory. You won't want to continue in sin. Instead you will find every sinful urge gradually leave until they all leave for good. You will embark on an upward cycle of lasting transformation!

Practice Returning to Grace

My wife Wendy and I have met so many women—wives and mothers—who've come to us and shared how right believing in God's amazing grace has set them free of daily struggles in their relationships with their spouses and children. They told us how entrenched mind-sets that used to trip them up and bring tension into their family life just began to inexorably dissolve when they let the grace of God wash over them and began to believe in His goodness. Things they had tried for years to change on their own, like an explosive temper or perpetual anxiety over their performance as a parent, just disappeared effortlessly. Many also expressed how, as they tasted and rested in their heavenly Father's love for them, the guilt and frustration that came with the stress of daily parenting simply gave way to peace, to a permanent sense of God's joy, and subsequently to healthier relationships with their husbands and children.

My dear reader, whether you're trying to quit an addiction or want to be a more loving and forgiving spouse or parent, your answer is found in the person of grace and in returning to His grace every time you feel weak or fail. That's what true repentance is all about. When you've made a mistake, remember and receive afresh the forgiveness and righteousness that Jesus has provided for you at the cross. Believe He is still with you, loving you, and working in you to walk in His victorious and abundant life. This is how you practice returning to His grace. The Lord's amazing grace will bring deliverance, a fresh start, and new ways of living and loving that will radically transform your life, your marriage, and your parenting for His glory.

CHAPTER 3

HEAR THE WORD OF HIS GRACE

Trembling at the thought of discovery, the man with leprosy crouched beneath a stone slab—one of the many that dotted the slopes of the picturesque hills that framed the Sea of Galilee. He had come to see the man they called Jesus, Who he had heard was a healer. The man's name had been on everyone's lips, and how He traveled with His band of disciples, teaching in synagogues and open spaces, was well known.

But mostly the people had talked about how Jesus healed—how everyone who had gone to Him for healing, whether from the Decapolis, Galilee, Jerusalem, or east of the Jordan River, received their healing. He turned none away. Whatever their conditions—fevers, paralyses, deaf ears, or demonic oppression—He healed them all.

Jesus turned none away. Whatever their conditions—
fevers, paralyses, deaf ears, or demonic oppression—
He healed them all.

All. That little word gave him hope that perhaps even he might be made whole. And so he had listened for where he might find Jesus. And that was how he had heard that Jesus was heading to the hills surrounding the Sea of Galilee.

By the time this man reached the hills, a large multitude had gathered on the slopes to listen to Jesus teach. Desperate to be healed of his terrible condition, yet terrified of being seen and stoned by the crowds, he had decided to hide himself.

God Is Willing and Able

This poor diseased man couldn't see Jesus from where he was hiding in fear, a safe distance from the crowds. But because of the unique acoustics of the hills, he could hear every word that Jesus was speaking to the multitudes:

"That is why I tell you not to worry about everyday life—whether you have enough food and drink, or enough clothes to wear. Isn't life more than food, and your body more than clothing? Look at the birds. They don't plant or harvest or store food in barns, for your heavenly Father feeds them. And aren't you far more valuable to him than they are?" (Matt. 6:25–26 NLT).

He listened attentively—the timbre of Jesus' voice and every word He spoke carried an immeasurable depth of understanding and empathy for his everyday fears. Embers of hope that he had thought long dead suddenly flared to life, fanned by the authority of Jesus' words. Whereas he had initially trembled from fear of being exposed, now he began trembling with a different emotion that made him listen even more fervently to Jesus' next words:

"And why worry about your clothing? Look at the lilies of the field and how they grow. They don't work or make their clothing, yet

Solomon in all his glory was not dressed as beautifully as they are. And if God cares so wonderfully for wildflowers that are here today and thrown into the fire tomorrow, he will certainly care for you" (Matt. 6:28–30 NLT).

As the meaning of Jesus' words sank in, the man with leprosy began to weep. For the first time in years, he wondered, *Is this possible? That God wants to be a Father to me? A heavenly Father Who would clothe me much better than the lilies, which are better clothed than Solomon in all his glory—if I put my trust in Him? Is it possible that God is reaching out to me with kindness, acceptance, and love, and inviting me to taste and receive His goodness?* After all the years of being rejected and living as an outcast, something deep within his heart broke at these new thoughts and brought on a fresh flood of tears.

Galvanized by the unmistakable compassion in Jesus' voice that caused hope to race along every still-intact nerve in his body, the man crawled out of his makeshift shelter the moment Jesus finished speaking. All thoughts of staying hidden were gone. All he wanted to do was to go to Jesus and ask Him to take his disease away.

As he began to make his way to Jesus, he heard footfalls and movement just ahead of where he was. There, coming down the hill, a man walking slightly ahead of a few others caught his eye. He realized it was Jesus, coming straight toward him. Instead of having gone straight down to the crowds after preaching to them, the Lord had turned another way to go toward the lone, afflicted man, as if He already knew all about the man's need and where he was. Unable to hold back his feelings, the man fell at Jesus' feet and worshiped Him.

In a voice still choked with tears, he whispered, "Lord, if You are willing, You can make me clean." Without hesitation, as if that was exactly why He was there, Jesus reached out and touched him. "I am willing," He said, with the same compassion and warmth the man had heard earlier in His voice. "Be cleansed" (see Matt. 8:2–3).

As he felt the touch of Jesus' warm hands, the man closed his eyes involuntarily and his body shuddered under that touch. It had been *so* long since he had felt the touch of another human being, let alone a warm and loving touch. Then he opened his eyes to look at Jesus, and found Him smiling at him with love in His eyes. Sensing that something was different about his body, the man looked down at his hands, which a moment ago had been covered with open sores and had ended in stubs for fingers. His eyes beheld healthy hands with fingers fully formed and skin completely whole. Like one in a dream, he began lifting the sleeves and hem of his robe and watched in amazement as the cloth rolled upward to reveal smooth, unblemished skin covering his arms, legs, and feet. He was cleansed! The power of Jesus had, in an instant, swallowed up his uncleanness.

He looked up into the face of the One Who had made him whole, overcome with gratitude. Even as he turned to go, the man knew he would never forget the compassion and encouragement he had seen in our Lord Jesus' face, nor His warm and affirming touch.

He has not just healed and cleansed me, the elated man thought as he walked away in wonder. *He has given me back my life!*

Come Out of Your Hiding

When I visited the Mount of Beatitudes in Israel some time ago, the Lord opened my eyes to see for the first time *how* He had met the man with leprosy. After preaching to the multitudes, our Lord didn't go down the mountain toward them, otherwise the Bible would not have said that the multitudes "*followed* Him" (Matt. 8:1, emphasis mine).

Our Lord had actually walked down the mountain in another direction, very likely toward Capernaum, because after His preaching on the mountain, the gospel accounts tell us that He entered that city (see Matt. 8:5).

As I took a path down the mountain toward Capernaum that day, I saw slabs of stone strewn along the foot of the mountain. These stone slabs are just the right size for a man to crawl under to find shelter. Right then and there, I had the revelation of how the man with leprosy could have hidden under one of these slabs for fear of being discovered by the people, and how our Lord Jesus had known the man was hiding there and deliberately gone to seek him before the crowds caught up with Him.

In Jesus' day those with leprosy were ostracized and isolated in accordance with the law of Moses. Because they were conscious of how unclean they were and what the law required of them, their natural response was to withdraw and hide.

But hiding didn't get the man with leprosy in Matthew 8 the healing and restoration he needed. Fortunately, hearing about the goodness of God—how God wanted to be a loving Father to him and take care of all his needs—got him out of hiding and into seeking the Lord for his miracle. It changed his mind from seeing a God Who ostracized and condemned unclean people to seeing a God Who loved them no matter what their condition. This change of mind lit his faith and put courage in his heart to seek and receive the healing he so desperately wanted.

Like the man with leprosy at the start of his story, could you also be hiding from God today? Maybe you've been struggling with an addiction or cycle of defeat that you can't seem to get out of. Maybe you've been a victim of sexual abuse and you blame yourself for it. Maybe you've had a failed marriage or business, or made a bad decision that has led to loss. And maybe your failure has caused you to avoid God, avoid going to church, and avoid people in general. Beloved, whatever may be causing you to feel "unclean" or disqualified today, God wants you to change your mind about Him and, instead of hiding from Him, run to Him!

What Are You Hearing about God?

How does one change from hiding from God to running to God? Well, the Bible tells us that "faith comes from hearing, and hearing by the word of Christ" (Rom. 10:17 NASB). The man with leprosy had enough faith to come out of his hiding place and head straight for Jesus because of the gracious words he had heard from Jesus. If our Lord had preached a hellfire-and-brimstone message of condemnation, do you think the man would have dared to approach Him for healing? Of course not. He would have walked away fearful of punishment, and feeling more condemned and hopeless than ever. But because he heard words of grace—how God wanted to be a loving Father to him and provide for all his needs—faith arose in his heart, giving him the confidence to approach the Lord Jesus for his miracle.

My dear friend, what you hear about God is of utmost importance. It can mean the difference between receiving your miracle and remaining where you are in your lack or bondage. It can draw you close to God, or drive you further away from Him. Faith comes by hearing, but fear also comes by hearing. If you've been hearing about a God Who is mostly angry and out to get you for your sins, how can you have faith to look to Him for help? If you've been hearing that He gives people (even believers) sicknesses and punishes them with horrible accidents for their sins, how can you look to Him for healing? If you've been hearing that He wants you and your family poor to keep you humble, how can you believe Him for financial breakthroughs or deliverance from mounting debts? How can you possibly trust God for anything good if all you've been hearing are sermons that make you feel more condemned and fearful of His judgment?

It's sad, but the things I've just mentioned are the very things people are hearing about God. Just look at the movies made about God today—God is always portrayed as mean, judgmental, petulant, destructive, and even murderous! How they've perverted Who God really is—"compassionate and merciful, slow to get angry and filled with unfailing love" (Ps. 103:8 NLT)! Don't misunderstand me. God does have anger, but the Bible never defines God as wrath; it defines God as *love* (see 1 John 4:8, 16). Did our Lord Jesus ever condemn the prostitutes and tax collectors, those despised and rejected by society? No, He was a friend of sinners! Did He ever take away from the poor, or inflict the sick with more diseases? No, He fed a hungry multitude, with twelve baskets full of leftovers, and healed everyone who sought Him for healing, wherever He went!

The Bible never defines God as wrath; it defines God as love.

The Bible tells us that Jesus "went about doing good and healing all who were oppressed by the devil, *for God was with Him*" (Acts 10:38, emphasis mine). What does that tell us? God wants to do good, not evil, to us! If this were not true, God would not have been with Jesus, backing Him up. Jesus said, "He who has seen Me has seen the Father.... Do you not believe that I am in the Father, and the Father in Me? The words that I speak to you I do not speak on My own authority; but the Father who dwells in Me does the works" (John 14:9–10). If you want to know what God is really like (and not what man portrays Him to be), look at Jesus in the Gospels. He is God's will in action, and He went about doing *good*—saving, delivering, healing, restoring, providing, guiding, and loving the unlovable. That's our God!

Faith Comes by Hearing the Word of Christ

Beloved, if you want to have faith for your breakthrough, make sure you are hearing and believing right about God through the word of Christ. By the way, it is the word of *Christ*, not the word of *God*, as written in some Bible translations. The Greek word used in Romans 10:17 is *Christos* for Christ. What's the difference? The word of Christ refers to the word of the *new covenant*, the word of *His grace*.

To have faith for your breakthrough, make sure you are hearing and believing right about God through the word of Christ.

In the book of Acts, the apostle Paul says, "So now, brethren, I commend you to God and to the word of His grace, which is able to build you up and give you an inheritance among all those who are sanctified" (Acts 20:32). What is able to build you up and give you an inheritance among the saints? It is the word of His grace or the word of Christ. The Bible exhorts us to "Let the word of Christ [*Christos*] dwell in you richly in all wisdom" (Col. 3:16).

So if you're feeling discouraged today, I encourage you to keep hearing messages full of the grace and finished work of our Lord Jesus. Whatever your circumstances, keep hearing about how your sins have all been forgiven through Christ, and how you are today the righteousness of God in Christ. Whatever the prognosis you've heard, keep hearing about how much God loves you and wants to be a loving Father to you, to watch over you, provide for you, and deliver you from all your fears and afflictions.

My friend, when you give priority to this daily, you will have the word of Christ dwelling richly in you. And it is this word of His grace that will impart faith and hope to you. When you know God's love for you, it will cause you to run to Him instead of hiding from Him. His love upon you and in you will make you strong. It will cause you to overcome every temptation and fear, slay your giants, and live life with greater boldness and victory!

When you know God's love for you, it will cause you to run to Him instead of hiding from Him.

Freedom Comes When You Hear about His Grace

Let me share with you the personal story of Calli from Florida. As painful and heartrending as her experiences were before she encountered the person of Jesus, much greater was the Lord's restoration to her when she began to hear the word of His grace:

> *Throughout the years I was raised in church and studied at a Bible college, legalistic teachings had led me to believe that my sin was greater than the grace of our Lord Jesus Christ and His finished work on the cross. As a result, I lived in constant fear that I would lose my salvation every time I sinned. My past*

haunted me and I could never seem to outrun it as the torment simply overwhelmed me.

I was sexually abused and threatened into silence when I was younger. This caused me to live in shame, guilt, and a cycle of violence, abusive relationships, rape, drug abuse, insanity, suicidal tendencies, and self-mutilation. I was also tortured and beaten by my first husband when I married him at the age of twenty-three.

Consequently, I developed multiple personalities and post-traumatic stress disorder (PTSD). I was admitted to a state institution and hospitalized in psychiatric wards thirty-eight times over a span of twenty-nine years. I was also bound to an addiction to cigarettes and drugs for over thirty-six years.

I was hopelessly enslaved by the chains of addiction and insanity for many years. I was considered permanently and totally mentally disabled, and was in a day treatment program for the chronically mentally ill. Churches started developing "compassion fatigue" and got tired of praying for me. I was even told, "Perhaps your schizophrenia is your cross to bear."

Since they gave up on me, I immersed myself in a world of bondage and sadomasochism. Still, I was not content and I wanted to go home to my heavenly Father, even though I thought that He did not want me anymore. I felt like I was the beaten leftovers of the church.

But oh, thank You, Jesus! He did not give up on me! I had begun watching Joseph Prince Ministries' broadcast on television. And as I listened to Pastor Prince teach on grace, the Lord began to open my heart, and for the first time, all the head knowledge of Scriptures I had memorized since I was a child began to bring illumination to my mind when I saw them through the lens of God's grace, and hope and faith began to spring in my heart.

Then one day, I heard Pastor Prince share on how Noah never fell out of the ark even though the ark was tossed about in the water, and how Jesus said nothing could take us out of His hands. As I listened, the Lord spoke to me. I heard Him in my heart, calling my name, and telling me, "My child, I have held you in the palm of My hands all these years that you have stumbled, fallen, and wandered. I have called you, and waited for you to turn and hear My voice. You are Mine."

I realized then that just hearing about Jesus and His grace had broken through all my chains of darkness, insanity, and addictions. I shouted "HALLELUJAH!" in my apartment, and I broke down and wept. For the first time in my life, I felt all my shackles fall off. After that, it was as though I had never picked up a cigarette or drug in my life, and all the insanity was gone!

I now take no medication for schizophrenia or PTSD. I no longer have fourteen personalities. My doctor, who had worked on me for almost twenty years, has seen the changes— and has declared that I am no longer a mental patient.

Praise God for the grace message that Pastor Prince is preaching—the same gospel that Apostle Paul preached in the Scriptures! This gospel is indeed the power of God unto salvation! I am living proof and am now in a church where I am giving my testimony and sharing with others the hope that they too can find peace and deliverance from the chains that have them bound! Praise the name of Jesus!

What a glorious testimony! Thank you so much, Calli, for sharing it and encouraging countless others. Transformed lives like Calli's are living proof that the word of His grace is the power of God unto our salvation. When we know God's love and grace toward us, we overcome whatever the enemy throws at us. Instead of hiding from God, we run to Him Who is our help, and we find grace and strength to come out of the darkest pit, to become shining testimonies of God's goodness.

Knowing God's Love Strengthens You

Knowing God's love for you makes you strong. It makes a champion out of you. The book of Daniel tells us that "the people who know their God shall be strong, and carry out great exploits" (Dan. 11:32). Daniel himself started out as a young captive taken from Jerusalem to serve in the courts of Babylonian and Medo-Persian kings. Yet Daniel stood out among his peers. Over his lifetime he interpreted dreams by the wisdom of God and demonstrated an "excellent spirit" people around him could see (see Dan. 6:3). He always found favor in the eyes of the Gentile kings he served and experienced supernatural deliverance when there seemed to be no way out. Daniel walked out of the lion's den unharmed, because he knew his God, His power, and His heart for him.

Dear reader, is this what you desire today—to walk in strength, wisdom, and favor that is undeniable and irresistible? Do you desire to see the God-kind of miracles and breakthroughs in your life? Then I encourage you to keep hearing and growing in your knowledge of God's grace and mercy toward you. In Daniel's story, the Lord, through an angel, addressed him as a "man greatly beloved" (Dan. 10:11). So the more you hear about and are confident in His love for you, the more you will live life with boldness and a different, excellent spirit that sets you apart from others and testifies of His power in your life.

The more you hear about and are confident in God's love for you, the more you will live life with boldness.

Consider also young David, the shepherd boy who was bold enough to challenge and take down Goliath when others were cowering in fear. David knew God as a covenant-keeping God Who loved him. David would have been reminded of God's love for him every time he heard his own name, for David's name means "beloved," the beloved of the Lord. I believe David became such an amazing worshiper, a leader beloved by His people, and a man after God's own heart because he knew and was conscious of how much the Lord loved him. Even when David failed, I believe it was his revelation that he was still beloved of the Lord that kept him going. Beloved, when you know how much God loves you, you will bring down the giants in your life, and your life will testify of His goodness and glory!

Can I give you one more example? Do you remember Gideon, who saw himself as least in his family and who was threshing wheat in a winepress for fear of being seen by the Midianites? We read his story in the book of Judges and see how he overcame his insecurities and fears and single-handedly saved Israel from the Midianites, because he first heard gracious, encouraging words from the Angel of the Lord: "The LORD is with you, you mighty man of valor!...Surely I will be with you, and you shall defeat the Midianites as one man" (Judg. 6:12, 16).

When he began to see how the Lord saw him, and believed that the Lord was with him and for him, he fulfilled his destiny!

If, like Gideon, you feel small and powerless in the face of your challenges, I encourage you to keep hearing how because of Jesus' sacrifice and finished work, nothing can separate you from God's love. I want you to know right now that He has already made you more than a conqueror in Christ (see Rom. 8:37–39). When you know who you are in Christ and believe in God's love for you, you will become strong and you will see God do great things in and through you. When you know that God is with you and for you, who or what can stand against you (see Rom. 8:31)? You will surely win the fights of life and live out the amazing destiny God has prepared for you!

When you know who you are in Christ and believe in God's love for you, you will become strong and you will see God do great things in and through you.

Know His Love in Your Heart

My dear friend, do you have a revelation of God's personal love for you today? His love has to be experienced in your heart. Head knowledge—just knowing intellectually that God loves you because He loves everyone—isn't going to cut it. It is when you really encounter the person of Jesus and His grace, and really know in your heart that He loves *you*, that positive and profound changes begin to happen in your life.

Is there a scriptural basis for saying this? Yes, there is. The Bible tells us clearly, "Grace and peace be multiplied to you in the knowledge of

God and of Jesus our Lord" (2 Pet. 1:2). The word for "knowledge" here is the Greek *epignosis*, which refers to a heart experience of what and Who God is, rather than mere intellectual knowledge of facts about Him. It is a knowledge that is gained through an intimate and personal relationship with God.[1] In other words, when you hear and hear until you know *in your heart* that the Lord loves you and is for you, you will experience His unmerited favor and supernatural peace in the area of your challenge. That is when you will find His strength, wisdom, and supply multiplied tangibly in your life.

John, the apostle of love, wrote, "Herein is love, not that we loved God, but that he loved us, and sent his Son to be the propitiation for our sins" (1 John 4:10 KJV). I pray that as you continue to read the word of His grace in this book and listen to messages of His great grace, you will come to truly know the Lord's love for you and embrace it heart and soul. His love will make you strong and cause you to do great exploits!

CHAPTER 4

RECEIVE THE GREATEST BLESSING

The key to living with greater confidence and boldness is knowing, first and foremost, that all your sins are forgiven. Today, as a beloved child of God, know that your heavenly Father is not angry with you. He is not mad at you. All your sins have been judged and punished in the body of Jesus at the cross.

> *The key to living with greater confidence and boldness is knowing, first and foremost, that all your sins are forgiven.*

Do you have this assurance that all your sins have been forgiven? There are many believers battling guilt, fear, and condemnation because they are not confident that *all* their sins have been forgiven once and for all. They inadvertently hide from their heavenly Father when they fail, instead of coming boldly to His throne of grace to obtain mercy and find grace to help them when they need it the most (see Heb. 4:16 NLT). They hide, as Adam and Eve hid in the Garden of Eden, downcast with shame and fear.

How to Break Out of the Cycle of Defeat

If you are hiding from God today, I want to encourage you with this heartwarming testimony that I received from Joni, who lives in Texas:

Wow! Where do I begin? I am a thirty-seven-year-old whose heart has just been renewed by God. He has given back to me lost years and a sense of peace I cannot explain.

I am a preacher's daughter who was raised under legalistic teaching. I always saw God as another authority figure in my life, Who loved to point out my mistakes.

During a difficult season in my life, I suffered a major seizure. I thought I was dying at that moment and realized how completely helpless we are as humans. Right after that episode, my sister-in-law gave me one of your books. Believe me, I had enough grief over "churchianity" up until then and so was not looking forward to reading the book at all. However, I read it just to shut my sister-in-law up.

After the second chapter, something started to sink in! I began repeating, "I am righteous in Christ," even though that was SO far from how I felt at that moment. As I continued reading, I knew changes were happening in me. I started to see what Daddy God was all about—peace, love, faith, truth, and most of all, FORGIVENESS! I discovered that my sins were on that cross with His Son, so I could move on from all my failures. I did not have to drag them around anymore.

Since then, I have truly asked Christ to take over my heart and life. I was rebaptized and truly knew that my sinful flesh was circumcised from my spirit when I was immersed in the water. I was made NEW!

I was addicted to alcohol and cigarettes in the last two years as well. Today, I am delivered from both—not by my own strength, but because of Christ. I just kept repeating, "I can't, but You can."

People who have known me for a number of years can see the difference in my life! I am just resting in Christ! I don't have to work for Him to love me. I just crawl into His lap and let Him love me.

Relationships with my children, parents, and even with myself are healed because of Christ Jesus and His perfect sacrifice! Because of bad choices and sinful decisions in the past, I'd lost a few important things in my life, but God is restoring them to me sevenfold! The overwhelming sense of peace has been the greatest. Sometimes, I also feel Daddy God taking time to tell me He is thinking of me!

My youngest child also just got baptized. Part of her testimony to the church was how "Mom went through a really tough time and God got her through it. Now, I see my mom as a really big Christian and that made me see what power God has!" Wow! That from an eleven-year-old!

Thank you, Pastor Prince, for allowing God to speak through you!

You are most welcome, Joni, and thank you for taking the time to share your story.

Do You Have the Assurance of Forgiveness?

You can see from Joni's sharing how her life began to turn around when she received the revelation that all her sins, mistakes, and bad decisions are forgiven. For you to live above defeat and experience lasting breakthroughs, it is vital for you to have the assurance of forgiveness.

For you to live above defeat and experience lasting breakthroughs, it is vital that you have the assurance of forgiveness.

The moment you invited Jesus into your heart as your Lord and Savior, all your sins were forgiven. Your past sins, your present sins, and your future sins. The Word of God tells us, "In Him we have redemption through His blood, the forgiveness of sins, according to the riches of His grace" (Eph. 1:7). Once you are born again, you are in Christ. You do not have to try to get forgiveness. You *have* the forgiveness of sins, and this forgiveness of sins that you have is not according to what you have done, but according to the riches of God's grace— His unmerited, unearned, and undeserved favor!

The Bible tells us that "the wages of sin is death" (see Rom. 6:23). In other words, the punishment for sin is death. It also tells us that "without the shedding of blood there is no forgiveness" (Heb. 9:22 NIV). Blood is thus necessary for the forgiveness of sins. That is why, under the old covenant of law, sin was covered temporarily through the blood of sacrificial animals.

The good news of the gospel is that our Lord and Savior, Jesus

Christ, came down from heaven to earth and sacrificed Himself at the cross. His perfect, sinless blood provided forgiveness for all our sins. You and I cannot pay for our own sins, so He did it for us. Now whosoever believes in Him will never die but will receive the gift of eternal life. Hallelujah!

Notice how David describes the blessedness of a man whose sins are forgiven:

> *"Blessed are those whose lawless deeds are forgiven, and whose sins are covered; blessed is the man to whom the* Lord *shall not impute sin."*
>
> *—Romans 4:7–8*

Now read it in the New Living Translation:

> *"Oh, what joy for those whose disobedience is forgiven, whose sins are put out of sight. Yes, what joy for those whose record the* Lord *has cleared of sin."*

Oh, what joy and what a blessing it is to receive the forgiveness of sins! Conversely, when believers start to question if they are truly forgiven, it leads to all kinds of insecurities, fears, and destructive bondages. Fear and insecurity cannot exist in a healthy relationship with God. In a marriage relationship, if a wife never feels secure in her husband's love for her, she will never draw strength from or find joy in her marriage. Instead of thriving, that marriage will disintegrate over time. Similarly, our heavenly Father does not want us to live trapped in perpetual insecurity because we are never sure of our forgiveness.

Know the Value of Jesus

The apostle Paul tells believers who have been born again in Christ that God the Father "has delivered us from the power of darkness and conveyed us into the kingdom of the Son of His love, in whom we have redemption through His blood, the forgiveness of sins" (Col. 1:13–14). Notice that there has been a *change of location*. You used to be under the power of darkness. But the moment you believed in Jesus, you were moved and placed under the blood of Jesus, where there is perpetual forgiveness of sins.

To understand the total forgiveness of sins, we have to understand the value of the person Who sacrificed Himself on the cross for us. He alone, because He was sinless, could pay for all the sins of every man. When our Lord Jesus died at Calvary, He took all of humanity's sins with one sacrifice of Himself at the cross. He took the judgment, punishment, and condemnation for all sins upon Himself. That's the value of the one Man, Jesus. He is an overpayment for all our sins.

To understand the total forgiveness of sins, we have to understand the value of the person Who sacrificed Himself on the cross for us.

Only One Way to Receive God's Forgiveness

Now, does that mean that everyone is automatically forgiven? Of course not! Read this carefully. While everyone's sin is paid for, every individual needs to make a personal decision to receive the forgiveness of all their sins by receiving Jesus as their personal Lord and Savior. Jesus is the only way to salvation. There is no other way except through Jesus and His shed blood. Listen to what God's Word says:

> *If you confess with your mouth the Lord Jesus and believe in your heart that God has raised Him from the dead, you will be saved. For with the heart one believes unto righteousness, and with the mouth confession is made unto salvation. For the Scripture says, "Whoever believes on Him will not be put to shame." For there is no distinction between Jew and Greek, for the same Lord over all is rich to all who call upon Him. For "whoever calls on the name of the LORD shall be saved."*
>
> *—Romans 10:9–13*

There is no ambivalence in Scripture as to how a person becomes a born-again believer in Christ. To be saved, you have to confess with your mouth that Jesus is your Lord and believe in your heart that God raised Him from the dead. Therefore, anyone who tells you that everyone's sin is automatically forgiven and that you don't need to receive Jesus as your Lord and Savior in order to be saved is scripturally inaccurate. Such teachings are heretical and are lies from the pit of hell. There is no salvation without Jesus. There is no forgiveness without the cleansing blood of Jesus Christ. There is no assurance that all our sins have been forgiven without the resurrection of Jesus.

There is no assurance that all our sins have been forgiven without the resurrection of Jesus.

How Do You Know Your Sins Are Forgiven?

The apostle Paul proclaims, "If Christ is not risen, your faith is futile; you are still in your sins!...But now Christ is risen from the dead, and has become the firstfruits of those who have fallen asleep. For since by man came death, by Man also came the resurrection of the dead. For as in Adam all die, even so in Christ all shall be made alive" (1 Cor. 15:17, 20–22).

Now, is Christ risen? Yes, absolutely! And according to the Bible, because He is risen, you are no longer in your sins. Jesus' resurrection is the living proof that all your sins have been completely and totally forgiven. You cannot preach grace without preaching the resurrected Christ. We are saved by grace through our faith in our Lord Jesus Christ:

> But God, who is rich in mercy, because of His great love with which He loved us, even when we were dead in trespasses, made us alive together with Christ (by grace you have been saved), and raised us up together, and made us sit together in the heavenly places in Christ Jesus, that in the ages to come He might show the exceeding riches of His grace in His kindness toward us in Christ Jesus. For by grace you have been saved through faith, and that not of yourselves; it is the gift of God, not of works, lest anyone should boast.
>
> —*Ephesians 2:4–9*

Our forgiveness is not contingent upon us and what we have or have not done, so no one can boast that they earned their forgiveness through their own efforts. Through faith in Jesus' finished work at the cross, we have received the gift of salvation. Salvation is a gift. When something is a gift, it means that you cannot work for it, earn it, or merit it. A gift is lavished upon the recipient by the giver, and Jesus gave of His own life to ransom yours.

Jesus gave of His own life to ransom yours.

He Has Secured Forgiveness for You

But Pastor Prince, I don't deserve it.

You are absolutely right. We deserve punishment for all the sins we have committed and will commit in our lifetime. We deserve death, but Jesus took that death for us and gave us eternal life. He took what we deserved and gave us what we didn't deserve. That is why we are saved by grace—His unmerited, unearned, and undeserved favor—through faith.

Now, always remember this: How are you saved? *By grace through faith.* How have all your sins been forgiven? *By grace through faith.* How have you been made righteous? *By grace through faith.* This is your unshakable foundation, built upon the finished work of Jesus Christ. Don't allow any teaching to diminish the cross of Jesus in your life and make salvation, forgiveness, and righteousness things you have to work at in order to maintain and keep. You received salvation, forgiveness, and righteousness by grace through faith in Jesus' finished work, and they are secured by His obedience to the Father at the cross:

*Therefore, as through one man's offense judgment came to all
men, resulting in condemnation, even so through one Man's
righteous act the free gift came to all men, resulting in justification of life. For as by one man's disobedience many were
made sinners, so also by one Man's obedience many will be
made righteous.*

—*Romans 5:18–19*

Righteousness is not about right doing. Righteousness is about
right believing. You are made righteous in God's eyes when you put
your faith in Christ and His sacrifice for you. It is through Jesus' obedience that we have been made righteous and justified from all our
sins. Justification is our Lord Jesus removing all the guilt and penalty
of sin and proclaiming that we have been made righteous by His shed
blood.

---

*Righteousness is not about right doing. Righteousness is
about right believing. You are made righteous in God's eyes
when you put your faith in Christ.*

How Can "Future Sins" Be Forgiven?

*Pastor Prince, if all my sins are forgiven, that means my future sins are
too. But how can my future sins be forgiven?*

That's a great question. The reality is, when Jesus died on the cross
two thousand years ago, *all* our sins were in the future.

There are people who argue that there is no Scripture that says all
our future sins are forgiven. They teach that when we receive Jesus, all

our past sins are forgiven, but our future sins are only forgiven as we confess them and ask God for forgiveness.

First let me address those who claim that there is no Bible verse stating that our future sins are forgiven. Let me put it to them that there is no Bible verse stating that only our past sins are forgiven! But there is a Scripture that clearly states, "In Him we *have* redemption through His blood, the forgiveness of sins, according to the riches of His grace" (Eph. 1:7, emphasis mine). In the original Greek text, the verb for "have" is in the present tense, which indicates *durative action*, meaning *we are continually having forgiveness of sins*, including every sin we will ever commit.[1]

Furthermore, 1 John 2:12 says, "I write to you, little children, because your sins are forgiven you for His name's sake." The Greek perfect tense is used here for "are forgiven," meaning this forgiveness is a definite action completed in the past, with the effect continuing into the present.[2] This means that God's forgiveness avails for you in your present, and continues into your future.

Let me give you another clear Scripture that states that all our sins, including our future sins, have been forgiven:

> *You were dead because of your sins and because your sinful nature was not yet cut away. Then God made you alive with Christ, for he forgave* all *our sins. He canceled the record of the charges against us and took it away by nailing it to the cross.*
> —*Colossians 2:13–14* NLT *(emphasis mine)*

Jesus forgave *all* our sins! The word "all" in the above Scripture is the Greek *pas*, meaning "every kind or variety…the totality of the persons or things referred to."[3] It refers to "all, any, every, the whole."[4] So "all" means *all*. God's forgiveness of our sins covers *every* sin—past, present, and future! When we received the Lord Jesus as our Savior, we received the total and complete forgiveness of all our sins.

In Hebrews 10:11–14, the Bible says, "And every priest stands ministering daily and offering repeatedly the same sacrifices, which can never take away sins. But this Man, after He had offered one sacrifice for sins forever, sat down at the right hand of God, from that time waiting till His enemies are made His footstool. For by one offering He has perfected forever those who are being sanctified."

Now, according to this Scripture, as a believer, for how long are you perfected?

Forever!

How can you be perfected forever, if your future sins are not forgiven?

Does Total Forgiveness Mean Right Behavior Isn't Important?

Many believers are worried that when the truth of the gospel is told like that, people will take advantage of the revelation of their total forgiveness in Christ and go on to lead godless lives. They are worried that such teaching places no emphasis on sanctification or the desire to live holy, God-glorifying lives. So allow me to explain here that while you have been justified and made righteous by the blood of Jesus or perfected forever, the truth is that sanctification is ongoing in your growth as a Christian. This is why the author of the book of Hebrews says that we are *being sanctified* even though we are *perfected forever* by Christ's one act of obedience at the cross (see Heb. 10:14).

As a believer you cannot become more righteous, but you can

become more sanctified or holy in terms of how you live your life. Justification by faith happened instantaneously. The moment you received Jesus, you were forgiven, cleansed, perfected in righteousness, and saved. You were also sanctified *in Christ* (see Heb. 10:10). However, it is important to understand that the revelation and outworking of your sanctification in Christ is progressive. This means that the more you grow in your relationship with the Lord Jesus, the more holy you will become in every area of your life.

I remember a precious brother writing to my ministry describing how the revelation of our forgiveness in Christ brought him into an intimacy with God that he had previously only dreamed about. "Previously, when I was *trying* to be a good Christian," he said, "I was only *crawling* along, inch by inch. But now that I've got hold of grace, I'm *running* in my relationship with God! The more I learn about God's amazing grace, the more I desperately want to glorify Him with my life!"

What a beautiful, true-life picture of what really happens when a person sits under teaching that uncovers the undiluted gospel of grace! My dear friend, we know that "all Scripture is given by inspiration of God, and is profitable for doctrine, for reproof, for correction, for instruction in righteousness" (2 Tim. 3:16), so how can we say that behavior is not important? But contrary to what many people imagine, the revelation of forgiveness does not detract from, nor is it at the expense of, right living. Instead it is the fuel that makes right living happen.

The revelation of forgiveness does not detract from, nor is it at the expense of, right living. Instead it is the fuel that makes right living happen.

Merriam-Webster Online describes *sanctification* as "the state of growing in divine grace as a result of Christian commitment after conversion."[5] You see, it is all about growing in grace. Establish yourself in the gospel of grace. Paul told Timothy to be "strong in the grace that is in Christ Jesus" (2 Tim. 2:1). Peter encouraged believers to build a strong foundation with these closing words in his last epistle: "Grow in the grace and knowledge of our Lord and Savior Jesus Christ" (2 Pet. 3:18).

Precious believers all around the world are today growing in the grace and knowledge of our Lord Jesus Christ. I have observed that the more I focus my preaching on unveiling the person of Jesus in the gospel of grace, the more my ministry office receives testimonies from people who have found freedom from the power of sin! Today they are so in love with Jesus and so filled with His peace and life that they begin to lose the desire to dabble in self-destructive behaviors!

You see, grace produces true holiness. The more you grow in grace—the more you are washed, again and again, by the water of the word of God's grace—the more you grow in sanctification and holiness, and the more you allow the Holy Spirit to correct habits and thinking that keep you in bondage. Beloved, when you experience the grace of our Lord Jesus, the allure and passing pleasures of sin fade in the light of His glory and grace. Victory also begins to come into previous areas of struggle, weakness, and defeat.

When you experience the grace of our Lord Jesus, the
allure and passing pleasures of sin fade in the light of
His glory and grace.

Forgiven and Free to Reign

Listen to this heartwarming praise report that I received from Reese, who lives in California:

> *While surfing television channels one evening, I came across Joseph Prince's broadcast. What I heard blessed me so much that on the following Friday at 9:00 p.m., I was glued to the TV as I listened to him preach again.*
>
> *I decided to purchase two of Pastor Joseph Prince's CD sermons on grace and righteousness, and listened to them many times over. Never in my whole life had I heard such preaching. I was born into a Christian family, personally received Christ at age twenty-two, yet felt I was hearing the gospel for the very first time. My heart jumped within me and bore witness that what I heard was the real gospel.*
>
> *I grew up being told that I had to keep God's laws to make it to heaven. I was also told that I had to be approved by God in order to have my prayers answered. God was presented to me as a mean old man in heaven, looking and waiting for me to make one mistake so He could discipline me. I was also told that righteousness and salvation had to be worked for by keeping the old covenant laws and living a holy life. What I was taught made me fearful, unstable, and confused all my life. I kept repeating the cycle of falling into sin and repenting. The Christian life was very hard for me.*
>
> *To hear the true gospel of grace—how grace means unmerited, undeserved favor—and that righteousness is a gift that I*

received when I got saved and didn't have to earn, was much-needed water and nourishment to my soul.

I have since bought all of Joseph Prince's books and many of his sermons on CD. I also listen to his broadcast every day. Everything that Joseph Prince preaches has been so liberating to me, especially his sermons on God's gift of no condemnation. There is nothing as liberating as knowing that all my sins—past, present, and future—are forgiven and that God does not see any sin in me because He saw them all judged on the body of Jesus Christ. Therefore, God does not—and will not—condemn me anymore. I can't describe the freedom that I feel, and the joy and peace of knowing that God is cool with me. This is so sweet.

The revelation of grace I received through Joseph's teaching has resulted in so many blessings: My relationships with people have improved. I have been healed from a seven-year struggle with high blood pressure and from insomnia. Moreover, God miraculously provided the finances to buy a three-bedroom town house. He provided the money even though I was laid off from work the same year. Six months after the lay-off, I got the kind of job that I had always wanted to have, in an industry that I had always wanted to work in, along with a very good salary despite the economic downturn. On top of that, I recently received a promotion with a good pay increase.

Now I see God's favor all around my family. I am emotionally much more stable and I face every day confident in Christ. My husband tells me that I have become "solid." We are no longer fighting the way we used to because God has also blessed our marriage.

May all the glory be unto Lord Jesus, my Savior!

What a precious testimony. Thank you for sharing your journey of faith, Reese. I celebrate and rejoice with you.

My friend, you can have the same joy, security, and amazing restoration that Reese is enjoying today. Like Reese, you can go from being trapped in "the cycle of falling into sin and repenting," with no real difference resulting from such repentance, to walking in victory and freedom in a greater and greater measure every day. True repentance is turning to the cross when you have failed and returning to God's grace. You no longer have to be burdened by confusion and fear, guilt, and condemnation in your Christian walk. Come to your loving Savior and receive His grace and the assurance of His total forgiveness of your sins. He has paid for it all with His blood. It will set you free to have the kind of relationship you've always longed for with God, one that is intimate, powerful, and full of peace, joy, and good fruit!

CHAPTER 5

BEGIN LIVING WITH CONFIDENCE

My dear friend, when you understand the power of Jesus' ever-cleansing blood, it changes your life forever. Fear and depression give way to indescribable peace and joy. No longer do you feel insecure in your salvation, because you now possess the blessed assurance that Christ's eternal and efficacious blood has cleansed you and continues to cleanse you of every sin!

When you understand the power of Jesus' ever-cleansing blood, fear and depression give way to indescribable peace and joy.

Frances Ridley Havergal, a famous English hymn writer of the nineteenth century, was someone who experienced this very life-changing experience. Frances wrote more than eighty hymns, including the well-loved *Like a River Glorious* and *Take My Life and Let It Be*. Born to devoted Christian parents, she was a beautiful, bright, and energetic child. So full of life was she that her father fondly called her his "Little Quicksilver."[1]

Frances was also an extremely gifted child, able to read simple books at the age of three. At four years of age, she could write well and read the Bible and other books for grown-ups. Later she studied in England and Germany and mastered Latin, French, German, Hebrew, and Greek. At the age of twenty-two, she knew by heart the four gospel books, the epistles, and the books of Psalms, Isaiah, and Revelation!

The Continually Cleansing Fount of
Christ's Blood

But there was something about Frances that few people know. Despite her gifts and despite having received Christ as her Savior at a young age and loving the Lord, Frances was very unhappy. On the outside she was a cheerful, active Christian, but deep within she battled fear, insecurity, and depression. She was convinced her "great wickedness of heart" impeded a full and intimate walk with the Lord.[2] Frances spent her days longing for a deeper, fuller experience with Jesus, one in which she could have continuous enjoyment of abundant life. Most of all, she wanted to be able to trust Jesus fully for complete forgiveness of sins, enjoy intimacy with God, and have a rock-solid assurance of her salvation.

As I was reading about her experience, I was curious—*So how did she find that deeper, fuller experience in which joy was continuous? How did she come to trust Jesus fully for her complete forgiveness of sins and be free from sin-consciousness and depression?* As I read on I discovered that it was a revelation of 1 John 1:7—of how the blood of Jesus continuously cleansed her from all sin—that lifted her out of the doldrums and the depths of despair:

But if we walk in the light as He is in the light, we have fellow-
ship with one another, and the blood of Jesus Christ His Son
cleanses us from all sin.

—1 John 1:7

Because Frances knew the Greek language well, she understood that the Greek word for "cleanses" in 1 John 1:7 is in the present tense, which means that Jesus' blood *continually cleanses or keeps on cleans-ing.*[3] His blood, shed two thousand years ago, continues to have an ongoing cleansing power!

When asked about how she came to this revelation, Frances said,

I was shown that "the blood of Jesus Christ His Son cleanseth us
from all sin," and then it was made plain to me that He Who had
thus cleansed me had power to keep me clean; so I just utterly
yielded myself to Him and utterly trusted Him to keep me....

Have we not been limiting the cleansing power of the pre-
cious blood when applied by the Holy Spirit, and also the
keeping power of God? Have we not been limiting 1 John 1:7,
by practically making it refer only to "remission of sins that
are past" instead of taking the grand simplicity of "cleanseth
from all sin"? "All" is all; and as we may trust Him to cleanse
us from the stain of past sins so we may trust Him to cleanse us
from all present defilement; yes, all!

If not, we take away from this most precious promise, and,
by refusing to take it in its fullness, lose the fullness of its appli-
cation and power.... It was that one word "cleanseth" which
opened the door of a very glory of hope and joy to me. I had
never seen the force of the tense before, a continual present,
always a present tense, not a present which the next moment

becomes a past. It goes on cleansing, and I have no words to tell how my heart rejoices in it. Not a coming to be cleansed in the fountain only, but a remaining in the fountain, so that it may and can go on cleansing.[4]

You Can Enjoy Perfect Peace

Following Frances's powerful revelation that caused her heart to rejoice greatly, she wrote two well-loved hymns, one of which was *Like a River Glorious*. Read the lyrics of this beautiful hymn and see how her revelation of the ever-cleansing blood of Jesus ushered the richness of God's perfect peace into her heart and mind:

Like a river glorious, is God's perfect peace,
Over all victorious, in its bright increase;
Perfect, yet it floweth, fuller every day,
Perfect, yet it groweth, deeper all the way.

REFRAIN:
Stayed upon Jehovah, hearts are fully blest
Finding, as He promised, perfect peace and rest.

Hidden in the hollow of His blessed hand,
Never foe can follow, never traitor stand;
Not a surge of worry, not a shade of care,
Not a blast of hurry touch the spirit there.

Every joy or trial falleth from above,
Traced upon our dial by the Sun of Love;

We may trust Him fully all for us to do;
They who trust Him wholly find Him wholly true.[5]

Frances's last words before she went on to be with Jesus were, "It is all perfect peace. I'm only waiting for Jesus to take me in." What a way to enter into glory—possessing a perfect assurance of salvation, because she knew in her soul that all her sins were forgiven, and that every moment of her life she stood forgiven before God!

My friend, if you're living life in the valley of despair today, believing that your sins are separating you from intimacy with the Lord and miring you in defeat, I want you to know that because you have put your faith in Christ, you are under the fountain of the ever-cleansing blood of Christ! Every sense of defilement or stain of sin will be washed away from your conscience when you know and believe what Frances discovered.

Because Jesus' blood continually cleanses you, you cannot bounce in and out of the light of Christ, in and out of being seated in the heavenly places in Christ, in and out of being forgiven, justified, and made righteous, or in and out of fellowship with God. It is not a sometimes-yes-sometimes-no salvation, but a salvation that has secured a *yes* to all of God's promises because of the blood of Jesus (see 2 Cor. 1:19–20)!

Lose All Your Guilty Stains

There is another hymn about the cleansing blood of Jesus that I love to sing in church. Written by William Cowper, it is the beloved hymn *There Is a Fountain Filled with Blood.* William was a sensitive intellectual who for most of his life battled deep depression triggered by the traumatic experience of losing his mother at age six. Even after a glorious conversion later in life, William would at times doubt the love of God and his security as a believer.

Not long before his death in 1800, William penned the beautiful words to *There Is a Fountain Filled with Blood*. The lyrics stand as a testament to the peace he found with his Savior, after realizing how Christ's blood has completely atoned for all his sins. The anointed words have led countless saints as well as sinners to find their peace with God, which as the hymn declares is found by those who come under "a fountain filled with blood, drawn from Immanuel's veins":

> *There is a fountain filled with blood,*
> *Drawn from Immanuel's veins;*
> *And sinners plunged beneath that flood*
> *Lose all their guilty stains.*
> *Lose all their guilty stains,*
> *Lose all their guilty stains;*
> *And sinners plunged beneath that flood*
> *Lose all their guilty stains.*
>
> *The dying thief rejoiced to see*
> *That fountain in his day;*
> *And there have I, though vile as he,*
> *Washed all my sins away.*
> *Washed all my sins away,*
> *Washed all my sins away;*
> *And there have I, though vile as he,*
> *Washed all my sins away.*[6]

Beloved, see yourself perpetually beneath the fountain of Jesus' blood. See His blood continually cleansing you and you will lose every guilty stain, every sense of defilement. When you believe right in the efficacy of Jesus' ever-cleansing blood, and see how you have forgiveness of every sin through this blood, you cannot but live life with greater peace, joy, and boldness. You can go freely and boldly to the throne of grace to enjoy the Lord's embrace, to talk to Him about anything, and to receive His help and mercy in time of need.

When you see how you have forgiveness of every sin through Jesus' blood, you cannot but live life with greater peace, joy, and boldness.

The Biblical Way out of Sin

But Pastor Prince, doesn't such preaching just make believers feel that it is all right to go on sinning?

Let me ask you a question: when a truly born-again believer knows that he is forgiven of all his sins, does he go, "Yippee! Now I can go sin all I want"?

I submit to you that no true believer of Jesus is looking for an excuse to sin. Many may be struggling with sin, but they are looking for a way out. They know that what they are doing is self-destructive and not glorifying to their Lord and Savior.

Oh, Pastor Prince, I know of so-and-so, who says he is under grace, and now he has left his wife to be with his mistress.

Friend, let me be the first to tell you that this person isn't living under grace. The Word of God tells us in no uncertain terms that "sin shall not have dominion over you, for you are not under law but under grace" (Rom. 6:14).

This Scripture shows us that when a person is truly under grace, he is not ruled by sin, nor does he happily continue to live a sinful lifestyle. Notice that it also tells us that the way to be liberated from sin's dominion is to come under grace.

The way to be liberated from sin's dominion is to come under grace.

Just see how Jesus dealt with the woman caught in adultery in the Gospel of John. To the Pharisees who had flung her at His feet, He said, "He who is without sin among you, let him throw a stone at her first." One by one they dropped their stones and left. After the last of her accusers had left, Jesus asked the woman, "Woman, where are those accusers of yours? Has no one condemned you?" She replied, "No one, Lord."

Now, listen carefully to what Jesus said next: "Neither do I condemn you; go and sin no more" (see John 8:7–11).

Let me ask you this: did Jesus compromise on God's holiness? Absolutely not! His first words were: "He who is without sin among you, let him throw a stone at her first." He treated sin as something that had to be severely dealt with. Sin demands punishment, and Jesus knew that He would take on the punishment for all her sins at the cross. Sin *is* destructive. Sin tears marriages, families, and loved ones apart. And in the case of adultery, when there are children involved, it is these innocent ones who suffer the most. This is why the Bible warns strongly about the destructiveness of adultery: "Do not let your heart turn aside to her ways, do not stray into her paths; for she has cast down many wounded, and all who were slain by her were strong men. Her house is the way to hell, descending to the chambers of death" (Prov. 7:25–27).

So let me make this absolutely clear: sin is horrible! Sin comes with damaging consequences. I am against sin and that's why I preach *God's grace*! His grace is the only answer to overcoming sin!

Let's learn from the account in John 8 how Jesus helped this woman out of the sin of adultery. Did He recite the law of Moses to her? Did He command her to repent and confess her sin? You and I know that Jesus didn't do either of the above. Yet that is what is being taught as the answer to sin in many places today.

My friend, to the adulteress at His feet, our beautiful Lord Jesus simply showed her grace that she didn't deserve. He drove her accusers away with the same law of Moses they had come to impose on her. And He gave her the gift of no condemnation, which liberated her and enabled her to "go and sin no more." Jesus *never* endorsed her sin! But in giving her the gift of no condemnation, He showed her the way out of her sin.

Can Believers Sin Willfully and Lose Their Salvation?

Whenever I preach on the total forgiveness of our sins and assurance of salvation, someone will say, *But Pastor Prince, doesn't the Bible say in Hebrews 10:26 that if we sin willfully, we can lose our salvation?*

Many believers are taught that when they sin deliberately, they are committing what Hebrews 10:26 warns against, and that they can expect God's "judgment, and fiery indignation" (Heb. 10:27). As a result, these believers become sin-conscious—always mindful and worried about their "willful sins," and God's judgment to come. When something bad does happen to them (they blow a tire on the road or contract a disease, for example), they immediately attribute it to God's judgment of their mistakes. My dear reader, having this fear and perpetual judgment-consciousness is not how God the Father wants us to live.

I submit to you that almost every sin we commit after being saved (the exceptions being sins we commit unconsciously) is committed willfully. So this can't be what Hebrews 10:26 is talking about, or we should live each day expecting God's judgment and fiery indignation! What does it mean, then, to "sin willfully"? Is it something that a believer can do? Well, let's look at the context of Hebrews 10:26 to find out, and resolve this issue in our hearts once and for all:

> *For if we sin willfully after we have received the knowledge of the truth, there no longer remains a sacrifice for sins, but a certain fearful expectation of judgment, and fiery indignation which will devour the adversaries. Anyone who has rejected Moses' law dies without mercy on the testimony of two or three witnesses. Of how much worse punishment, do you suppose, will he be thought worthy who has trampled the Son of God underfoot, counted the blood of the covenant by which he was sanctified a common thing, and insulted the Spirit of grace? For we know Him who said, "Vengeance is Mine, I will repay," says the Lord. And again, "The LORD will judge His people." It is a fearful thing to fall into the hands of the living God.*
> *—Hebrews 10:26–31*

Whom Is the Warning For?

The first thing we need to understand is that the book of *Hebrews* was written to the Hebrews, or Jewish people (which included believers as well as nonbelievers). Hebrews 10:26, in particular, is addressing

Jewish nonbelievers who had heard preaching on Jesus being their
Messiah, but who were still going back to the temple to offer animal
sacrifices. This was an insult to the Spirit of grace, because they were
flatly rejecting the Lord Jesus, Who in His great grace had offered
Himself as the perfect and final sacrifice for their sins at Calvary. In
addressing these people, the apostle Paul (I believe that he is the writer
of the book of Hebrews) compares the imperfect priesthood of the
law and its repeated temple sacrifices with the perfect priesthood and
once-for-all sacrifice of Christ.

For example, in Hebrews 10:1, you find Paul talking about how the
animal sacrifices that the Jews offered continually at the temple could
not make them perfect. In contrast Jesus, "after He had offered one
sacrifice for sins forever, sat down at the right hand of God.... For by
one offering He has perfected forever those who are being sanctified"
(Heb. 10:12, 14). Paul goes on to say that because their sins have been
remitted through Christ's one perfect sacrifice, "there is no longer an
offering for sin" (Heb. 10:18).

In other words, Paul was telling these Jews that there was no use
going back to the temple to offer repeatedly the same sacrifices, which
can never take away sins. He was telling them that the Lord Jesus had
already become their final sacrifice, putting an end to all temple sacrifices. Can you see how the verses preceding Hebrews 10:26 contrast
the imperfect efficacy of the blood of the yearly temple sacrifices to
remove sins, and the Lord Jesus' one perfect sacrifice for sins forever?
Paul was showing the Jews what a perfect work our Lord Jesus had
accomplished.

I find it astonishing that instead of rejoicing at these faith-assuring
Scriptures in Hebrews 10, some believers choose to focus on verses 26
and 27, without understanding the context in which they were written. Clearly, in context, to "sin willfully" is to commit the *specific sin* of

knowing that Jesus is the final sacrifice, and yet choosing not to accept His finished work and turning back to the temple sacrifices. It is not referring to the deliberate sins a believer commits after he or she is saved.

Believers Have Nothing to Fear

Paul was certainly not addressing genuine believers when he warned about sinning willfully in verse 26. When he writes, "For if we sin willfully after we have received the knowledge of the truth, there no longer remains a sacrifice for sins," he is referring to his Jewish brethren who had received "the *knowledge* of the truth," but never received this truth (the Lord Jesus and His finished work) *into their hearts*. They heard the truth about Jesus, but chose not to depend on His perfect offering for their salvation. There is a massive difference between the two.

So Paul was in essence telling these Jews, "When you know the truth and still turn your back on the final sacrifice of Jesus, there remains no more sacrifice for sins." And in constantly rejecting in their hearts the final sacrifice of Jesus and returning to the offering of animal sacrifices in the temple, they "trampled the Son of God underfoot, counted the blood of the covenant...a common thing, and insulted the Spirit of grace" (Heb. 10:29).

From the context of Hebrews 10:26, it is clear that this verse is not targeted at believers at all. Genuine believers in Christ cannot commit this sin, simply because they have already believed in Jesus' sacrifice and put their trust in the Lord's finished work, and they are certainly not going back to any temple to offer animal sacrifices. The verse does not refer to Christians who are "backsliding" or "going astray"; nor does it refer to Christians who sin in a moment of weakness or temptation.

My friend, don't let anyone preach this verse out of its context and rob you of your security in Christ today. Just look at how the chapter ends: "But we are not of those who draw back to perdition, but of those who believe to the saving of the soul" (Heb. 10:39). Paul states clearly that believers are not like those who have rejected the Lord Jesus to their own destruction, but are the ones who have believed and are saved. Read that verse again and truly know this in your heart: as believers, all of us have believed to the saving of our souls for all eternity. Hallelujah!

Believers Will Not Come into Judgment

Now, if Paul was addressing the Jews of his day, especially those who were rejecting Jesus as the final sacrifice and returning to temple sacrifices, does Hebrews 10 have any application today? Yes, Hebrews 10:26 can today be applied to unbelievers who hear the truth of the gospel of grace, and with open eyes turn their backs on our Lord Jesus and the salvation He offers. Just imagine: God offers His salvation and all of His blessings in His hands to someone who, having knowledge of the magnitude of these blessings, slaps His hands away. That is what it means to sin willfully today and insult the Spirit of grace. And for such a person, as long as he keeps rejecting Jesus' perfect sacrifice and finished work, there no longer remains a sacrifice for his sins. He has rejected the only sacrifice God accepts. In the end this unbeliever will have to face God's judgment for his rejection of the Lord.

But what is God's Word when it comes to judgment and *His children*? Let me show you what the Scriptures *do* say to establish your heart in the security of your salvation in Christ. The Greek word for "judgment" in Hebrews 10:27 is *krisis*, which means a sentence of "condemnation and punishment."[7] Now turn with me to John 5:24

and read Jesus' own words: "Most assuredly, I say to you, he who hears My word and believes in Him who sent Me has everlasting life, and shall not come into judgment [*krisis*], but has passed from death into life." The same word for "judgment" (*krisis*) used in Hebrews 10:27 is used here in this Scripture regarding believers.

Can anything be more clear and transparent? What is it that God wants us to be assured of? That we believers will never come into *krisis* judgment! We have passed from death into life. True believers need never fear the Lord's judgment, as all of the fire of judgment fell fully on our Lord at Calvary. Today you can have full assurance of salvation in Christ your Savior. Amen!

Dealing with Sin in the Church

As Jesus extended His forgiveness and gift of no condemnation to the woman caught in adultery, so I preach the same grace that Jesus exemplified and offered. As a preacher of our Lord Jesus' grace, I never endorse or excuse anyone's sin. However, my job is not to point them to more laws, but to our Lord Jesus.

If either my pastoral team or I am involved in counseling anyone who is living in adultery, we will tell the person in no uncertain terms that they are not living under grace. Since sin is having dominion over them, how can they be living under grace?

We will point the person to the grace of our Lord Jesus, but we will also make it very clear to them that sin comes with destructive consequences, and that it is not acceptable for them to continue in their sin. Then we will tell the person to go back to their spouse and family, and most times the person will!

The point is, we are here to help those who are struggling with sin and who have a genuine desire to be helped. But for those who are bent on living a lifestyle of sin, we don't ever endorse or condone their lifestyles. Do we love them? One hundred percent. And we will be there for them in a heartbeat if they genuinely want to be helped.

We've found that many times, the individual who is insistent on living a lifestyle of sin will stop attending church by his or her own choice. Interestingly, it appears that the few who persistently want to live in sin find that they can't remain too long in a church that is preaching the true gospel of grace. It's hard to keep sinning against a loving Savior.

I'm sharing all this to tell you how a grace church is to be pastored. We don't make light of sin. As shepherds we have a responsibility to protect God's precious flock from wolves. The church opens its doors and welcomes everyone. However, if there is predatory behavior, we have to step in to ensure that our congregation and their children are safe. We see how a good shepherd protects his sheep in the example of David in the Old Testament. Even as a young shepherd boy, David went after the lion and the bear that took his sheep, and rescued his sheep right out of the mouths of those predators (see 1 Sam. 17:34–36). In the same way, we don't back down from sinful behavior that is hurting our flock, and we act to protect our "sheep." I have no doubt that you would do the same to protect your family and loved ones.

What about Confessing Our Sins for Forgiveness?

When I preach that all our sins have been forgiven and that we are perpetually under the fountain of the ever-cleansing blood of Jesus, another question I'm often asked is, *What about the confession of sins spoken of in 1 John 1:9? The verse says clearly, "If we confess our sins, He is faithful and just to forgive us our sins and to cleanse us from all unrigh-teousness." Don't we have to confess our sins in order to be forgiven and cleansed of all unrighteousness?*

My friend, you are looking at someone who went all the way with the traditional interpretation and understanding of this verse. As a young adult earnestly wanting to live a holy life and please God, I started confessing my sins all the time when I received that teaching. I didn't want to spend even one minute not being "right with God." So when just one wrong thought crossed my mind, I would confess that sin immediately. I would cover my mouth and whisper my confession, even if I was in the middle of a soccer match with my friends!

Needless to say, I appeared weird to my friends. I was also per-plexed as to why my Christian friends weren't confessing their sins as I was. Why weren't they serious about wanting to be 100 percent right with God?

The constant, unceasing confession of my sins made me extremely sin-conscious. I became so aware of and troubled by every nega-tive thought that I believed there was no more forgiveness for my sins. I even began to believe that I had lost my salvation and was going to hell! The enemy took advantage of my obsession with need-ing to confess every sin and placed me under constant condemnation. The oppression grew so heavy that I felt as if my mind was about to snap!

I've shared more extensively about my past struggle with 1 John 1:9 and what the verse is actually about in my book *Unmerited Favor*.[8] So let me give you just a quick understanding of the subject here:

- The first chapter of 1 John was not written to believers but to Gnostics who did not believe that Jesus came in the flesh, hence the uncharacteristic opening in the first epistle of John.

There was no greeting to believers, unlike what we find in his
second and third epistles. Instead, the apostle John opens up
his first epistle with a direct address to the serious heresy of the
Gnostics—"That which was from the beginning, which we have
heard, which we have *seen* with our eyes, which we have *looked
upon*, and our hands have *handled*" (1 John 1:1, emphasis mine).
John was telling them that Jesus had indeed come in the flesh, as
he and his fellow disciples had heard, seen, and touched Jesus.

- It is only in chapter 2 of John's first epistle that you see the phrase
  "My little children" for the first time, intimating that from that
  chapter on, the apostle John was addressing believers.

- The Gnostics also believed that they had no sin. So the apostle
  John was telling them that if they would acknowledge and confess
  their sins, God would forgive them and cleanse them from all
  unrighteousness (see 1 John 1:8–9).

- The early Christians did not have the book of 1 John for some
  fifty years, so their getting "right with God" could not have
  been through the confession of sins.

- Apostle Paul, who wrote two-thirds of the epistles to the
  churches, never once taught on confession of sins. In fact, in
  his letter to the Corinthian Christians, many of whom were
  committing sins like visiting temple prostitutes, he didn't tell
  them to go and confess their sins to get right with God. Rather
  he reminded them of who they were in Christ—"Know ye
  not that ye are the temple of God, and that the Spirit of God
  dwelleth in you?" (1 Cor. 3:16 KJV)

- Our being "right with God" is not based on the imperfect
  confession of sins by imperfect man, but on the riches of God's
  grace and the perfect sacrifice of His Son.

- Those who believe that 1 John 1:9 is telling believers to confess their sin every time they sin need to realize that *every* sin needs to be recognized and confessed (otherwise, based on that verse, one is still unrighteous). You cannot pick and choose what to confess or confess only the sins you remember. And it is not humanly possible to confess *every* sin in thought, word, and deed.
- The word "confess" in 1 John 1:9 is the Greek *homologeo*, which means "to say the same thing as" or "to agree with."[9] To confess our sins, therefore, is to say the same things about our sins as God does: that it is sin, and that our sins have been forgiven and washed away by the blood of our Lord Jesus Christ (see Rev. 1:5). When you have sinned and realize you have sinned, true confession is agreeing with God's Word and expressing your gratefulness to Him for the reality of your forgiveness in Christ.

To the theologian, I want to share with you a fresh and powerful revelation that the Lord just opened my eyes to. (This is so fresh that at the time of this writing, I have yet to preach this in my church.) In my study, He asked me to examine the word *sins* in 1 John 1:9 and to see if it is a noun or verb in the original Greek text. Are you ready for this?

In the two instances where we see the word "sins" in 1 John 1:9, it is the Greek noun *hamartia* that is used. According to well-known Bible scholar William Vine, *hamartia* ("a missing of the mark") indicates "a principle or source of action, or an inward element producing acts...a governing principle or power."[10] In other words, it refers to the sin principle, or our sinful state on account of Adam's sin. By using the noun form of this word, John was clearly not referring to our committing of individual acts of sin, or he would have used the verb form, *hamartano*.

In the light of this, can you see how 1 John 1:9 is not talking about confessing our sins every time we sin in thought or in deed? John was speaking of the need to acknowledge and confess to God that we are sinners because of Adam's sin, as well as to receive the total forgiveness for all our sins through Jesus' finished work. How often do we need to do this? Only once. That's why 1 John 1:9 is primarily a salvation verse, one that encourages the sinner to acknowledge and confess his sinful state or "sinnerhood," get born again by faith in our Lord Jesus Christ, and have his sinful state through Adam replaced with a new righteous state through Christ. The heretical Gnostic doctrine did not subscribe to a belief in man's sinful state. John was addressing this heresy directly in the first chapter of 1 John and encouraging the Gnostics to confess their sinful state and receive the Lord's complete forgiveness and total cleansing from all their unrighteousness through His finished work at the cross.

Now, what does the apostle John say then, about our committing of sins after we've become believers? Just two verses later in the second chapter of 1 John, John answers this question as he begins his address to believers: "My little children, these things I write to you, so that you may not sin. And if anyone sins, we have an Advocate with the Father, Jesus Christ the righteous" (1 John 2:1).

This time, the words "sin" and "sins" are the Greek verb *hamartano*. John is now referring to believers' committing of sins—their sinful thoughts and deeds. What does John say regarding this? He reminds us that when we fail as believers, we have an Advocate with the Father—Jesus Christ.

Because of our Lord Jesus and what He has accomplished at the cross, we have forgiveness and we still stand righteous before God even when we've missed it. As the apostle Paul reminded the Corinthian believers who had failed that they were still the temple of the Holy Spirit, John reminds us of who we are in Christ and who we have representing us at God's right hand.

Can you see that the Bible's answer to overcoming sin is always to remind believers of their righteous identity in Christ? This is not to encourage us to sin but to encourage us to look to our Lord Jesus, to see our sins punished at the cross and to live victoriously and gloriously for Him. That is what true repentance is all about— turning to the cross and returning to His grace! When you fail today, know that you can talk to God honestly about your failing, but do it with a revelation of the cross of our Lord Jesus. See your sins punished in His body and receive afresh His forgiveness and unmerited favor to reign over your sins.

Do We Confess Our Sins under Grace?

Once, when I was preaching in Italy, a prominent psychiatrist to whom I had been introduced shared with me something heartbreaking. He told me that he has counseled many sincere Christians who are living defeated lives, some even in mental asylums, because they believe that being right with God hangs on their ability to confess every sin.

My friend, can you see how dangerous this teaching is? Without the assurance of complete forgiveness, these believers are sin-conscious, burdened with guilt and shame, condemned by the enemy, joyless, and totally insecure about their salvation.

Yet the truth is that every believer has total forgiveness in Christ,

Whose eternal blood keeps on cleansing them from all sin. The moment they know this truth, heaven comes into their souls, as in the case of Frances Havergal. And the effect this produces in their lives is not a desire to go out and sin, but a desire to live a life that glorifies their Savior. He who knows that he is forgiven much—forgiven of all, actually—will love much (see Luke 7:47 NLT).

So is Joseph Prince against a Christian's confessing his sins? Let me say this clearly: I do believe in the confession of sins and I do confess my sins still. But there's a big difference now—I confess my sins knowing that all my sins are *already* forgiven. I don't confess my sins to *be* forgiven. Because I have a close relationship with my heavenly Father, I can be honest with Him when I've done wrong. I can talk to Him about it, receive His grace for my weakness, and move forward knowing full well that He has already forgiven me through His Son's sacrifice. And I no longer worry about the fact that I can't possibly confess every sin, because I know it's not my confessions that save me, but the blood of Jesus.

Beloved, our forgiveness was purchased perfectly with our Lord's precious blood. It is not contingent on how perfectly we are able to confess our every sin. How can our forgiveness be dependent on the consistency, frequency, and quality of our confessions? That is bound to fail! Our forgiveness is dependent on our faith in the quality of our Lord's sinless blood that was shed at the cross. There is a world of difference between these two bases for our forgiveness, and it results in a world of difference to your peace of mind!

Dear reader, grace doesn't make light of sin; it is the power to break free from sin! And this is the *present truth* of grace in which God wants us to be established (see 2 Pet. 1:12)—that concerning the confession of sins, we confess our sins because we *are already* forgiven, not *to obtain* God's forgiveness. The more conscious you are of how forgiven you already are in Christ, the more you will truly live above every defeat.

Start Walking in Boldness Today

Beloved, it is the blood of Jesus Christ that continually cleanses you from all sin, not your continuous confession of sins. You have remission and forgiveness of every sin through His shed blood. You have the assurance of forgiveness according to the riches of His grace, not according to the diligence of your confessions. Your assurance is founded upon what He has done, not what you need to keep doing.

Your assurance is founded upon what Jesus has done, not what you need to keep doing.

Those who insist that 1 John 1:9 is proof that the Christian must *keep confessing his sins in order to be forgiven and made righteous* will find it inconsistent with 1 John 2:12: "I write to you, little children, because your sins are forgiven you for His name's sake." We saw in the previous chapter how "are forgiven" here is in the perfect tense in Greek, indicating that our forgiveness is a definite action completed in the past with continuing, ongoing effect. So if Apostle John really wrote 1 John 1:9 for the Christian to practice, then he was engaging in double-talk! No, my friend, there is no double-talk in Scripture. We *are* forgiven of *all* through Jesus' blood.

It is this revelation of the cleansing power of Jesus' shed blood that is the launching pad to living life with greater boldness and confidence. The Scriptures tell us clearly:

And so, dear brothers and sisters, we can boldly enter heaven's Most Holy Place because of the blood of Jesus. By his death, Jesus opened a new and life-giving way through the curtain into the Most Holy Place. And since we have a great High Priest who rules over God's house, let us go right into the presence of God with sincere hearts fully trusting him. For our guilty consciences have been sprinkled with Christ's blood to make us clean, and our bodies have been washed with pure water.

—Hebrews 10:19–22 NLT

Do you see? Boldness comes when you realize that because of Jesus' cleansing blood, you don't need to hide from God, afraid that He is out to get you for your sins. You can have boldness to enter into the holiest presence of God with a heart that fully trusts Him, and with a conscience that is free of guilt and condemnation.

Boldness comes when you realize that because of Jesus' cleansing blood, you can enter into the holiest presence of God with a heart that fully trusts Him, and with a conscience that is free of guilt and condemnation.

This is the new and life-giving way God wants you to live by, one where you can confidently approach His throne of grace at any time to receive His mercy, favor, help, blessings, and life! My friend, whatever your challenges, if you will actively possess your perfect and complete forgiveness in Christ, you can overcome them and enjoy life at a whole new level, with greater boldness and confidence!

PART TWO

BUILD A FOUNDATION FOR LASTING BREAKTHROUGHS

CHAPTER 6

WHY PREACH GRACE?

I wrote this book to help you build a strong foundation for lasting breakthroughs. Whatever defeat you may be struggling with now, I want you to really anchor yourself in God's grace by receiving and understanding the gospel of grace from His Word. Don't base your understanding of God's heart toward you on hearsay or man's opinion. Base it on the unshakable and eternal foundation of His Word. My heart's desire is to see you live a glorious and victorious life, not a life entangled with sin, doubt, apprehension, and defeat.

You may have made many mistakes. You may think that it is too late now for God to turn things around for you. You may even think that you deserve to be in the mess you are in and that God has given up on you. My dear friend, those hard thoughts are not God's thoughts about you. His Word proclaims that His thoughts toward you are good:

> "For I know the plans I have for you," says the LORD. "They are plans for good and not for disaster, to give you a future and a hope."
> —Jeremiah 29:11 NLT

God has an amazing plan, purpose, and destiny for your life. Your past need not determine your future. No matter what your story may be, your greatest and best days are ahead of you. I believe that the more you build a rock-solid foundation in your relationship with the Lord Jesus and press in to understand His gracious heart of love and passion toward you, the more you will find security and experience lasting breakthroughs in life.

Your past need not determine your future. No matter what your story may be, your greatest and best days are ahead of you.

In the last few chapters, we focused on how to live with greater confidence and boldness. I centered my teaching on helping you to grow by showing you the importance of knowing beyond any doubt that when you become a believer of Jesus Christ, all your sins are forgiven. Forgiven people are not looking for an excuse to sin. Forgiven people find freedom and liberty from sin by coming to the Savior whenever they fail. Repentance is all about turning to the cross and returning to God's grace, and allowing His words to wash and renew your mind.

Many sincere but depressed people are living in deep remorse and regret over their past mistakes. But instead of running to the Lord, they are running away from Him. They find other ways to numb their pain or escape from it. Why are they doing this? Because they don't understand God's heart of grace. That is why we need to preach His glorious grace with boldness. Precious lives are imprisoned in crushing defeat not because victory isn't available to them, but because they don't know how victory can be theirs!

Let the Gospel Change Your Life

Anyone who says that the preaching of God's grace produces a license to sin probably doesn't fully grasp the power of God's transforming grace. Grace lifts a person who is struggling in sin out of their life of defeat. Grace produces true holiness. By true holiness, I mean holiness that is lasting. Not an outward form of holiness that is transient, but an enduring holiness that is birthed from a transformation that begins in the person's heart. Grace doesn't *condone* sin; it provides lasting freedom *from* sin. How can anyone think that to come under grace is to turn a blind eye to sin, when grace opens our eyes to see that it was our sins that put Jesus on the cross and cost Him His life?

Grace doesn't condone *sin; it provides lasting freedom*
from *sin.*

I have shown you from Scripture after Scripture the Father's heart in forgiving us of our sins. The bold preaching of the gospel of grace from this ministry has resulted in testimony after testimony of many precious lives being set free from sin, from addictions, and from all kinds of religious bondages. The testimonies of the people who have taken the time to share their astonishing breakthroughs attest to the power of God's amazing grace. And I know very well that the only reason these wonderful testimonies flood our ministry office every single week is that the gospel of Jesus Christ is being preached. Grace is not just an academic or theological subject to be pontificated about in a Bible seminary. Grace is the gospel itself and the preaching of the gospel changes lives!

This is what our Lord Jesus Himself proclaimed would happen. When He was in Nazareth, He said, "The Spirit of the LORD is upon Me, because He has anointed Me to preach the gospel to the poor; He has sent Me to heal the brokenhearted, to proclaim liberty to the captives and recovery of sight to the blind, to set at liberty those who are oppressed; to proclaim the acceptable year of the LORD" (Luke 4:18–19).

Listen closely to the words of our Lord. Notice how the Spirit of the Lord and His anointing are upon those who preach the gospel! The word "gospel" is the Greek *euangelion*, which means "good tidings"[1] or good news. Luke 4:18 uses the verb *euangelizoo*, meaning "to bring good news, to announce glad tidings."[2] Now, look at the results when the good news of Jesus is preached: the curse of poverty is destroyed, broken hearts are mended, prisoners and the oppressed are set free, and the sightless receive sight! Through the preaching of God's amazing grace, all these effects are what we are witnessing in our church and ministry. If you are a pastor or minister of God's Word, you can have the same results in your ministry when you preach the good news of Jesus.

The Liberating Truth of Grace

Here is a Scripture that I want you to get deep inside your heart:

> *For the law was given through Moses, but grace and truth came through Jesus Christ.*
>
> —*John 1:17*

The law that was given through Moses refers to the Sinaitic covenant, named after Mount Sinai, where the Ten Commandments were given. So whenever I talk about "the law" I am referring to the Ten Commandments given at Mount Sinai. For starters, let me make this clear: the Sinaitic covenant was a covenant that was made between God and Israel. Just ask any Jewish person. It was not a covenant that was made between God and the church. Our covenant is the new covenant of grace, which began at the cross of our Lord Jesus. Notice in John 1:17 that the Ten Commandments were *given* through a servant, Moses, but that grace and truth *came* through God's own Son, Jesus Christ.

Now, don't let anyone tell you that the "truth" here is the Ten Commandments. The verse is clearly contrasting the Ten Commandments with grace and truth. We see the Mosaic law on one side and grace and truth on the other side. In the verse, we see that truth is on the side of *grace*, not the Ten Commandments. In the original Greek text, the words for "grace" and "truth" are followed by a singular Greek verb for "came,"[3] which means that "grace" and "truth" are regarded as one item. Grace is the *truth* and this truth that sets people free is *grace*! So you cannot separate grace and truth—they are a composite whole. Let me say it again: grace is the truth and the truth is grace. Why is knowing this so important? Because grace, not the law, is the truth that sets you free and transforms you (see John 8:32).

Grace, not the law, is the truth that sets you free and transforms you.

When Jesus said to the woman caught in adultery, "Neither do I condemn you; go and sin no more" (John 8:11), that was grace and truth as a composite whole in action. Grace does not condemn the sinner but it also does not condone the sin. Grace pardons the undeserving sinner and the result of grace is the power to go and sin no more. Isn't that beautiful? That's Who our Lord Jesus is. He loves the sinner and releases him or her with the power and strength to go and sin no more. A person whose heart is full of the love of Jesus doesn't need to find love in an adulterous relationship. All your need for security, affirmation, and love is fully met in the person of Jesus. You don't have to settle for a life trapped in sin when you know that Jesus has such a beautiful and glorious future for you!

The Defeated Life—Trapped in a Cycle of Sin

How do born-again believers, who sincerely want to live holy lives, still end up trapped in a cycle of sin and living a defeated life? I believe that it is because they receive condemnation for their failings, and do not know or believe that God Himself does not condemn them because of the cross of Jesus. Show me someone who lives under constant condemnation and I will show you someone who is always struggling with sin. You see, the more believers live in condemnation, the more they actually become entrenched in a vicious cycle of sin, condemnation, and defeat.

Let me explain what I mean with a simple illustration. Let's say a believer is surfing the Internet one day when he chances upon pornographic images and looks at them longer than he should. Before he knows it, lustful thoughts tumble across his mind. At the same time, since he is a born-again Christian, he starts to feel guilty and condemned. He tells himself, "I shouldn't have looked at the images. I shouldn't be having all these unholy thoughts. Oh, I'm such a lousy Christian. God must be so disappointed with me."

The more he heaps guilt and condemnation on himself, the more he reasons, "What's the point of resisting? I'm a terrible Christian and since I'm already guilty and fellowship with God is broken, I might as well go all the way." What does he do? He clicks on one of the image links, which takes him to a pornographic website, and he indulges his fleshly desires. Now he feels all the more guilty and condemned, and even more convinced that God is angry with him and has distanced Himself from him.

All this guilt and alienation from God just make him more susceptible to fail the next time he faces a similar temptation. There is no power to overcome subsequent temptations, and his indulgences quickly develop into an addiction that imprisons him in perpetual guilt and self-condemnation. He knows he has a problem, but is just too ashamed of his secret sin to approach anyone for help. This is basically how many sincere believers end up trapped in a cycle of sin and condemnation. You can see this represented in the Cycle of Defeat diagram on page 97.

Can you see how the cycle of defeat is perpetuated? Feelings of guilt and condemnation do not empower a believer, no matter how sincere he is, to overcome his sin. In fact, they leave him more weak and vulnerable to the next temptation. The truth is, those who are under constant guilt and condemnation have no strength to overcome temptation, and end up repeating their sins and living a painful life trapped in a cycle of defeat.

In the countless testimonies my ministry has received over the years, many sincere believers shared how guilt, condemnation, and fear of God's judgment only perpetuated their sins and addictions. My friend, if this describes you today, and you are living under a heavy yoke of guilt and condemnation and struggling with sin, your answer is found in the Lord Jesus and His grace. It is when you are under the Lord's grace, not the law, that sin has no dominion over you (see Rom. 6:14). So let Him be your Savior. Don't hide from Him. Come to Him and allow Him to set you free!

The Victorious Life—Breaking the Cycle of Defeat

So how do we go from a place where like the apostle Paul we lament, "I want to do what is good, but I don't. I don't want to do what is wrong, but I do it anyway.... Oh, what a miserable person I am!" (Rom. 7:19, 24 NLT), to a place of lasting victory?

My dear reader, the first step to victory is to realize and believe that because the Lord Jesus has already taken the punishment for all your sins at the cross, you don't have to be bound and driven by guilt, condemnation, or fear. Every failure of yours has already been punished in Jesus' body and *you have perpetual* forgiveness and intimacy with God through Christ's blood! This is the power of right believing in the gospel that will lead you to inside-out transformation and lasting breakthroughs.

So when the next temptation comes, right in the midst of that temptation, believe and say this from your heart: "Therefore *there is now no condemnation* for those who are in Christ Jesus" (Rom. 8:1 NASB, emphasis mine). Instead of believing that you are a failure of a Christian and that God is angry with you, begin to believe in and proclaim His grace. Begin to believe and declare boldly, "I *am* the righteousness of God in Christ Jesus! Because I am in Christ Jesus Who bore all the punishment for my sins, there is therefore now *no* condemnation for me! Fellowship with my heavenly Father is *not* broken and I am *still* His beloved child—highly favored and deeply loved by Him!"

This is exactly how all those people who wrote in to my ministry broke free of their addictions for good. Let me, however, qualify that I am addressing those who *sincerely* want to be free from their addictions, not those who just want to excuse and justify their indulgences and sins.

Why is believing and declaring that you are righteous so important? Because sin cannot take root in you when you are full of the consciousness of your right standing in Christ. The more you are established in God's gift of righteousness, the more you will walk in victory over sin and addiction. The Bible says it like this: "Awake to righteousness and sin not" (1 Cor. 15:34). It is this awakening, in which you freely receive God's abundant grace and gift of righteousness, that empowers you to reign over sin (see Rom. 5:17)!

Look at the Cycle of Victory diagram on the next page and see how, in contrast to the Cycle of Defeat diagram, righteousness-consciousness ultimately propels a believer out of the cycle of sin to increasingly live a life above defeat.

When Temptation
Comes

A Life
of Increasing
Defeat

**Cycle
of
Defeat**

Guilt and
Condemnation

Give In to Sin

Cycle showing the defeated life.

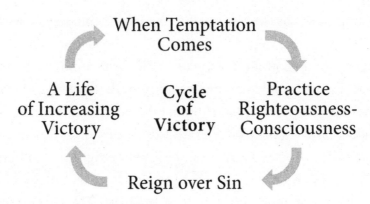

Cycle showing the victorious life.

Beloved, as the gospel of grace continues to be preached, precious folks around the world are breaking out of the cycle of defeat and starting to live in the cycle of victory. In fact, they find that as they grow in the revelation of their forgiveness, righteousness, and no condemnation in Christ, the temptations of the past no longer trigger any desires in them to sin. That's how the apostle Paul came out of his own struggle. He said, "Therefore there is now no condemnation for those who are in Christ Jesus" (Rom. 8:1 NASB). Are you in Christ Jesus? Then there is no condemnation for you, but acceptance from God and His empowerment to be free from sin and defeat.

My dear friend, whatever your struggle today, it is this revelation of no condemnation and awakening to righteousness that will set you free. This is what happened to Neil from the United Kingdom, who wrote to my ministry about his liberation from a forty-year struggle with a sexual addiction:

> *While reading a book by Pastor Prince, I was delivered from a forty-year addiction to pornography. In the past, I had tried to break free from this addiction by my own power and in my own strength, but failed every time.*

Throughout that time, the devil used this addiction to heap fear, guilt, and condemnation on me. This fear and shame kept me from asking for help from the pastors of the various churches I attended over the forty-year period. I had even held leadership positions in some of these places.

Through reading Pastor Prince's book, I got a fresh revelation of who I am in Christ—I am the righteousness of God in Christ Jesus—and how there is no condemnation for those who are in Christ Jesus. It was through this fresh revelation that the grip of this addiction was broken off my life forever.

I now wear a ring on my left middle finger to remind myself that I am righteous, as righteous as Jesus, that there is no condemnation for me because I am in Christ Jesus, and that I am perfect and holy in God's sight. Every time the devil tries to tempt me to view pornography, I just have to look at the ring to remind myself that I am the righteousness of God in Christ, and the temptation loses any hold on me.

Hallelujah! This is what I'm talking about. Beloved, however long you've struggled with a certain temptation or addiction, the same victory Neil had and is still enjoying can be yours today. It's yours when you know what Jesus' finished work has accomplished for you and you receive His gift of no condemnation.

He Has Paid for It All

I preach the gospel of grace because the good news of Jesus changes lives. The Spirit of the Lord and His anointing, favor, and blessings are upon those who preach the gospel. The gospel is the good news that the moment you receive Jesus into your life and make Him your Lord and Savior, all your sins are forgiven and you receive the gift of eternal life. You are justified and made righteous through your faith in Jesus Christ. Your righteousness is a gift from Him. In Christ you have perfect standing before God, paid for by the precious, eternal blood of His Son. There is no more judgment, punishment, and curse for you because the full judgment, punishment, and curse for all your sins fell upon our Lord Jesus at the cross. He paid for it all!

In Christ there is no more judgment, punishment, and curse for you because the full judgment, punishment, and curse for all your sins fell upon our Lord Jesus at the cross.

The Word of God tells us this:

Anyone who belongs to Christ has become a new person. The old life is gone; a new life has begun! And all of this is a gift from God, who brought us back to himself through Christ. And God has given us this task of reconciling people to him. For God was in Christ, reconciling the world to himself, no longer counting people's sins against them. And he gave us this wonderful message of reconciliation. So we are Christ's ambassadors; God is making his appeal through us. We speak for Christ when we plead, "Come back to God!" For God made Christ, who never sinned, to be the offering for our sin, so that we could be made right with God through Christ.

—*2 Corinthians 5:17–21* NLT

The New King James translation of the last verse, verse 21, says, "For He made Him who knew no sin to be sin for us, that we might become the righteousness of God in Him."

I encourage you to read and reread this beautiful passage of Scripture. I highly recommend that you meditate on the verses and feed on them. You will find so much nourishment, joy, and peace from them. Just writing about this causes my heart to be ignited with a new passion to preach the gospel of grace with greater authority and boldness!

Receive God's Power to Live Whole

What does preaching the gospel, the good news of our Lord Jesus Christ, do? The apostle Paul tells us in Romans 1:16 that it releases "the power of God" to bring His salvation into your life. The word "salvation" does not just mean being saved from hell to go to heaven. "Salvation" is the ultra-rich Greek word *soteria*, which means "deliverance, preservation, safety, salvation."[4] It covers any area of your life that needs saving so that you can enjoy wholeness and well-being in your body, soul, and spirit.

Now, where do you find this salvation? In the gospel of Christ. Not in the old covenant of law. It is the gospel of Jesus Christ that unleashes the power of God to save you and make you whole. It is this gospel that brings protection, healing, deliverance, and soundness to every area of your life. It is no wonder the enemy brings opposition to anyone who preaches the gospel of Christ. He doesn't want the power of God to come into people's lives. By the same token, if you want the well-being and wholeness of God to come into your areas of challenge, then make sure you are hearing the gospel of Christ, which is "the gospel of the grace of God" (Acts 20:24).

What Makes the Gospel So Powerful?

But what is it about the gospel of grace that makes it so powerful? We find the answer in Romans 1:17—"For in it the righteousness of God is revealed from faith to faith; as it is written, 'The just shall live by faith.'"

The gospel is so powerful because in it is the revelation that you have been made righteous by the work of Christ, not by your works. This is the glory of the gospel, the good news that when God looks at a man who has put his faith in what Jesus has done, God sees him perfect, complete, and righteous in Christ. It is knowing this that unleashes the power and salvation of God in all its richness into all areas of our lives.

Notice what the apostle Paul said in Romans 1:17—"The just [or righteous] shall live by faith." You cannot walk in faith, talk in faith, or live a life of faith when you don't understand that you have been made righteous by faith. But once you realize that God is not counting your sins against you, because of what Christ has done, peace and joy settle in your heart. Fear flees and hope springs forth. Faith for every blessing Christ purchased for you just erupts in you and activates the power of God to overcome every obstacle in your life!

Once you realize that God is not counting your sins against you, because of what Christ has done, peace and joy settle in your heart.

The Revolution Began with Jesus

Dear reader, I didn't invent the gospel of grace and I certainly didn't start the grace revolution. The grace revolution began with Jesus! He Who never sinned became the offering for our sins so that we who believe in Him can become the righteousness of God in Him. Our Lord Jesus then entrusted the gospel of grace to the apostle Paul.

Now, listen to how Paul describes the gospel of grace: "But I make known to you, brethren, that the gospel which was preached by me is not according to man. For I neither received it from man, nor was I taught it, but it came through the revelation of Jesus Christ" (Gal. 1:11–12).

Paul received the gospel directly from our Lord Jesus. And everything I preach today about the gospel of grace is based entirely on what Paul first preached. The gospel *is* God "reconciling the world to himself, no longer counting people's sins against them" (2 Cor. 5:19 NLT). Isn't that what we have been establishing in this book?

Come Back to God

How necessary it is to have a confident assurance that all your sins have been forgiven! Old covenant prophets bring your sins to remembrance (see 1 Kings 17:18), but new covenant ministries bring Jesus' forgiveness to your remembrance (see Luke 24:47). The ministry that God has placed in our hands is the ministry of reconciliation! Today we are God's ambassadors of grace. We are called to proclaim with boldness the gospel of grace from the rooftops of the world. This is the message we are proclaiming to the world: "Come back to God! God is not angry with you. Come back to a Father Who loves you and gave up His beloved Son to ransom you from all your sins." This is the good news!

God is not angry with you. Come back to a Father Who loves you and gave up His beloved Son to ransom you from all your sins. This is the good news!

And to the believer bound in religious legalism and condemnation, we also preach, "Come back to God!" No more hiding in fear, no more struggling with sin, no more living in dread of punishment and the curse descending on you, and no more pretenses of self-righteousness. Come boldly to the throne of grace and receive from God all the help, peace, healing, joy, deliverance, and saving you need (see Heb. 4:16).

My friend, whatever you may be struggling with today, come back to the Father's loving embrace and grace. He loves you. Receive the good news that you are a new creation in Christ; old things are gone. You have been reconciled to God through Christ's perfect work at the cross. You are righteous in God's sight (even when you fail) and are empowered to overcome every failing through His gift of no condemnation. Let this good news of our Lord Jesus take hold in your heart. And in your every area of challenge, you will begin to experience lasting victory and a multiplication of His grace and peace in your life.

CHAPTER 7

WILL THE REAL GOSPEL PLEASE STAND UP?

A life that is founded upon the gospel of Jesus Christ is unshakable. When you build your life upon the gospel, you are building on a strong foundation that will give you stability and the power of God for lasting breakthroughs (see Rom. 1:16).

A life that is founded upon the gospel of Jesus Christ is unshakable.

You may be going through an extremely difficult season right now. Perhaps you have just received a negative medical report, or maybe you are surrounded by some challenging circumstances at your place of employment. I want to encourage you to say this by faith: "I am too blessed to be stressed." Now invite our Lord Jesus into your situation. Involve Him in your area of need. Whether it is a healing, provision, or relationship breakthrough that you need, see and believe that the Lord is with you.

My dear friend, don't put your trust in your own understanding. Instead lean wholly on the one Who is more interested in your success than you are. The book of Proverbs tells us, "The name of the LORD is a strong tower; the righteous run to it and are safe" (Prov. 18:10). Run to Him and cast all your cares upon Him, for He cares for you. I speak this promise of God into your situation right now: " 'No weapon formed against you shall prosper, and every tongue which rises against you in judgment you shall condemn. This is the heritage of the servants of the LORD, and their righteousness is from Me,' says the LORD" (Isa. 54:17). Amen and Amen! Meditate on the last line of this powerful Scripture. In the new covenant of grace, your righteousness is from the Lord Jesus Himself. Now, the more you understand your righteousness in Christ, the more you will experience His promise in Isaiah 54:17.

The opposite holds true. When God's people are not established in their righteous identity in Christ, they become susceptible to the weapons of the enemy. Weapons like sickness, lack, guilt, condemnation, fear, depression, and all kinds of disorders and addictions. That is why it is so important to be sure that you are listening to the real gospel. God's Word proclaims that none of these weapons, even if they have already been formed, shall prevail against you. And every unfounded accusation, every malicious lie, and every false allegation you shall condemn! The enemy doesn't have a hold over your life. God does, and He holds it together.

When God's people are not established in their righteous identity in Christ, they become susceptible to the weapons of the enemy.

A New Generation Sounding the Ram's Horn

I see a new generation of God's people emerging as the grace revolution sweeps the globe. As the word of His grace is preached around the world today, I see more and more believers, many of them dynamic church leaders, leaving the old covenant of law and embracing fully the new covenant of grace. They are realizing that only grace, found in the person of Jesus Christ, can lead them into the promised land.

The truth is that Moses, who represents the law, is dead (see Josh. 1:2). And only Joshua (*Yehowshua* in Hebrew), a type of Christ, can bring us into the promised land. We can't enter it based on the obsolete Mosaic covenant. We can't inherit it based on our efforts to be justified through keeping perfectly the Ten Commandments. We can inherit it only through faith in the grace of our Lord Jesus. It is not by our works that we inherit God's promises, but by Christ's perfect, finished work.

How did the wall of Jericho that stood between God's people and the promised land come crashing down? Did God's people have to use their own might to push down the wall? Did they have to fight an army? No, at just the blast of the rams' horns and a great shout, God caused the wall to crumble. The ram's horn is a beautiful picture of the death of our Lord Jesus. The ram had to die for the horn to be obtained. The sounding of the ram's horn is thus a proclamation of our Lord's death and finished work. At the cross, when Jesus had paid fully for all our sins with His blood, He proclaimed, "It is finished!" (John 19:30).

The walls of Jericho falling at the sounding of the rams' horns.

Freedom through Jesus' Blood

It is the shed blood of Jesus that brings us out of captivity and into the promised land. What the ten plagues of Moses could not do, the blood of Jesus did. It was the blood of Christ, typified by the lambs' blood applied to the lintels and doorposts of the Hebrew homes, that caused Pharaoh, a type of Satan, to finally release God's people. God threw down His trump card—the blood of His Son! So it was His Son, the true Lamb of God, Who brought them out of Egypt, and it was also His Son Who brought them into the promised land. It is all Christ and Christ alone!

Why couldn't the miracles of Moses free God's people? Because they were miracles of judgment. Judgment and condemnation will not free you. Only the love and grace of our Lord Jesus, Who shed His blood at Calvary for you, can do that. My friend, are you hearing about the judgments of the law today, or are you hearing the ram's horn being blown? One condemns and brings death, the other liberates and gives life. One causes you to remain in bondage to sin and live a defeated life, the other empowers you to break free and reign in life. Make sure you are hearing the true gospel today!

Judgment and condemnation will not free you. Only the love and grace of our Lord Jesus, Who shed His blood at Calvary for you, can do that.

I am so glad I am seeing a new generation of people who are sounding the ram's horn. They have moved their pulpits from Mount Sinai to Mount Zion, and are now preaching the unadulterated gospel of grace of our Lord and His finished work. The result? Countless lives are being set free from Satan's grip and ushered into their promised land! Pastors and leaders, I encourage you to blow the ram's horn in your preaching and teaching! Proclaim with boldness the finished work of our Lord Jesus. Every Sunday at the pulpit, that is what I endeavor to do. That is what makes bondages and addictions crumble, as the walls of Jericho did, and fall away from people's lives.

The Crux of the Real Gospel

So what is the gospel? How do we know if we are hearing the real gospel? What sets the true gospel apart from every other "gospel"?

To answer this question, let's go to the book of Jude. Apostle Jude tells us to "contend earnestly for the faith which was once for all delivered to the saints" (Jude 1:3). What is "the faith" here that the church is to contend earnestly for? My dear reader, when you hear the word *faith* mentioned in the New Testament, it refers to "justification by faith"—how one is made righteous before God based solely on his faith in Christ Jesus. This is the crux of the gospel of Jesus Christ. This is what sets it apart from all the false gospels.

Unfortunately, there are believers today who are departing from this core, defining truth of the gospel. If you hear them teach the Bible, you will find that justification by faith is not their emphasis or priority. They see it as elementary, as basic, as something that believers need to move on from in order to grow in their Christian walk. For them it is just not the crux of the gospel.

What they prefer to preach and teach is doing right or living right. You'll hear about all sorts of things that you need to do for God in order to live right. You'll hardly hear anything about how you are justified or made righteous by faith in Christ. Now, I'm not against right living, but that is *not* the gospel. Right living is certainly important, but it comes by believing right. When you believe right, you will live right.

Right living comes by believing right.

The crux of the gospel is not right living or good works, but justification by faith. And the apostle Jude tells us to contend earnestly for this. We are told not just to contend for this, but to *contend earnestly*. That term is translated from one Greek word, *epagonizomai*,[1] from which the English word *agony* is derived. In other words, *epagonizomai* literally means "to agonize for." We are to *agonize* for the faith! We are to fight for the truth that we are justified by faith and not works. This is the real gospel. This is the good news.

Justified and Blessed by Faith in Christ

Sadly, what you hear today is hardly good news, because justification by faith has been subtly replaced with justification by works. Yes, they may tell you that you are saved by grace through faith, but then in the same breath, they corrupt the simplicity of the gospel by saying that you stay saved or get blessed through works. If you go to the streets and ask Christians today what justifies them and releases God's blessings into their lives, most of them will tell you, "Obeying God's laws and living a good life." Rarely will you hear, "I'm justified and blessed by faith in Christ."

But what does the Bible actually say about the gospel we are to preach? The answer is found in Romans 1:17—"For in it the righteousness of God is revealed from faith to faith; as it is written, 'The just shall live by faith.'" What is supposed to be revealed in this gospel? Not our sins, but the righteousness of God! Have you been hearing fire-and-brimstone preaching that focuses on your sins, or have you been hearing preaching that shows you that you are the righteousness of God through faith in Christ? Only hearing about the grace of God and how you are righteous by faith in Christ will set you free from your struggle with sin, addiction, and bondage.

How to Live from Faith to Faith

Romans 1:17 tells us that this righteousness of God that we have in Christ is revealed from "faith to faith" and that the just "shall live by faith." Can you see this powerful truth? It's not this idea that once you are saved by grace through faith, you move on to works and watch your performance to maintain your salvation. Many Christians experience abundant joy when they are saved, only to lose that joy quickly when they are told, "Now that you're saved, you need to work to please God in order to stay saved."

These sincere believers try their best to do this, only to feel discouraged and condemned when they fail time and again. Because of hearing a perverted gospel, they are not going from faith to faith, but from faith to works. No, my friend, it's from faith to faith to faith to faith... all the way until we see Jesus face-to-face!

This doesn't mean that there is no place for good works or living a holy life. These are by-products of living from faith to faith. They will be evident in your life when you live believing that you are justified, made righteous, and blessed through faith in Christ.

I love how the New Living Translation puts it: "This Good News tells us how God makes us right in his sight. This is accomplished from start to finish by faith" (Rom. 1:17 NLT).

So if someone comes to you and tells you that they are preaching the gospel, don't just swallow everything, hook, line, and sinker. Discern for yourself if what you are hearing about righteousness is accomplished from start to finish by faith in our Lord Jesus Christ.

The True Gospel Makes All the Difference

Let me share with you a testimony that demonstrates how hearing the true gospel can make all the difference to your life. It comes from Sally, who lives in New Jersey. She wrote:

I used to listen to teaching that contained a mixture of condemnation and grace. The longer I stayed under that teaching, the more condemned I felt. It came to a point where I was so afraid that I prayed to God to get me out of the grip of condemnation.

The Lord miraculously gave my husband an outrageously generous, out-of-this-world job offer in the United States (US). So my husband and I moved from Hong Kong all the way to the US.

Although I stopped listening to those legalistic messages, I remained severely depressed for a long time. The voice of condemnation did not stop. Whenever I thought about it, tears would run down my face for hours. The stress was too much to bear. I couldn't find comfort in reading the Bible because I would remember the way the Scriptures were taught to me—always condemning, fault-finding, and accusatory. I prayed to God for a way out.

One day, as I was surfing the Internet to do some research for my music assignment, I came upon the word JUSTIFIED. The passage I was reading had nothing to do with faith but yet, the word stirred something inside me and immediately, I was crying nonstop. I started to have this little argument with God: "I don't believe You. Don't tell me that I'm justified. This is not what my previous church told me. They said that I have to obey to perfection in order to be justified!"

I continued crying until I was tired out and then, in the silence following, I heard the word justified spoken to me softly yet very affirmatively in my spirit. I didn't argue anymore but just accepted it, even though I still didn't understand what God seemed to be saying to me.

I asked the Lord to reveal to me what was going on and shortly after that incident, I stumbled upon Pastor Joseph Prince's preaching on YouTube. At that time, I didn't know him and I have no idea how I ended up clicking on his sermon. Just as I was about to click away, I heard Pastor Prince speaking on the subject of justification! My goodness! The Lord was revealing the answer to my prayer so I listened on.

In his message, Pastor Prince explained how the lamb was used as a sacrifice in ancient Israel to justify those who broke the law. I was crying as I heard it. I finally understood, without a doubt, that I am justified by the blood of the Lamb of God, Christ—even though I am still not perfect in my conduct!

My life changed so dramatically after that episode. I began to watch all of Pastor Prince's sermons on whatever media they were made available because the Spirit in me kept bearing witness that all that he was preaching is truth.

Now, the Bible has become so dear to me. Every time I read it, I get revelation after revelation of God's grace and loving-kindness. The fulfillment that comes from reading and hearing His Word is so satisfying.

Experiencing Wholeness through Seeing Jesus' Beauty

Sally's blessings didn't stop there. She goes on to share the following:

The years of living under condemnation had caused me to age very quickly. But I am now looking more and more youthful and energetic. I've learned to rest in Jesus and the pain and discomfort I was feeling all over my body disappeared without me realizing it. Pastor Prince's preaching of Jesus and His loveliness has caused me to focus on the Lord Himself. I became so preoccupied, so captivated by His beauty that I forgot about the pain, and the pain left on its own.

Since I started to pursue His righteousness instead of mine, I'm also always at the right place at the right time to experience miracles. They are too many for me to include here but they range from big issues like buying and selling our house and finding a new job, to small, trivial matters like getting our cat temporary lodging during our move. It no longer matters whether we are able to do everything the right way as all things work together for our benefit. We always end up getting the best price, best house, best job offer—the best of everything beyond our imagination, all of which we do not deserve.

It is just amazing to live a life under the abundance of His grace and gift of righteousness! I want to thank Pastor Prince for expounding on the beauty of Christ and the perfection of His finished work. It is the knowledge of Jesus Himself that lifted me out of deep depression and despair onto a path of joy, peace, and hope. It's the best thing that has ever happened in my life!

Thank you, Sally, for sharing your wonderful testimony. I rejoice with you and have no doubt your story will encourage many people and set them on the road to freedom.

My dear friend, if you are experiencing the condemnation and misery that Sally experienced, hear these precious, reassuring words from your heavenly Father: "You are JUSTIFIED through faith in My Son's sacrifice." Be set free from the voice of condemnation and, like Sally, begin to live life full of joy, peace, and hope!

God's Power for Lasting Breakthroughs

It is so important you hear the right gospel—the one that tells you that you are forgiven and justified by faith—because the gospel is the power of God unto salvation. Let's look again at this vital truth that the apostle Paul taught to the early church:

> *For I am not ashamed of the gospel of Christ, for it is the power of God unto salvation to everyone that believeth; to the Jew first, and also to the Greek.*
> —*Romans 1:16 KJV*

As we established in the previous chapter, "salvation," besides the wonderful blessing of being saved from hell to go to heaven, also encompasses whatever deliverance, preservation, and safety you need in the here and now.

What do you need saving from today? Are you suffering from a debilitating sickness? Are you in the grip of anxiety, panic attacks, or deep depression that keeps you imprisoned at home? Perhaps you feel the heavy burden of guilt and condemnation because of a long-term addiction. My friend, I am here to tell you that your deliverance, your preservation, your answer is found in the gospel of Jesus Christ—*the* power of God unto your salvation.

Your deliverance, your preservation, your answer is found in the gospel of Jesus Christ—the power of God unto your salvation.

The gospel of our Lord's grace is what will free you and keep you free. The Bible doesn't say that medicine, psychology, money, or the Internet is the power of God unto your salvation. These are good and have their place, but they are not the power of God that frees you and gives you lasting breakthroughs. Only the true, unadulterated gospel of His grace can accomplish that.

So whatever your challenge, don't give up, dear reader. God knows exactly what you are going through. He cares for you and wants you free in every area of your life. That is why He has placed this book in your hands. Just keep reading. Just keep hearing the true gospel that reveals to you your total forgiveness, your everlasting righteousness or justification in Christ, and His unconditional love for you. And I have no doubt that God's power will break those chains and open those prison doors for you!

Don't Let Your Zeal Be Misdirected

The devil is a cunning adversary. He gets people to depart from the simplicity of the gospel into works because he knows that many believers are sincere in wanting to please God. He knows that they have an enthusiasm or zeal for God. But he also knows that man has something called pride. So what does he do? He takes advantage of their pride and misdirects their zeal by using the law. He tells them, "You want to get right with God and please Him? Then here are His laws to obey and obey perfectly." In the book of Romans, Paul talks about this misguided zeal, which was prevalent among his Jewish brethren:

> *Dear brothers and sisters, the longing of my heart and my prayer to God is for the people of Israel to be saved. I know what enthusiasm they have for God, but it is misdirected zeal. For they don't understand God's way of making people right with himself. Refusing to accept God's way, they cling to their own way of getting right with God by trying to keep the law.*
>
> —*Romans 10:1–3* NLT

The same thing is still happening today. Many believers, in their zeal for God or their pride, are trying to please God and become righteous through trying to keep the law. They don't understand that God makes an individual righteous solely by grace through faith. They reject God's way and cling to what they think makes them righteous—their obedience to God's laws.

Yet the irony of it all is that in trying to keep God's laws to be righteous, people produce works of the flesh such as adultery, fornication, hatred, heresies, and drunkenness (see Gal. 5:18–21). Why? Because "the strength of sin is the law" (1 Cor. 15:56). The law arouses or stirs up the sinful passions within our flesh (see Rom. 7:5).

We see a classic example of this truth being played out in the Old Testament. At Mount Sinai, when God's people presumed that they could be righteous before God by obeying His laws (see Exod. 19:8, 24:3), it produced a work of the flesh. They built a golden calf and worshiped it, breaking God's very first commandment not to have any other god (Exod. 32:1–8). In the New Testament, we have the case of Paul. He said, "I would not have known sin except through the law. For I would not have known covetousness unless the law had said, 'You shall not covet'" (Rom. 7:7).

My friend, this is the result of coming under the law and trying to obey God's laws to be made righteous. Works of the flesh are produced, as opposed to the fruit of the Spirit.

Grace Produces Fruitfulness

Galatians 5:22–23 lists the fruit of the Spirit as "love, joy, peace, long-suffering, kindness, goodness, faithfulness, gentleness, self-control." Notice that Paul mentions the fruit of the Spirit only in the fifth chapter. In the first four chapters he talks about grace, contrasting it with the law and contending earnestly for justification by faith, because the Galatian Christians were going back under the law. Paul was essentially bringing them back under pure grace, before talking to them about the fruit of the Spirit.

Can you see how the fruit of being under grace is the fruit of the Spirit? Notice also how Paul calls it the *works* of the flesh and the *fruit* of the Spirit. What's the difference between "works" and "fruit"? Works are a result of *self-effort* that comes from being under the heavy demands of the law. *Fruit* is a result of life! Just as a tree will naturally produce good fruit when it is well watered and receiving the right amount of sunlight, so a Christian will produce good fruit without self-effort when he or she is well watered by the word of His grace and exposed to the sunshine of God's love.

Beloved, if you want to exhibit the fruit of the Spirit, make sure you are not hearing the law preached, but the unadulterated grace of our Lord Jesus. Make sure you are hearing the ram's horn being sounded from the pulpit to remind you that you are justified by faith in the Lamb Who died for you. This will help you to build your life upon the solid Rock of Christ and the firm foundation of His finished work. Contend earnestly to hear and to live by the real gospel, by grace through faith. It will usher you into the promised land, for the gospel is the power of God unto your salvation in every area of your life.

CHAPTER 8

FREEDOM FROM SELF-CONDEMNATION

Cruel words spoken in anger. A betrayal of trust. Promises broken. A destructive relationship you knew you should not have entered into.

Have you been down those dark paths before? So many people are living in the shadow of guilt and condemnation. The mistakes of their past haunt them and it is a painfully lonely and arduous journey for them.

Perhaps the paralyzed man who was let down through the roof by his four faithful friends in the book of Mark understood a little of this. The Bible tells us he was paralyzed to the point where he could only lie on a mat, which was how his friends carried him to the house Jesus was in. With the man lying inert on his mat, his four friends lowered him through the roof, right in front of Jesus—the only way they knew to bring their crippled friend before Jesus and secure his healing. Scripture tells us that when Jesus saw their faith, He said to the paralytic, "Son, your sins are forgiven you" (Mark 2:5).

To all who were watching this scene unfold that day, that must have been a very strange thing for Jesus to say—"your sins are forgiven you." The man was clearly paralyzed. He was obviously there for healing. What had forgiveness to do with his condition or healing?

But Jesus knew it was exactly what this poor man needed to hear for his healing to manifest. And indeed, at Jesus' next words, "Stand up, pick up your mat, and go home," the paralyzed man "jumped up, grabbed his mat, and walked out through the stunned onlookers" (Mark 2:11–12 NLT). What had transpired? Jesus saw, when no one else could, that the man needed to hear he was forgiven, that God was not condemning him. And those words opened the door to his healing and broke him loose from his paralysis. No wonder the onlookers were stunned—the man went from being immobile and helpless to being active, strong, and completely whole right before their eyes!

My beloved friend, if you are paralyzed by a heavy sense of condemnation over something in your past, I want you to know beyond any doubt that God is not withholding your breakthrough from you. He loves you, understands your pain and suffering, and has forgiven you through the cross. He wants you to know that your past does not have to poison your future. God has amazing plans for your future. No matter how many dark days you have experienced, your brightest and most glorious days are still ahead of you.

Your past does not have to poison your future. God has amazing plans for you.

And this is why I am so sure: the living Word of God declares, "Eye has not seen, nor ear heard, nor have entered into the heart of man the things which God has prepared for those who love Him" (1 Cor. 2:9). This means that God has prepared many wonderful open doors of opportunity, favor, and success for you to walk through in the days ahead.

So Clean, God's Spirit Lives in You

The Scripture goes on to say that even though you may not be able to see right now the good things that God has for your future, "God has revealed them to us through His Spirit.... Now we have received, not the spirit of the world, but the Spirit who is from God, that we might know the things that have been freely given to us by God" (1 Cor. 2:10, 12). Isn't that just the best news? The Holy Spirit is in us to reveal to us the things that God has freely given to us. These are precious and priceless gifts, such as the gift of forgiveness, the gift of no condemnation, the gift of righteousness, the gift of eternal life, and the different gifts of the Spirit that God has placed in all our lives!

Because you are a believer in Jesus Christ, not only have all your sins been forgiven, but you have also been justified by faith and made righteous by His blood. And the Holy Spirit lives *in* you! You have something that the patriarchs of the Old Testament never had. Abraham, "the friend of God" (James 2:23), never had it. Moses, who led the children of Israel out of Egypt, never had it. And even David, whom the Bible calls "a man after [God's] own heart" (Acts 13:22), never had it. They had the Spirit *on* them, but not *in* them. Back then the Holy Spirit would come and go (see 1 Sam. 16:13–14, Ps. 51:11). You and I, however, have been so perfectly cleansed by the blood of Jesus—once and for all—that the Holy Spirit now lives *in* us and abides with us *forever* (see John 14:16–17)!

Because you are a believer in Jesus Christ, not only have all your sins been forgiven, but you have also been justified by faith and made righteous by His blood.

The apostle Paul tells us that when we believed in Jesus, He identified us as His own by giving us the Holy Spirit. The Holy Spirit is God's guarantee that He will give us the inheritance He has promised and that He has purchased us to be His own people (see Eph. 1:13–14). My friend, when you believed the gospel and got saved, you were sealed with the Holy Spirit of promise. The Holy Spirit is God's seal upon your life to attest that you have been given the free gift of righteousness and the gift of eternal life through Jesus' finished work. That is why when you hear the purity of the gospel of grace being preached, the Holy Spirit in you responds with great joy and great peace.

Feeling Born Again, All Over Again

I have received so many testimonies from people who shared that when they first heard me preaching on the love of God and His beautiful grace, they felt as if they were getting born again, all over again. When they heard the gospel being preached, the shackles of Christian religion, legalism, self-righteousness, and years of toilsome condemnation started to break off one by one. Precious intimacy with the Lord Jesus was restored. Fear was replaced with His perfect love, insecurities with His assurance of grace, and self-doubt with His strong embrace of affirmation. That's what the preaching of the gospel of grace does. It changes lives!

Listen to this praise report by Pete from Oklahoma, who shares,

> *When I heard one of Pastor Joseph Prince's sermons for the first time, I knew that this message of grace was what I'd been seeking my entire Christian life. I felt like I was born again, all over again!*

Since then, I've been listening to and feeding on the word of grace daily. I think I cried every day as the understanding that all of my sins are forgiven began to sink in. My faith has shot through the ceiling and my life has been radically transformed!

My wife and my four kids have also been listening to Pastor Prince's sermons and we are forever "ruined" by this incredible message of grace. This truth has borne fruit in our lives and caused us to be blessed beyond anything we could ever think of!

Grace—the Final Jigsaw Piece

Let me share another precious testimony, from Daphne from the United Kingdom. I have no doubt you will be greatly blessed by it:

I am a recovered alcoholic who received Jesus Christ five years ago. At that time, even after being saved, I was still full of self-condemnation and found it hard to believe that Jesus really cared about me. I thought He was very angry with me and that I needed to try to be good. For us alcoholics who have been very ill with addiction, this self-condemnation and the belief that we are never going to be able to do what God expects of us often send us back to drink, develop an addiction to drugs, and even die as a result of complications.

But when I heard Pastor Joseph Prince preach on television, suddenly, the final jigsaw piece fell into place. It was the first time I had heard about God's grace. After that, I bought and read Pastor Prince's books. Grace and truth in the

*person of Jesus came and made all the difference. The changes
happened in me once I understood and believed that everything had already been done for me at the cross, and that Jesus
wanted to heal me and pour His grace into my life.*

Helping Others Experience Lasting Sobriety

Today Daphne sponsors many alcoholic women through a twelve-
step recovery program and even runs a retreat for them. But she runs
the program "with God's grace at the forefront so that it is not a legalistic program." She says,

*When I help the women begin their journey with the program,
I give them my copies of Pastor Prince's books to read. I also
show them clips of Pastor Prince's messages.*

*These women now have a much better chance at lasting
freedom. Before receiving the message of grace, they had the
same wrong beliefs I had. Like me, they believed that they
could never live up to what an angry God of judgment expects
of them. Without right believing about the true God and His
grace, lasting sobriety is just not possible for any of us and we
would all have gone back to drinking.*

*Since listening to the gospel of grace, I now believe that the
Lord wants to help us all because He loves each one of us. I
love seeing people recover from their addictions. It's His grace
alone that has given my friends and me true freedom. I have
also been able to forgive others and myself.*

Seeing Restoration in Relationships

Not only did Daphne experience the above breakthroughs, but her relationship with her only son was also restored. It actually began when she was hospitalized for an infection in her gallbladder. She shares the following:

> *I thank Jesus that I was admitted on time, or I would have lost my life. It was a long illness because the doctors could not operate to remove my gallbladder until the infection subsided two months later.*
>
> *Looking back, I now see how good God was because during the period of waiting for my operation, my thirty-one-year-old son came from the other end of England to look after me. Our relationship, which had been so damaged due to my alcoholism, was rebuilt during that period. While he was caring for me, my son also gave up his use of drugs without me having to say anything! My son could see the change in me and I believe the Lord is ministering to my only son—he has opened up to the fact that there could be a loving being (God) out there Who wants to look after us.*
>
> *By believing right in the Lord's grace, I have experienced massive healing in my body and my family in a way I never thought possible. I am seeing more miracles around me. The Holy Spirit is healing and teaching others through me—I see more people no longer drinking and indulging in other addictions after finding freedom in Jesus and His grace. There are so many girls aged twenty to sixty who are learning the true meaning of grace. Jesus loves us all so much!*

Thank you, Daphne, for taking the time to share your powerful story. I agree with you 100 percent. When these precious girls, or others with addictions, experience true grace, they will find freedom from condemnation and their crippling bondages.

A Dangerous and Vicious Trap

Can you see from Daphne's story how it is so vital that you believe in God's love for you? Because of His superabundant grace, your past doesn't have to determine your future. In Christ you have a new life, a new beginning, and a new future. What God did for Daphne, He can and wants to do for you too.

In Christ you have a new life, a new beginning, and a new future.

So don't allow self-condemnation to get the better of you. It's a dangerous and vicious trap. Listen to how Daphne describes the dangers of this trap: "For us alcoholics who have been very ill with addiction, this self-condemnation and the belief that we are never going to be able to do what God expects of us often send us back to drink, develop an addiction to drugs, and even die as a result of complications."

Condemnation kills! Whatever addiction you may be battling today, condemnation will keep you enslaved to it. Condemnation is a snare that keeps you imprisoned. It eats at you from the inside out.

Self-Condemnation Can't Be Willed Away

You can't just will away self-condemnation. You can't just tell yourself to forget about the mistakes and bad choices you have made. You can try your best to forget about your past, but it will always creep back to haunt you. Been there before? Our sins demand an answer. They demand a resolution. They can't simply be swept under the carpet.

The Bible tells us that the soul who sins shall die (see Ezek. 18:20) and that the wages of sin is death (see Rom. 6:23). Our conscience cries out against us and demands that punishment for our sins be meted out. That is why you need to have an unshakable revelation of your righteous identity in Christ. At the cross Jesus took your place of punishment and condemnation and became the full payment for all your sins. And when you believed in Jesus, you were justified by faith! The cross of Calvary has made all the difference. It's the only answer that will satisfy your guilty conscience.

The cross of Calvary has made all the difference. It's the only answer that will satisfy your guilty conscience.

The Foundation for Lasting Breakthroughs

Now—and this is an important question—what does this justification by faith produce? Look at Daphne's testimony. When she received the gospel of grace, she shared that "changes happened in me once I understood and believed that everything had already been done for me at the cross, and that Jesus wanted to heal me and pour His grace into my life." When did change and freedom happen for her? The moment she understood the power of the finished work of Jesus Christ our Lord and how she is totally justified by faith. The cross, my dear reader, is the foundation for lasting breakthroughs and genuine inside-out transformation!

The cross is the foundation for lasting breakthroughs and genuine inside-out transformation!

I submit to you that many people are unable to experience lasting freedom from their fears, addictions, and bondages because they don't yet understand the gospel of grace. You can evaluate how well you understand what Jesus accomplished at the cross for you by looking at how free you are in Christ today. Are you constantly struggling with thoughts of fear, doubt, guilt, and condemnation? Are you persistently entangled in a sinful habit or addiction?

If that is you, you need to experience what Daphne experienced. You need to study, meditate upon, and feed on the gospel of grace. Don't back away from grace; be strong in the grace of God extended to you. Be strong in understanding that your sins are forgiven. Be strong in the knowledge that you are justified by faith through grace. Be strong in the revelation that today, you are the righteousness of God in Christ.

When you are strong in the gospel of grace, you will produce a godly, holy, and glorious life! In the same way that you can't touch water and not become wet, you can't "touch" grace and not become holy. And this holiness is a true holiness that comes from the inside out. It is a holiness that flows from a heart that has been emancipated from self-condemnation. We are not talking about superficial outward changes. We are talking about changes that happen in the deepest recesses of a person's heart, motivations, and thoughts. Real change in a person whose heart is washed by the precious blood of Jesus and touched by His grace brings lasting breakthroughs.

In the same way that you can't touch water and not become wet, you can't touch grace and not become holy.

When Daphne received the revelation of the gospel of grace and learned that all her sins are forgiven, did it result in her feeling that she now had a license to sin more? Did it produce a desire to go back to being an alcoholic? Of course not. True grace doesn't produce a license or desire to sin. True grace produces the power to sin no more. True grace doesn't produce the desire for adultery. True grace produces the desire to build a strong marriage.

Grace produced in Daphne lasting freedom from alcoholism and self-condemnation, but it didn't stop there. It also produced in her a desire to help other precious ladies who are struggling with alcoholism and condemnation. In other words, her faith produced good works. You must understand that she doesn't *have* to volunteer her time to help these women. She doesn't have to, but she *wants* to. That's what grace does in a person's life. It transforms the person from the inside out. Grace makes a person gracious, kind, and generous. The gift of righteousness in you will produce fruits of righteousness.

But Aren't We Justified by Our Works?

I have been establishing over the last few chapters the good news that you have been justified by faith in our Lord Jesus, because it not only frees you from self-condemnation and bondages, but also produces true holiness and good works in your life.

The good news that you have been justified by faith in our Lord Jesus produces true holiness and good works in your life.

But Pastor Prince, what about the book of James, which says that one is justified by works and not just faith?

That's an excellent question and I am going to answer it here for you. It's important that believers understand what James means, or they will fall back into trying to be justified by works and end up in self-condemnation when they fall short.

I believe you are referring to this Scripture from James: "You see then that a man is justified by works, and not by faith only" (James 2:24). Now, I believe that there is no contradiction between what James says and what the apostle Paul teaches. What many people don't realize is that what James is referring to here is *justification before men*.

Jesus said, "Let your light so shine *before men*, that they may see your good works and glorify your Father in heaven" (Matt. 5:16, emphasis mine). Who sees your good works? Men. James said, "If a brother or sister is naked and destitute of daily food, and one of you says to them, 'Depart in peace, be warmed and filled,' but you do not give them the things which are needed for the body, what does it profit? Thus also faith by itself, if it does not have works, is dead" (James 2:15–17). Notice how the good work of giving to the needy is done before men and to men?

You see, people can't see with their physical eyes that you have been justified by faith. They can't see that God has made you righteous.

They condemn or justify you based on what you do. You may tell your friends, "God has justified me and made me righteous through faith in Christ," but they are not necessarily going to believe you or give weight to your words until they see your good works. In her testimony, Daphne described how her son could see the change in her, which in turn prompted him to be more open to the Lord and give up his use of drugs. Not only was Daphne finally sober, but she was also joyful and forgiving, and on top of that, she was dedicating her life to helping other women break free from alcoholism and drugs. Her good works justified her in her son's eyes.

How Good Works and Good Fruit Really Come

The problem with the church today is that we are focusing on works. We want to see good works and we want to see them *now*! No wonder so many new believers end up in self-condemnation when they can't meet the expectations, and give up on church.

How often have we expected new converts to produce good fruit overnight? The moment they are saved, we expect them to stop cussing immediately and to use all the right words. Or we expect them to stop smoking or drinking right away, and to quickly begin reading the Bible and praying an hour each day. It's like the little boy whose father expects him to grow a beard overnight—"Where's your beard, boy!" And try as he may, the poor boy can't grow a beard. But given time, just because he is his father's son, he will grow a beard. And he will have this beard that keeps growing for the rest of his life no matter how many times he shaves it!

The truth is that once a person has been born again, once God has justified him based on his faith in Christ, good works will follow because he knows how much he is forgiven and loved by God. That forgiveness and love experienced will overflow to others (see 1 John 4:19 NLT). It may not happen right away, but the grace that God has placed in him will one day produce good fruit in his life (see 2 Cor. 9:8). That's why I preach grace so strongly. Grace is the cause; good works are the effect. Focus on the cause and the effects will eventually come.

Pastors and leaders, I encourage you to establish your people in the grace of God. Help them grow well in that grace and the good works *will* come. For some the good works may come quickly; for others they may take a little longer, but the good works will come as your people grow in grace through the knowledge of our Lord Jesus (see 2 Pet. 1:2). We have to be patient and give people time to grow. Let God do His deep, lasting work in them. Our part is to keep pointing them to Jesus.

We have to be patient and give people time to grow. Let God do His deep, lasting work in them. Our part is to keep pointing them to Jesus.

Give People Time to Produce Good Works

Let's look at the two examples of good works that James gives: "Was not Abraham our father justified by works when he offered Isaac his son on the altar? ... Likewise, was not Rahab the harlot also justified by works when she received the messengers and sent them out another way?" (James 2:21, 25).

James cites Abraham's offering of Isaac and Rahab's assistance to the two Israelite spies as their good works. Christians like to quote these examples and say, "So where are your good works? Don't you know that faith without works is dead?" What they don't realize is that between the justification of these two Bible characters and their good works is a *long* time!

Isaac was around seventeen years old when Abraham offered him on Mount Moriah. Some believe that he was older—around thirty years old. Even if we take the younger age, that's still more than seventeen years between Abraham's justification and the manifestation of his good work. And we expect new believers to exhibit good works overnight!

Abraham was justified by faith even before Isaac was born. In the book of Genesis, we see how God brought Abraham outside and said, "Look now toward heaven, and count the stars if you are able to number them. So shall your descendants be." Abraham believed the Lord and "He accounted it to him for righteousness" (Gen. 15:5–6). That's when Abraham was justified. Isaac wasn't even conceived in Sarah's womb yet. And only after Isaac was born and grew up to be a young man did Abraham perform the good work of offering him to God. It didn't happen overnight.

What about Rahab? Scripture tells us that she went to the spies she had hidden on her roof and told them, "I know the LORD has given you this land.... We are all afraid of you.... For we have heard how the LORD made a dry path for you through the Red Sea when you left Egypt. And we know what you did to Sihon and Og, the two Amorite kings east of the Jordan River, whose people you completely destroyed. No wonder our hearts have melted in fear!... For the LORD your God is the supreme God of the heavens above and the earth below" (Josh. 2:9–11 NLT).

Notice how Rahab used the term "LORD" or *Yahweh*, and declared to the spies that He was "the supreme God of the heavens above and the earth below." She was already a believer in *Yahweh*. That's why she was willing to help the Israelites and even begged them to spare her and her extended family when the Israelites came into Jericho (see Josh. 2:11–13 NLT). She had no doubt that the same Lord Who had opened the Red Sea and defeated the two Amorite kings for them would also give them the land of Jericho. Rahab must have grown up hearing about how the Lord had dried up the Red Sea for the Israelites, and she'd believed then in the Lord, that He was surely the supreme God of heaven and earth. So if you think about it, as in the case of Abraham, there must have been a good many years between her believing God and her good work!

One last thought for those who love pointing to the two examples of good works that James gives: if you consider the acts that "justified" both Abraham and Rahab—attempted murder and lying, respectively—these are hardly moral acts or good examples of obeying the law. Clearly James was not talking about our justification before God, or the basis of our receiving blessings from Him.

You Will Bear Fruit in Grace Ground

Many of us, despite our best intentions, have made mistakes and bad decisions. And despite our failures, God in His grace continues to be patient with us.

There's a beautiful Scripture that says, "A bruised reed He will not break, and smoking flax He will not quench" (Matt. 12:20). Reeds can be made into flutes that produce beautiful tunes. Flax is used as wicks in lamps. My friend, when you've lost your song, when the fire in you is dying, God is not going to break you or snuff you out and throw you aside. No, He will not give up on you. He will love you back into wholeness so that there is a song in your heart once more. He will reignite your passion to live for Him and His glory as you see His love for you.

God will love you back into wholeness so that there is a song in your heart once more.

You will also find, like so many of the precious folks who write to my ministry, that when you know and believe you are justified by faith, it is a matter of time before you produce good works and live a life that glorifies Him. Just let your roots go deep into the healthy ground of His grace and stay in the bright sunshine of His love, and His glorious presence in your life will be evident to all!

CHAPTER 9

EXPERIENCE FREEDOM FROM FEAR

Fear is a destructive bondage. Fear paralyzes you and prevents you from fulfilling the amazing destiny that God has for you. Fear makes you feel inadequate and insecure, and comes with unhealthy side effects ranging from panic attacks to sleep disorders. Fear is irrational. Fear is a spiritual condition, which is why you can't reason fear away. You can't simply tell someone who is struggling with fear and gripped by panic attacks to just stop being fearful. A spiritual condition cannot be remedied naturally. Fear can be eradicated only by a personal encounter with the person of Jesus. The Word of God tells us, "There is no fear in love; but perfect love casts out fear, because fear involves torment" (1 John 4:18).

Beloved, if what I just described about fear is all too familiar to you, I want you to know that it is not your heavenly Father's heart for you to live tormented by fear. There is no fear in God's love. His perfect love drives out all fears.

There is no fear in God's love. His perfect love
drives out all fears.

I don't know if you have ever experienced God's love, but my desire is that TODAY you will catch a revelation of His love for you in a deep and personal way. And as His love floods your heart, I pray that every fear that has you bound will forever be cast out of your life.

John 3:16 tells us, "For God so loved the world that He gave His only begotten Son, that whoever believes in Him should not perish but have everlasting life."

Oh, how clearly this verse proclaims that God SO loves you. And if you only knew how much He esteems and treasures His beloved Son, you would catch a glimpse of how much He loves you, because He gave up His Son for you. That is why I preach and write about the gospel of grace. The gospel of grace is all about unveiling God's perfect love—a love whose length and depth and height were demonstrated at the cross. A love that gave up the Son of God as a sacrifice. A love that bore your sins and mine, so that we can receive His everlasting life and live free of any bondage.

Do You Know God's True Nature?

How we see God is important, because a faulty perception of God can result in a lifetime of fear and bondage. Too many people have a wrong impression of God, because for generations people have portrayed Him as demanding and easily provoked to anger. They have made Him appear hard, angry, unfeeling, and condemning, just waiting for man to trip up. These portrayals of God cause many sincere people to have an unhealthy fear of God. And when they believe that God is against them and out to punish them, they find it impossible to break out of their sins, addictions, anxieties, and fears.

My friend, if you've been shown a God of judgment and anger all your life, let the Scriptures reveal to you His true nature:

- "God is love" (1 John 4:8).
- "But you, Lord, are a compassionate and gracious God, slow to anger, abounding in love and faithfulness" (Ps. 86:15 NIV).
- "The Lord our God is merciful and forgiving" (Dan. 9:9 NIV).
- "O LORD, Your tender mercies and Your lovingkindnesses... they are from of old" (Ps. 25:6).

This is our God! Our God is love! He is slow to anger, gracious, and patient. He is full of forgiveness, loving-kindness, and tender mercies. This is the very opposite of how the world (and even Hollywood movies) likes to portray God. Thank God we can go to the Holy Word for the truth!

Our God is love! He is slow to anger, gracious, and patient. He is full of forgiveness, loving-kindness, and tender mercies.

See Jesus, Friend of Sinners, and See God

If you want to further understand the true nature of God, just look at Jesus. He said, "He who has seen Me has seen the Father.... The words that I speak to you I do not speak on My own authority; but the Father who dwells in Me does the works" (John 14:9–10). Have you ever seen Jesus provoked and angry with sinners? Was He ever mad at the prostitutes or tax collectors? Did He berate the woman at the well who had five husbands, or the woman who was caught in adultery? Now, He was at times angry with the self-righteous, hardhearted, grace-resisting scribes and Pharisees, but He was always kind and loving toward the sinners and outcasts of society. That's the nature of your heavenly Father!

Jesus was always kind and loving toward the sinners and outcasts of society. That's the nature of your heavenly Father!

Jesus demonstrated such graciousness that His haters sarcastically labeled Him "a friend of sinners" to cast aspersions on His integrity (see Matt. 11:19). The same type of accusation is hurled against my ministry today when I preach about God's grace and His fatherly heart of love. People call me all kinds of horrible names. I have been accused of condoning sin, giving people a license to sin, and even giving people an excuse to leave their wives to marry their secretaries! This cannot be further from the truth. If you have been reading this book and my other books, you know my position on sin. Sin brings destructive consequences and I am 100 percent against sin. But carrying the heart of our Lord Jesus, I love the sinner and I love every believer even if they are struggling with sin.

Those who hated Jesus called Him a friend of sinners. But what was intended to be a derogatory label is really a beautiful picture of His grace. Grace doesn't shun the sinner; grace *pursues* the sinner. Grace doesn't picket against those who fall short; grace embraces them into wholeness and brings about real inward transformation for them. Grace does not condemn those struggling against sin; grace produces holiness in them.

Grace doesn't picket against those who fall short. Grace embraces them into wholeness and brings about real inward transformation for them.

Like my Lord Jesus, I want to be known as a friend of sinners. Sinners found only despair, judgment, and condemnation in the law, but they found hope, joy, and liberty in Jesus. He showed them His grace and His grace transformed them from living a life of sin to living a life of holiness. He never condoned their sins. A thousand times no. How could He, when He gave His life to save them from their sins!

We see an example of our Lord's love for sinners when He befriended the corrupt tax collector Zacchaeus. He invited Himself over to Zacchaeus's home, loved him, and showed him grace. Before the night was over, Zacchaeus stood in the presence of all his dinner guests and said to Jesus, "Look, Lord, I give half of my goods to the poor; and if I have taken anything from anyone by false accusation, I restore fourfold" (Luke 19:8). That's the power of grace! Grace changes people's lives from the inside out. Jesus gave Zacchaeus no commandments, no condemnation, no laws…just grace, grace, and more grace. And Zacchaeus's heart was forever transformed. Grace produces true holiness.

How Fear and Sorrow Enter

In the chapter before this story, we read about a rich young ruler who came to Jesus saying, "Good Teacher, what shall I do to inherit eternal life?" (Luke 18:18). Now listen closely to how Jesus replied: "Why do you call Me good? No one is good but One, that is, God" (Luke 18:19). Jesus knew that this rich young ruler didn't see Him as God but only as a "teacher." Isn't that still true of the world we live in today? There are many people who see Jesus as a great man, a great philosopher, and a great historical figure, but they don't see Him as their Lord and Savior.

Unfortunately, there are also believers who are saved, washed by the blood of Jesus, and made righteous by faith, but who now relate to Jesus only as a teacher and not their Savior. They believe that after they have been saved by grace, they are to be justified by their works through their keeping of the Ten Commandments. They forget that how God makes us right in His sight is "accomplished from start to finish by faith" (Rom. 1:17 NLT).

When we were born again in Christ, we were justified by faith. Until the day we see Jesus, we will continue to be justified by faith and not our works. Our justification is from faith to faith, not faith to works. The good news is that those who are justified by faith will produce good works and bear fruits of holiness. And not only will you find them obeying God's commandments unconsciously, but you will also find them exceeding outward fulfillment with inward motivation!

Our justification is from faith to faith, not faith to works.

However, for those who, like the rich young ruler, think that they can be justified by works and do something to inherit eternal life, our Lord Jesus will point them back to the law to bring them to the end of themselves. Jesus said to the rich young ruler, "You know the commandments: 'Do not commit adultery,' 'Do not murder,' 'Do not steal,' 'Do not bear false witness,' 'Honor your father and your mother.'" The young ruler (perhaps with a smirk) replied, "All these things I have kept from my youth." On hearing this, Jesus said, "You still lack one thing. Sell all that you have and distribute to the poor, and you will have treasure in heaven; and come, follow Me." When the rich young ruler heard this, he walked away sorrowful (see Luke 18:20–23).

When you come to the Lord to be justified by your works, He will point you to the law! No matter how perfectly you think you have kept the Ten Commandments, like the young ruler, you will be found lacking in one thing. For the young ruler, it was in the area of money. The very first commandment is, "You shall have no other gods before Me" (Exod. 20:3). Yet money was his god—he walked away sorrowful when the Lord asked him to sell all that he had.

Beloved, no man can meet the demands of the law and be justified. We can be justified only by faith in the blood of the Lamb. If you are not anchored in this truth and if your conscience is not washed by the Lamb's blood, you will always be fearful.

The Law Demands, Grace Supplies

I believe the Lord put these two stories side by side—one in Luke 18 and the other in Luke 19—to help us understand that we can be justified only by faith and not our works. Justification by faith produces hope, peace, joy, and a heart for Jesus that results in good fruit. Attempting to be justified by works produces fear, anxiety, and an inability to produce lasting fruit.

When the rich young ruler came wanting to be justified by his works, the Lord gave him the law and he left sorrowful. There is no record that he gave even one nickel to the poor. But look at what happened when Jesus invited Himself to Zaccheus's house. Not one commandment, just pure grace was given. And it resulted in Zaccheus's giving half his wealth to the poor and making a public commitment to repay fourfold everyone he had stolen from!

The law *demands*, grace *supplies.*

The law demands, and it results in fear, guilt, and sorrow. Grace supplies, and it produces generosity, holiness, and inward heart transformation. Now, you tell me, which gospel should we preach? Justification by works through the law? Or justification by faith through the power of God's grace?

The law demands, and it results in fear, guilt, and sorrow.
Grace supplies, and it produces generosity, holiness, and
inward heart transformation.

Unfortunately, because many have been taught and believe, like the rich young ruler, that they can be justified before God only by their works, they end up conscious of failing Him. They end up with a fearful expectation of God's punishment and judgment. Every bad thing that happens to them reinforces that fear. Even when things are going well, they are fearful of losing God's blessings or protection because of a mistake they may have just made. The result? Insecurity, dread, anxiety, and all kinds of fears become constant companions that rob them of the joy of living, let alone living life with boldness and confidence.

The Good News of No Condemnation in Christ

My friend, if that describes you, if you've been living in the abyss of fear for as long as you can remember, it is time for your liberty. You can begin this journey of freedom today by believing that God's heart is full of love, grace, and mercy toward you. Listen to your Father's heartbeat: "For God did not send His Son into the world to condemn the world, but that the world through Him might be saved. He who believes in Him is not condemned" (John 3:17–18). Do you believe in Jesus? There is no condemnation for anyone who calls upon the name of Jesus! All who call on Him and believe in Him are not condemned but saved. That is the good news of the gospel.

All who call on Jesus and believe in Him are not condemned but saved. That is the good news of the gospel.

Unfortunately, this good news of no condemnation from God is not being proclaimed from every housetop. Many believers are still living under the heavy yoke of condemnation and fear because they hear the Mosaic covenant being proclaimed and put themselves under the Ten Commandments.

Look at how the apostle Paul describes the Ten Commandments in 2 Corinthians 3:7–9: "But if the ministry of death, written and engraved on stones, was glorious... how will the ministry of the Spirit not be more glorious? For if the ministry of condemnation had glory, the ministry of righteousness exceeds much more in glory."

No one can argue that Paul was talking here only about ceremonial laws (like the killing of sacrificial animals) and not the Ten

Commandments, because only the Ten Commandments were "written and engraved on stones"—written by the finger of God Himself. And Paul calls them the "ministry of death" and "ministry of condemnation."

Paul then contrasts the Ten Commandments with the new covenant of grace by describing the latter as the "ministry of the Spirit" and "ministry of righteousness." Can you see the clear distinction that God makes in His Word? The Ten Commandments minister death and condemnation, whereas the gospel of grace ministers the spirit of liberty and the gift of God's righteousness.

What the Real Problem Is

Now, please understand this: the Ten Commandments are glorious! The problem has never been the Ten Commandments or God's perfect law. The problem has always been imperfect man's ability to keep God's perfect law. Based on the terms of the Mosaic covenant, if you kept God's law, you were blessed. But if you didn't, you were cursed, were condemned, and had a death sentence hanging over your head.

Man's only hope to be right with God once and for all is Christ.

The fact is that even under the old covenant, no man was able to keep the law perfectly. From the very beginning of the law, God made a provision of animal sacrifices so that man's curse, condemnation, and death sentence could be transferred to the sacrificial bull or lamb. What is this a picture of? This is a picture of Jesus at the cross! When

John the Baptist saw Jesus on the banks of the Jordan River, he said, "Behold! The Lamb of God who takes away the sin of the world" (John 1:29). So even in the law we see that man's only hope to be right with God once and for all is Christ.

The book of Hebrews explains this beautifully:

> *The old system under the law of Moses was only a shadow, a dim preview of the good things to come, not the good things themselves. The sacrifices under that system were repeated again and again, year after year, but they were never able to provide perfect cleansing for those who came to worship. If they could have provided perfect cleansing, the sacrifices would have stopped, for the worshipers would have been purified once for all time, and their feelings of guilt would have disappeared. But instead, those sacrifices actually reminded them of their sins year after year. For it is not possible for the blood of bulls and goats to take away sins.*
>
> *—Hebrews 10:1–4 NLT*

My dear reader, what could not be accomplished by the blood of bulls and goats was accomplished PERFECTLY by the blood of Jesus Christ. In Christ we have been purified once for ALL time. The curse, guilt, condemnation, and punishment for all sins have been fully met at the cross. In Christ we are no longer under the ministry of condemnation, but are under the glorious ministry of righteousness.

In Christ we are no longer under the ministry of condemnation, but under the glorious ministry of righteousness.

How Free Are You?

The book of Hebrews continues to explain, "He cancels the first covenant in order to put the second into effect. For God's will was for us
to be made holy by the sacrifice of the body of Jesus Christ, once for all
time" (Heb. 10:9–10 NLT).

Our Lord Jesus came not to abolish the law, but to fulfill it (see Matt.
5:17). The law was perfectly fulfilled at the cross when He cried out,
"Finished!" (see John 19:30). He met the demands of the first covenant,
which is the Mosaic covenant of the Ten Commandments, in order to
put the second, which is the new covenant of God's grace, into effect!

We are in the age of God's grace. That is why we preach the gospel
of grace! My friend, the cross of Jesus has made all the difference! You
no longer have to live in condemnation and fear under the old covenant of the law. You are now under the new covenant of grace, where
you are fully forgiven, justified, and made righteous by Jesus' blood to
reign in life.

When you realize you are justified by faith and not by your works
in the new covenant of God's grace, something liberating happens.
You become free from the ministry of condemnation and the death it
ministers—guilt, insecurity, dread, anxieties, and all sorts of debilitating fears. Condemnation robs you of peace in your heart and of joy
in your relationship with your Father. It robs you of faith and confidence in His love and ability to save you. But when you know and
believe you are not under the ministry of condemnation but under
the ministry of righteousness, you can come freely before your Father
in heaven and bring every concern on your heart to Him. You will
not be constantly fearful that your failures will cause Him to punish
you or withhold His blessings and protection from you, because you

know that Jesus bore the punishment meant for you upon Himself at the cross.

When you know and believe that you are not under the ministry of condemnation but under the ministry of righteousness, you can come freely before your Father and bring every concern on your heart to Him.

Dear reader, as you are reading these words, perhaps you know what it's like to battle fear every day. Perhaps you've been plagued by fears of being unable to cope with certain changes in your circumstances. Maybe fearful thoughts of losing your health, your job, your children, or your very life keep you awake at night. Perhaps you suffer from severe anxiety attacks and the very thought of going anywhere outside of your home fills you with suffocating fear. I want you to know that this is not the life God wants you to live. Through the sacrifice of His Son and the perfection of Christ's finished work, He has made a way for you to live free from the captivity of fear.

The Mother of All Fears

What I've shared with you so far in this chapter is foundational to your breaking free from every fear, bondage, and cycle of defeat that you may be in right now. I encourage you to take some time to go over the previous sections and really meditate on the liberating truths from the Word of God that I have shared with you. Meditate on how they apply to you personally. I believe that as you do, you'll personally experience every knot of fear dissolving as you see the Lord's perfect love for you.

In Christ you have been redeemed from all fears. You no longer need to live in fear of judgment, punishment, and condemnation from God for your sins. Because you are a believer in Jesus, the curse of the law and its ministry of death and condemnation no longer have a hold over you! His Word victoriously proclaims that "Christ purchased our freedom [redeeming us] from the curse (doom) of the Law [and its condemnation] by [Himself] becoming a curse for us, for it is written [in the Scriptures], Cursed is everyone who hangs on a tree (is crucified)" (Gal. 3:13 AMP). You have been redeemed!

Because you are a believer in Jesus, the curse of the law and its ministry of death and condemnation no longer have a hold over you!

Do you know what the mother of all fears is? I believe it is the fear of death. Why do believers come under the fear of death when they've been forgiven, justified, and redeemed? It's simple: when believers don't believe that all their sins have been punished and forgiven through the death of Jesus Christ at the cross, their consciences are never at rest. As a result, the wages of sin, which is death, continue to oppress them and keep them under bondage.

But here's the good news: God's Word tells us, "Because God's children are human beings—made of flesh and blood—the Son also became flesh and blood. For only as a human being could he die, and only by dying could he break the power of the devil, who had the power of death" (Heb. 2:14 NLT). Why did He do all this? To "release those who through fear of death were all their lifetime subject to bondage" (Heb. 2:15). Our Lord Jesus wants us free from the fear of death and from any bondage.

Read Hebrews 2:15 again and you'll see that the fear of death leads to other fears and bondages—"those who through fear of death were all their lifetime subject to bondage." People who fear death automatically fear falling sick, so they worry about their health all the time. Every little symptom causes them anxiety and keeps them running to doctors. Many times the fear of death is the root of people's fear of flying, driving, or simply going to the mall, because they imagine the worst things happening to them. For some people the fear of death is so severe that it interferes with their daily life. It consumes their thoughts and negatively affects the decisions they make.

If that's you today, I encourage you to take the time to anchor yourself in the truth of these two verses. Know beyond the shadow of any doubt that Jesus, through His death at the cross, has set you free from the fear of death, and with it every bondage you may be in right now. Hebrews 2:15 shows us clearly that the moment the fear of death is removed from your heart, your bondage is removed. Your very susceptibility to being in bondage is removed. Hallelujah! Jesus died on the cross to set you free. The more you are established in this truth, the more you'll experience the abundant life He came to give you.

Jesus, through His death at the cross, has set you free from the fear of death, and with it every bondage you may be in right now.

Finally Finding Freedom from Fear

Let me encourage you with Ursula's testimony. This precious sister from South Africa found freedom from all her fears, including her fear of death, when she simply began to understand the true nature of God and have a personal revelation of His love and finished work. Here is her story:

I grew up with a fear of dying. I remember being anxious about dying from a young age and even suffering from terrible nightmares from the age of six. I wanted to depend on God for my freedom, but I could not relate to or trust Him.

Because of the uncertainties I faced, I set out to create a perfect and completely safe house where I could live, work, and ultimately raise a family in peace and security. However, once I became a wife and mother, I found it increasingly stressful to keep my loved ones safe. I have three adventurous little boys and I felt increasingly out of control when faced with the unpredictability of life.

I started to isolate myself more and more, walled in by my unrealistic expectations and fear of exposing my vulnerabilities to the harsh judgment of others. I started experiencing dizziness, brain fog, and feelings of blacking out. Eventually, my anxiety increased to the point that I was paralyzed with fear.

I went for several tests with different specialists, but no one could pinpoint a particular cause for my symptoms. I felt like the woman with the issue of blood in the Bible who spent all her money seeking different cures, yet seeing nothing work.

Three and a half years ago, I was admitted to a hospital for nonstop panic attacks that lasted almost a week. It was a pit so deep and dark that I struggle to find words to adequately describe it. I felt like I had been buried alive in hell, completely disconnected from God and others.

But as I lay on that hospital bed, God penetrated the haze of my fearful thinking and lovingly showed me that He was not the source of my troubles as I'd come to believe, but my solution. Desperately, I hung on to that single truth and as I did, help began to come. God brought a counselor into my life who preached God's grace to me. Then, my husband happened to have lunch with someone in his office and this man's wife passed Joseph Prince's DVD to me via my husband.

As I watched the DVD, the truth of what was preached resonated deeply in my soul. From then on, I went online and downloaded more MP3s and have been listening to them nearly every day these past three years. As I embraced my Father's powerful love that He has made available to me in Christ, my heart was transformed and I began to blossom and thrive.

It has been three years since my hospital visit and God has progressively restored all that the locusts have eaten. I have been healed to the point that I no longer require antidepressant medication. Instead, I live enjoying an intimacy with God, my family, and friends that I could never have imagined before. Jesus has come into all the dark areas of my life to be with me, befriend me, and warm me with His presence. He shows me the love and forgiveness of God and restores my hope for the future!

I thank God for the ministry of Joseph Prince in revealing the truth of Who God is to people desperate for intimacy with their Daddy God, and for fearlessly preaching the good news of the gospel of grace!

What a glorious testimony of freedom from paralyzing fear! I love how Ursula is now enjoying an intimacy with God she never thought possible. When she didn't have a revelation of His love and forgiveness, she couldn't relate to God and trust Him for her freedom. In fact, she even believed that God was the source of her problems. You see, when your perception of and approach to God are based on the Mosaic law of the old covenant, you can't have an intimate relationship with Him, and you stay entrenched in your fears.

Conversely, when you have a revelation of God's love and you approach Him not through the law but by relying purely on His grace, you will have the intimacy with Him that you long for. And this intimacy will produce good fruit in your life. Whether it's fear of death, fear of rejection, fear of failure, a relationship issue, or a long-term addiction, you will find yourself overcoming your challenge as His love and power work mightily in you, through you, and for you. You cannot but thrive and blossom when you are basking in the glory of God's powerful love and amazing grace!

CHAPTER 10

GLORIOUS GRACE

Grace transforms lives.

I have received so many powerful testimonies from people all around the world who have awakened to their righteous identity in Christ and found freedom from their sins. The gospel of grace tears down the veil of Christian religion and brings people into an intimate relationship with God. The Word of God tells us, "Awake to righteousness, and sin not" (1 Cor. 15:34 KJV).

The grace revolution is this great awakening to righteousness. When people hear the real gospel being preached—the gospel that tells them how right Jesus' finished work has made them—they begin to grasp just how loved, valued, and precious they are in Christ. From then on, their lives will never be the same again. They begin to realize that they don't have to live in defeat, live bound to addictions, and live in failure. Instead of seeing someone worthless when they look in the mirror, they see a highly favored, greatly blessed, and deeply loved child of the Most High God!

When people hear the real gospel that tells them how right Jesus' finished work has made them, their lives will never be the same again.

Grace Removes Your Burdens

Kirk, who lives in Germany, shared this with me:

My wife had contemplated suicide because I kept failing to keep the promises I made to her. It seemed like the more I struggled to do things right, the more I ended up doing those things wrong. Eventually, she left me and in five months we were officially divorced. She then moved to Austria with our nine-year-old son.

I knew that my bad conduct was a thorn in my marriage, but I didn't know how to make things right. However, God knew, and that's why He pointed me to Pastor Joseph Prince.

The very first day I listened to Pastor Prince's preaching about God's grace, I felt as if a heavy burden was lifted off me. It was as if God knew about my burden more than I did and He made a way to set me free.

You see, I used to be very conscious of my weaknesses and shortcomings, believing that I would never escape God's curses and hellfire because of them. Every day, I made commitments to live right, but I found myself struggling to improve my behavior. I was tormented by fear and my powerlessness.

Despite attending church, Bible study, and prayer meetings regularly, I felt so empty that I wondered if I would make it to heaven. I was also confused because I thought God was gracious in giving to us, but would cause His wrath to fall on those who disobeyed Him. Trying to get myself fully right with God to avoid His wrath and get His blessings was like living under a curse.

Surrendering to the Power of Grace

Kirk's turnaround and restoration came as he kept hearing about God's glorious grace:

> *As I kept listening to Pastor Prince share the message of grace and the gift of righteousness, I began feeding on God's love for me. My life became more meaningful because I discovered that it is no longer I who live—Jesus is the One Who operates in me. The more I focus on His love for me, the more I fall in love with Him, and the more the Bible becomes a book about His love.*
>
> *It was during the times of separation and divorce with my wife that I surrendered completely to the power of God's grace because there was nothing more left for me to do other than to say yes to Jesus. Jesus turned the turmoil of my divorce into a breakthrough. I started experiencing life like never before as God kept showing up in my daily living, healing me, and fixing issues in my life—even issues that I had not asked Him to fix.*
>
> *At the same time, God was also healing my wife from the emotional breakdown and renewing love in her heart and mind. Gradually, she opened up to me and showed me her care and kindness.*
>
> *So miraculously, we got back together and we are one again by His grace. Now, I'm with my family every weekend—something that was never possible before. I was promoted in my company and with the promotion came a company car that makes it possible for me to spend more time with my wife and son.*

Besides mending my marriage, God also delivered me from a sexual sin. Prior to discovering the message of grace, I was watching pornography. However, since I started following Pastor Prince's ministry, the desire to watch pornography just died and I no longer indulge myself in that area. Jesus did it all for me even though I don't deserve it at all!

I thank God that He has raised Pastor Joseph Prince to bring the good news to those whom God loves, those beaten down by shortcomings, hopelessness, and addictions—those like me. Now, I am walking with boldness, knowing I'm fully safe and sound in Jesus Christ and that He is always there for me. Eternal life is my inheritance in Christ Jesus by faith, not by my self-works.

Wow. Isn't God good? Kirk's marriage was restored and he was also set free from an addiction to pornography. He is no longer "beaten down by shortcomings, hopelessness, and addictions." And it all happened because he "awoke to righteousness" and realized just how unconditionally and irrevocably loved he is by God. Hallelujah!

Genuine Grace Glorifies Jesus

But even as God restores the glorious truth of the gospel of grace to the body of Christ, be aware that the enemy also produces a counterfeit grace to try to confuse people and make them wary of the true ministry of God's grace. Why is there a counterfeit grace? The reality is, there are counterfeits of things only when they are of great value and greatly prized. You find counterfeit diamonds, but not counterfeit pebbles.

Now, don't be discouraged or afraid that you might be misled by counterfeit grace. Just be skillful in God's Word and learn how to discern what is scriptural by reading God's Word for yourself. Build a strong foundation on the true gospel of grace. The simplest way to know if someone is preaching the gospel of grace is to evaluate whether the teaching glorifies our Lord Jesus. Does the teaching cause you to want to live a life that glorifies Him? Does the teaching emphasize your works or the work of our Lord Jesus? Does the teaching cause you to be occupied with yourself or occupied with our Lord Jesus?

The simplest way to know if someone is preaching the gospel of grace is to see whether the teaching glorifies our Lord Jesus.

Some of you may have come across a teaching that claims *everyone* will ultimately be saved. This is called "universal reconciliation" and I want to say this from the outset: it is heresy. Such teachings do not exalt or glorify our Lord Jesus. You CANNOT talk about eternal salvation without the person of Jesus and His finished work at the cross. Jesus is the only way! Jesus said, "I am the way, the truth, and the life. No one comes to the Father except through Me" (John 14:6).

Is There Correction under Grace?

There are also those who teach that being holy is not important since we are under grace. They claim that under grace there is no correction and no need to grow in holiness. Let me just say this: such "teachers" are propagating error! The truth of the matter is that you cannot become more righteous, but you can become more holy. True grace produces true holiness. That is why the apostle Paul exhorts the Corinthian church to "awake to righteousness, and sin not" (1 Cor. 15:34 KJV). The more you are under grace—the more you are established in your righteousness in Christ—the more you will want to live a holy life and be open to God's correction.

The more you are established in your righteousness in Christ, the more you will want to live a holy life and be open to God's correction.

So is there correction under grace? Absolutely. But I want you to be established in the fact that under the new covenant of grace, God does *not* correct His children by using accidents, sicknesses, and diseases. Correction in the new covenant takes place through His Word. Paul tells us, "All Scripture is inspired by God and profitable for teaching, for reproof, for correction, for training in righteousness" (see 2 Tim. 3:16 NASB). Notice how correction through God's Word includes "training in righteousness," which is believing that you have been justified or made righteous by faith in our Lord Jesus. I have found that oftentimes the Holy Spirit uses God-appointed leadership to accomplish this (see Gal. 6:1, 2 Tim. 4:2, 2 Thess. 3:15)—to point you back to Jesus' finished work and who you are in Christ. That is why it is so vital that you be a part of a local church with good leaders.

Observe how the apostle Paul corrects those in the Corinthian church who got entangled in sin and sexual immorality:

Do you not know that your bodies are members of Christ? Shall I then take the members of Christ and make them

members of a harlot? Certainly not! Or do you not know that
he who is joined to a harlot is one body with her? For "the
two," He says, "shall become one flesh." But he who is joined to
the Lord is one spirit with Him. Flee sexual immorality. Every
sin that a man does is outside the body, but he who commits
sexual immorality sins against his own body. Or do you not
know that your body is the temple of the Holy Spirit who is in
you, whom you have from God, and you are not your own?
For you were bought at a price; therefore glorify God in your
body and in your spirit, which are God's.

—*1 Corinthians 6:15–20*

How did Paul correct them? In saying, "Do you not know that your
bodies are members of Christ?" he corrected them by firmly reminding them of their righteous identity in Christ. He then went on to
remind them that their bodies were temples of the Holy Spirit. What
does all this tell us? It tells us that anyone who is reminded of and has
a revelation of his or her righteousness in Christ will have the power
to overcome sin!

Anyone who is reminded of and has a revelation of his
or her righteousness in Christ will have the power to
overcome sin!

It is those who have forgotten or who are not established in their
righteous identities in Christ who get trapped by the destructive
forces of sin. Under grace we are called to walk in newness of life as
the righteous children of God. We are called to reign in life through
the abundance of grace and the gift of righteousness. We have been

purchased with a price, a heavy price at the cross, and are now called to live for the glory of our Lord Jesus!

Grace Frees You to Live a Christ-Glorifying Life

Earlier on I mentioned the importance of reading the Bible for yourself and being skillful in God's Word. Look at this passage from Romans 6:

> *Our old man was crucified with Him, that the body of sin might be done away with, that we should* no longer be slaves of sin. *For he who has died has been* freed from sin. *Now if we died with Christ, we believe that we shall also live with Him, knowing that Christ, having been raised from the dead, dies no more. Death no longer has dominion over Him. For the death that* He died, He died to sin once for all; *but the life that He lives, He lives to God. Likewise you also, reckon yourselves to be* dead indeed to sin, *but alive to God in Christ Jesus our Lord. Therefore* do not let sin reign *in your mortal body, that you should* obey it in its lusts. *And do not present your members as instruments of unrighteousness to sin, but present yourselves to* God *as being alive from the dead, and your members as* instruments of righteousness *to God. For* sin shall not have dominion over you, *for you are not under law but* under grace.
>
> —*Romans 6:6–14 (emphasis mine)*

There is an erroneous thinking that preaching the Ten Commandments can produce holiness in people. In reality, if you read the passage above closely, you will see that it is actually the preaching of the gospel of grace and the finished work of Jesus that gives people victory over sin! Because of the cross at Calvary, you are no longer "slaves of sin." You are "freed from sin" and "dead indeed to sin."

The preaching of the gospel of grace and the finished work of Jesus gives people victory over sin.

Also, in Christ, by the power of His glorious grace, you have the liberty and power to glorify your Lord by not letting "sin reign in your mortal body" and by presenting "your members as instruments of righteousness to God." You can know beyond a shadow of a doubt that "sin shall not have dominion over you, *for you are not under law but under grace*" (emphasis mine). That's the glorious gospel of grace! Grace produces glorious, victorious, and holy lives.

Now, if you know people who are living in sin and claiming that they are under grace, you know that they are most definitely *not* living under grace! How can they be when the Bible states that sin shall not have dominion over those who are under grace? Grace is the power to go and sin no more (see John 8:11). There is a grace revolution going on and it is liberating precious people from the power of sin!

Holiness Is a Fruit of God's Grace

There are people who think that preaching God's grace gives people a license to sin and endorses licentiousness. That is not what God's grace does at all! On the contrary, God's amazing grace transforms a person's heart and produces true holiness. By true holiness, I am referring to a holiness that isn't just outward, but also deep and intimate, beginning at the very core of a person's heart. Holiness is a fruit of God's grace.

God's amazing grace transforms a person's heart and produces true holiness.

The word "holiness" in the New Testament is the Greek word *hagiasmos*, which is sometimes translated also as "sanctification."[1] The moment you received Jesus as your Lord and Savior, you were justified by faith and made perfectly righteous. You were also made holy or sanctified, which is to be set apart unto the Lord. And as you grow in the grace and knowledge of Jesus, you are progressively transformed into His image from glory to glory (see 2 Cor. 3:18). Now, you cannot be more righteous, because you are already 100 percent righteous by Jesus' blood. But under grace you can grow in holiness in the way you live your life.

I am all for holiness and I am vehemently against sin. Where I differ from some preachers is in my focus on *how* we stop the power of sin and help God's people grow in holiness. For many preachers the answer to sin is preaching the Ten Commandments. I believe the answer is preaching Jesus and the gospel of grace.

When people experience Jesus' unconditional love, they fall in love with Him and inevitably out of love with sin. Why? Because when you are loved and in love, you desire to please, honor, and bring glory to the One Who loves you unconditionally. A woman who is loved by her husband, and who is in love with her husband, doesn't go around looking for ways to commit adultery.

In the same way, a church who knows she is loved by her Savior, and who is in love with her Savior, doesn't go around looking for ways to dishonor Him. That is why my mission every Sunday is to preach the gospel of grace in my church. My part is to unveil our Lord Jesus to the congregation and show them His beautiful grace in the Word of God. When they experience the undeserved, unmerited, and unearned favor of God, they will go on to live glorious, victorious, and holy lives.

A church who knows she is loved by her Savior, and who is in love with her Savior, doesn't go around looking for ways to dishonor Him.

We read in 1 John 4:10, "In this is love, not that we loved God, but that He loved us and sent His Son to be the propitiation for our sins." Now, which comes first? Our love for God, or God's love for us? God's love for us! Yet so many are still preaching that Christianity is about our love for God. My friend, Christianity is all about God's love for you. It is His love for and in you that results in inward heart transformation. Christianity is not a religion; it is a relationship. Christianity is not about a list of dos and don'ts; it is about intimacy, love, and a warm, beating heart. That is why you can't preach holiness and right conduct to someone who has not yet experienced and tasted the grace of God.

Holiness Is a Result of Growth

I can't demand a beard from my son, Justin, who is three years old at the time of this writing. Some things can come only with growth.

When Justin wakes up in the morning, I don't expect him to make his bed, brush his teeth, and change his diapers. Do I love him as my son even though his behavior is not "perfect"? Of course I do, but I recognize that some things come with growth.

Similarly, holiness is a result of growth. Holiness is the fruit and not the root. Apostle Paul says it this way: "But now being made free from sin, and become servants to God, ye have your fruit unto holiness, and the end everlasting life" (Rom. 6:22 KJV). Fruit comes with growth. You can't demand fruit from a juvenile tree. So how do you cultivate the tree to produce fruit? Simply by watering and nourishing it. In the same way, a believer who is well rooted and established in the gospel of grace will bear fruit in due time. The more he grows in the grace and knowledge of our Lord Jesus Christ, the more he will bear the fruit of holiness. Holiness is a by-product of grace.

A believer who is well rooted and established in the gospel of grace will bear fruit in due time.

Now I want to draw your attention to the next few verses:

Beloved, if God so loved us, we also ought to love one another.
—1 John 4:11

Husbands, love your wives, even as Christ also loved the church, and gave himself for it.
—Ephesians 5:25 KJV

Wives, submit yourselves unto your own husbands, as unto the Lord.

—*Ephesians 5:22 KJV*

Children, obey your parents in the Lord: for this is right.

—*Ephesians 6:1 KJV*

And be kind to one another, tenderhearted, forgiving one another, even as God in Christ forgave you.

—*Ephesians 4:32*

What is the common denominator in all these verses? The common denominator is the person of Jesus and His love, grace, and finished work at the cross. We have no ability to love one another, love our spouse, honor our parents, and forgive one another except if we have *first* experienced His love and forgiveness in our lives. Being occupied, consumed, and absorbed in the love of Jesus makes you holy. Jesus is your holiness!

We have no ability to love and forgive one another except if we have first *experienced Jesus' love and forgiveness in our lives.*

Love Is the Fulfillment of the Law

There are people who think that preaching the gospel of grace makes you someone who is against the Ten Commandments. How far from the truth that is! I have not told people to come against the Ten Commandments. What I have been preaching is that one cannot be justified by keeping the Ten Commandments. In the 1,500 years that God's people lived under the law, not a single man (apart from our Lord Jesus) could be justified by the Ten Commandments.

Now, listen carefully to what I am about to say. Under grace, when you experience the love of our Lord Jesus, you will end up fulfilling the law! Under grace you will end up being holy. Grace produces true holiness! As the apostle Paul boldly proclaims, "Love does no harm to a neighbor; therefore love is the fulfillment of the law" (Rom. 13:10).

When the love of Jesus is in you, you can't help but fulfill the law. When your heart is overflowing with God's grace and loving-kindness, you will have no desire to commit adultery or murder, bear false witness, or covet. You will have the power to love your neighbor as yourself. Where does this power come from? From your being firmly rooted and established in the grace of God. You have the power to love, because He first loved you! This is why the Bible declares in Romans 13:10 that "love is the fulfillment of the law."

In fact, when God's people are under grace, not only do they fulfill the letter of the law, they also exceed it and go the extra mile. The law commands you not to commit adultery, and there are people who can fulfill just the letter of the law and not commit adultery outwardly. However, inwardly they have no love for their spouses. Grace changes all that. Grace doesn't just deal with the surface; it goes deeper and teaches a man to love his wife as Christ loved the church. In the same way, the law can command a person not to covet, but it has no ability to make a person generous. Again, God's grace goes beyond the superficial to inwardly transform a covetous heart into a heart that is loving, compassionate, and generous.

When God's people are under grace, not only do they
fulfill the letter of the law, they also exceed it and
go the extra mile.

Remember the story of Zacchaeus? Not a single commandment was given. Yet when the love and grace of our Lord Jesus touched his heart, the once-covetous tax collector wanted to give half of his wealth to the poor and repay fourfold every person he had stolen from. The love of money died when the love of Jesus came.

Say Yes to Jesus and His Grace

I want to encourage you to be consumed with the person of Jesus. God's Word says that "you are in Christ Jesus, who has become for us wisdom from God—that is, our righteousness, holiness and redemption" (1 Cor. 1:30 NIV). Jesus Himself is your wisdom, your righteousness, and also your holiness! The Greek word used here for "holiness" is *hagiasmos*, the same Greek word used for "sanctification." Our holiness or sanctification is found in the person of Jesus. So whenever you have an unclean thought, a stirring in you, or a temptation to sin, stop for a while and look at Jesus. See the cross. See and experience His love, forgiveness, and grace for you afresh. Jesus is your victory over every temptation, addiction, and bondage!

There are people who believe that all you have to do is say no to temptation. But you know what? Your willpower is no match for sin. The reality is, the more you try to say no by your own efforts, the worse it becomes. The apostle Paul describes this very struggle, which he himself experienced: "For the good that I will to do, I do not do;

but the evil I will not to do, that I practice" (Rom. 7:19). So the answer is not to depend on your willpower to say no to temptation, but to depend on God's grace and say yes to Jesus!

Don't depend on your willpower to say no to temptation.
Depend on God's grace and say yes to Jesus!

In the midst of your struggle and temptation, say YES to Jesus. Say, "Lord Jesus, I thank You that You are my righteousness, my holiness, and my redemption." Turn every temptation into an opportunity to look to and praise Jesus! That's what Paul did. Just look at what he says in Romans 7:24–25: "O wretched man that I am! Who will deliver me from this body of death? I thank God—through Jesus Christ our Lord!"

Paul's answer for victory over sin is found in a *person*. His question is, "*Who* will deliver me?" He doesn't say, "*Which commandment* will deliver me?" Your liberty from every sinful habit is found in the person of Jesus! Say yes to Him! He is your righteousness and holiness. Let Him come into the areas where you feel the weakest and allow His grace to transform you from the inside out.

The War within Us

Now, please remember that there is nothing wrong with God's perfect law. In fact, Paul says, "For I delight in the law of God according to the inward man" (Rom. 7:22). However, he goes on to say, "But I see another law in my members, warring against the law of my mind, and bringing me into captivity to the law of sin which is in my members" (Rom. 7:23). Can you see? The law of God is holy, just, and good, but it has no power to make you holy, just, and good. By the law is the knowledge of sin (see Rom. 3:20)!

Paul explains this with great clarity:

Well then, am I suggesting that the law of God is sinful? Of course not! In fact, it was the law that showed me my sin. I would never have known that coveting is wrong if the law had not said, "You must not covet." But sin used this command to arouse all kinds of covetous desires within me! If there were no law, sin would not have that power. At one time I lived without understanding the law. But when I learned the command not to covet, for instance, the power of sin came to life, and I died. So I discovered that the law's commands, which were supposed to bring life, brought spiritual death instead. Sin took advantage of those commands and deceived me; it used the commands to kill me. But still, the law itself is holy, and its commands are holy and right and good.... Sin used what was good to bring about my condemnation to death.... So the trouble is not with the law, for it is spiritual and good. The trouble is with me, for I am all too human, a slave to sin.... And I know that nothing good lives in me.... I want to do what is good, but I don't. I don't want to do what is wrong, but I do it anyway.... I love God's law with all my heart. But there is another power within me that is at war with my mind. This power makes me a slave to the sin that is still within me. Oh, what a miserable person I am! Who will free me from this life that is dominated by sin and death? Thank God! The answer is in Jesus Christ our Lord.

—Romans 7:7–14, 18–19, 22–25 NLT

There is nothing wrong with God's perfect law. But when you combine God's perfect law with the flesh (the sin principle), the result is not holiness. It is, as Paul described, a life that is dominated by sin, condemnation, and death. Just as a spoon can be used to stir up sediment in a glass of water, so the law stirs up the sinful passions in our flesh. Those who preach strongly the Ten Commandments completely fail to acknowledge man's flesh and to understand what Paul describes in Romans 7.

In man's flesh dwells no good thing, and as long as we are in this mortal body, the sin principle in our flesh will continue to be stirred. That is why even after you have become a believer of Jesus, you still experience the temptation to sin. That is why, while God's law is glorious, God's Word calls it the ministry of death and condemnation. But praise be to our Lord and Savior, Jesus Christ, this doesn't have to end in misery and hopelessness. Because of what Jesus accomplished at the cross, Paul reminds us,

> *Shouldn't we expect far greater glory under the new way, now that the Holy Spirit is giving life? If the old way, which brings condemnation, was glorious, how much more glorious is the new way, which makes us right with God! In fact, that first glory was not glorious at all compared with the overwhelming glory of the new way. So if the old way, which has been replaced, was glorious, how much more glorious is the new, which remains forever!... But the people's minds were hardened, and to this day whenever the old covenant is being read, the same veil covers their minds so they cannot understand the truth. And this veil can be removed only by believing in Christ.... So all of us who have had that veil removed can see*

and reflect the glory of the Lord. And the Lord—who is the Spirit—makes us more and more like him as we are changed into his glorious image.

—2 Corinthians 3:8–11, 14, 18 NLT

My friend, it is clear from God's Word that the law stirs up our sinful nature, whereas grace produces true holiness! Holiness is all about becoming more and more like Jesus, and it comes about when the veil of the law is removed. When the veil is removed, we see our beautiful Savior face-to-face and His glorious grace transforms us from glory to glory. The glorious gospel of grace always produces glorious lives.

I pray that as you read through the pages of this book, you will have a greater revelation of just how wonderful your Savior is, just how perfect His work on Calvary was, and just how deeply loved YOU are. And as you behold Jesus, may you grow from glory to glory and shine as a testament to all of His goodness!

PART THREE

VALUE THE PERSON OF JESUS

CHAPTER 11

GROW IN GRACE BY HEARING HIM

There once was a wealthy man who loved his one and only son above all things. As father and son, they began to build an art collection together. Every spare minute they were out at auctions and sales acquiring rare works of art, everything from Picasso to Raphael.

Within a period of some ten years, they had built one of the rarest, most valuable collections in the world. Then war broke upon them and a letter came one day informing the son he had been drafted into the army. The son, feeling compelled to serve his country as his father and grandfather had before him, went off to war.

While he was away, the son wrote his dad every day. One day the letters stopped. The father's worst fears were realized when he received a telegram from the war department informing him his son had been killed while attempting to rescue another soldier.

About six months later there was a knock on the door. The father opened the door and saw a young soldier with a large package under his arm. The young soldier said, "Sir, you don't know me, but I am the man your son saved the day he died. While he was carrying me out of harm's way, he was shot through the heart and died instantly. Your son was my friend and we spent many nights just talking. He would talk about you and your love for art."

The young soldier held out his package and said, "I know this isn't much and I'm not much of an artist, but I wanted you to have this painting I've done of your son as I last remember him."

The father tore open the package and found himself gazing at a portrait of his one and only son. Fighting back tears, he said, "You have captured the essence of my son's smile in this painting and I will cherish it above all others." The father hung the portrait over his mantelpiece. When visitors came to his home, he always drew their attention to the portrait of his son before he showed them any of the other masterpieces.

When the father died, news went out that his entire collection of masterpieces was being offered at an exclusive private auction. Collectors and art experts from around the world gathered for the chance of purchasing one of them. They were a little surprised when the first painting on the auction block was the soldier's modest rendering of the man's son.

The auctioneer pounded his gavel and asked someone to start bidding. The sophisticated crowd scoffed and demanded the Van Goghs and the Rembrandts to be brought forth, but the auctioneer persisted: "Who will start bidding for this painting? One hundred dollars? Two hundred dollars?" The crowd, waiting to see the more serious paintings, continued to hiss for the auction to move on. Still the auctioneer asked, "The son! The son! Who will take the son?"

Finally a voice from the back said, "I'll bid ten dollars for the son." The bidder was none other than the young soldier whom the son had died saving. He said, "I didn't come with the intention to buy anything, and all I have is ten dollars to my name. But I'll bid my entire ten dollars for the painting."

The auctioneer continued seeking a higher bid, but the angry crowd shouted, "Sell it to him and let's get on with the auction." The auctioneer pounded the gavel and sold the painting to the soldier for the bid of ten dollars.

"Finally we can get on with the auction," someone from the second row bellowed. But right at that moment, the auctioneer announced, "The auction is now officially closed." The crowd was shocked and demanded to know how, when none of the "real" pieces had been sold, the auction could be over.

The auctioneer simply replied, "When I was called to conduct this auction, I was told of a stipulation in the will of the deceased. I could not divulge that stipulation until now. According to the wishes of the deceased, only the painting of the son was to be sold today. And whoever gets this painting gets it all—every piece of art in this collection. So today, for ten dollars, the young soldier has bought one of the world's most priceless art collections and the entire estate in which it is housed. The auction is closed." And with the swing of his gavel, he left the crowd sitting in stunned silence, staring at the young soldier.

Every time I think about this story,[1] I think of how, like the father in the story, God is looking for people who value and appreciate His Son. Whoever receives the Son receives all of God's blessings. To the one who values His Son, He gives every good thing He has. And how do we value His Son? One of the primary ways is by taking time to hear Him. Hear His word of grace to us and hear what He has done for us through His sacrifice at the cross.

God is looking for people who value and appreciate His Son. To the one who values His Son, He gives every good thing He has.

The psalmist says, "I will hear what God the LORD will say; for He will speak peace to His people" (Ps. 85:8 NASB). The Hebrew word for "peace" here is *shalom*, which means completeness, soundness, well-being in body and mind, safety, contentment, and peace in our relationships with people.[2]

My friend, if you desire to experience an increase in these blessings in your body, family, career, and ministry, then focus on hearing Jesus and growing in the knowledge of Him and His grace. The Bible tells us that grace and peace (and every good blessing) are multiplied to us when we grow in the knowledge of Jesus our Lord (see 2 Pet. 1:2).

Hear His Words of Grace

Not long ago the Lord opened my eyes to see, in the account of what happened on the Mount of Transfiguration, how important it is to hear God's Son and be established in His words of grace. Let's look at the story with an open heart to hear His now word to us.

In the accounts found in the Gospels of Matthew and Luke, we see how our Lord Jesus brought His disciples Peter, James, and John up a high mountain to pray. Scripture tells us that "as he was praying, the appearance of his face was transformed, and his clothes became dazzling white" (Luke 9:29 NLT). Then two of the most illustrious figures in the Jewish faith, Moses and Elijah, appeared and began talking with Jesus. The disciples, who had initially fallen asleep as Jesus was praying, woke up. Imagine their shock and awe when they saw these two great men—one representing the law and the other representing the prophets—appearing with Jesus in glory!

Peter, feeling he had to say something but not knowing what to say, blurted, "Master, it is good for us to be here; and let us make three tabernacles: one for You, one for Moses, and one for Elijah" (Luke 9:33).

Now, Peter didn't realize that by saying this, he was putting Jesus on the same level as Moses and Elijah, and the Father had to correct Peter. While Peter was still speaking, a cloud overshadowed them, and a voice came out of the cloud, saying, "This is My beloved Son. Hear Him!" (Luke 9:35). When the disciples heard this, they hit the ground, greatly afraid. Jesus came over to them, touched them, and said, "Arise, and do not be afraid" (Matt. 17:7). When they dared to look up, they saw no one but the Lord.

Now, imagine this: you've just been overshadowed by the bright cloud of the *shekinah* glory of God and heard the Father say from heaven, "Hear My Son, Jesus!" As you are facedown on the ground, absolutely terrified, don't you wonder what Jesus will say? What His first words will be? Then the Lord Jesus comes over to you, touches you in assurance and warmth, and says, "Arise, and do not be afraid."

Isn't that so beautiful, so like our Lord Jesus? His first words when His disciples were terrified were not words pertaining to a new law or commandment. They were words of grace. In fact, in the original Greek text, we get a fuller picture of how affirming and encouraging His words were. The word "arise" here is the Greek word *egeiro*, which means "to lift up."[3] Jesus, seeing Peter, James, and John flat on their faces, didn't just touch them—He literally lifted them up as He spoke reassuringly to them. This is the nature of our Lord. His presence and His words will always lift you up—spirit, soul, and body—when you are feeling down or in fear.

His presence and His words will always lift you up—spirit, soul, and body—when you are feeling down or in fear.

It's also significant that the Lord Jesus brought specifically these three disciples—Peter, James, and John—up the Mount of Transfiguration. Peter's name, *Petros* in Greek, means "stone,"[4] which is a picture of the law (see 2 Cor. 3:7 NLT). James is derived from the Old Testament name Jacob, which means "supplanter."[5] John's name in Hebrew, *Jochanan*, is derived from a root word that means "grace."[6] So if you put the three names Peter, James, and John together, there is a hidden message for us: *the stone (or law) has been supplanted (or replaced) by grace*! My friend, grace has come in the person of our Lord Jesus and replaced the law. Hear Him today. Hear His words of grace!

Whom Are You Hearing Today?

The Father said very clearly, "Hear *Him*," not "Hear *them*." On that mount of our Lord's transfiguration, Moses and Elijah were standing right there together with Jesus. Who was Moses? The lawgiver. Who was Elijah? Not just an Old Testament prophet, but also the law-restorer (in the Old Testament, when Israel went after other gods, Elijah came to the people as the restorer of the law).

For the believer, the law of Moses has served its purpose to bring man to the end of himself. The prophets have also served their purpose of reminding man of God's laws. Both have served their purposes. Now it is the day of grace. It is the day of the Son of God—not the *servants* of God, but the *Son* of God Himself.

Unfortunately, there are many believers today who put Jesus—grace—on the same level as the law of Moses. They see themselves as law-restorers and fight for the law of Moses to be restored. But that's not the heart of the Father. This is why the Father spoke and said, "Hear *Him*."

I believe that people who advocate bringing back the law of Moses don't realize that by the law is not the knowledge of holiness or God, but the "knowledge of sin"! Look at Romans 3:20–22:

> *Therefore by the deeds of the law no flesh will be justified in His sight, for by the law is the knowledge of sin. But now the righteousness of God apart from the law is revealed, being witnessed by the Law and the Prophets, even the righteousness of God, through faith in Jesus Christ, to all and on all who believe.*

Notice that in the above passage, Apostle Paul says, "But *now* the righteousness of God apart from the law is revealed" (emphasis mine). Do you want to live in the *now* or in the past? And do you want the latest revelation from God? Well, the latest revelation from God is grace! It's the revelation of the righteousness of God given to you as a gift apart from the law, and this revelation came through the Son. This is why Moses (the Law) and Elijah (the Prophets) were both witnesses to how we are to "Hear HIM," the Son—grace alone—today.

His Supply Flows When You Hear Him

Today, despite whatever you are facing in life, take time to hear Him. If you are concerned about symptoms in your body, keep hearing and hearing about how our Lord Jesus loved to heal and still heals today. Hear how He bore the cruel Roman lashes for you, so that by His stripes you are healed (see Isa. 53:5). Hear how He went about doing good and healing ALL who were oppressed (bodily, emotionally, and mentally) by the devil (see Acts 10:38, Matt. 9:35). Hear how when He saw the crowds waiting for His healing touch, He was moved with compassion—He didn't see them as people with impossible demands, but as sheep without a shepherd (see Matt. 9:36). And hear how He is the same yesterday, today, and forever (see Heb. 13:8). Faith will infuse your spirit, and His divine healing and health will flood every cell, organ, and system of your body!

Beloved, if you are anxious about the needs and demands of tomorrow, keep hearing how God is for you and not against you. Hear how He has freely given you ALL things through Christ (see Rom. 8:31–32), so that all you need to do is to freely receive ALL of His blessings, including the favor, wisdom, healing, and supply you need for whatever challenge you may be facing. Hear the Son remind you of your loving heavenly Father, Who knows your every need and promises He will take care of you as you cast your cares on Him and simply seek first His gift of righteousness (see Matt. 6:31–33). My dear friend, as you listen and become established in His grace toward you, every worry and anxiety will evaporate like mist as the morning sun comes up, and you will see His fresh supply of favor for every new need.

And if you've experienced the sting of betrayal, if you've been hurt by the words of people close to you, or if you are just feeling plain discouraged, hear the Lord's words of affirmation. Hear Him say to you, "I will never leave you nor forsake you." Let these words restore your heart, bring stability to your emotions, and give you the faith to boldly say, "The LORD is my helper; I will not fear. What can man do to me?" (Heb. 13:5–6).

My friend, to really grow in grace and see its fruit manifest in our lives, we need to keep hearing the Son and His words of grace, because it is so easy to slide back into being law- or demand-conscious, as opposed to being grace- or supply-conscious. Just look at what Peter, James, and John did after what happened on the Mount of Transfiguration.

To really grow in grace and see its fruit manifest in our lives,
we need to keep hearing the Son and His words of grace.

The Pull of Other Voices

In Matthew's account, the chapter ends with Peter and Jesus going to Capernaum (see Matt. 17:24–27). When they were there, the collectors of the temple tax came to Peter and asked if Jesus paid the temple tax. "Yes, He does," Peter replied confidently and without hesitation.

We then read that Jesus asked Peter, "What do you think, Simon? From whom do the kings of the earth take customs or taxes, from their sons or from strangers?"

To Jesus' question, Peter replied, "From strangers." Jesus said, "Then the sons are free."

Now what was all that about? You see, Peter had been very quick to say yes to the temple tax collectors and again had not quite known what he was saying. What was the issue really about? Under the law of Moses, the temple tax was for the maintenance of the temple, which was built for God. But Jesus as the Son did not have to pay the temple tax because He was greater than the temple. The Son of God had come and was right there.

Without being conscious of it, Peter had brought Jesus to the same level as Moses just as he had on the Mount of Transfiguration. Now, Peter's motive was good—he was doing it for Jesus' honor. He didn't want people to think that Jesus didn't pay the temple tax. But he was unconsciously looking at our Lord Jesus as a mere man and didn't know that in his earnest zealousness, he had actually lowered our Lord by bringing Him to the same level as the law.

Whom was Peter "listening" to? He was still thinking of Moses and what Moses had said about the temple tax. He didn't even ask or consult the Son. Earlier, on the Mount of Transfiguration, he had heard the Father say clearly, "This is My beloved Son, in whom I am well pleased. Hear *Him*!" And yet, before the chapter is over, you find that Peter again "listened" to Moses.

But look at our Lord Jesus. Was He offended? Look at what the Lord said to Peter: "Nevertheless, lest we offend them, go to the sea, cast in a hook, and take the fish that comes up first. And when you have opened its mouth, you will find a piece of money; take that and give it to them for Me and you."

Isn't the Lord wonderful? He patiently showed Peter that the temple tax did not apply to Him because He was the Son of the Father, and He was patiently telling Peter He would demonstrate this truth by summoning the wealth of the lake as the Creator. And as quickly as Jesus had revealed Who He was, He humbled Himself and paid the temple tax for Himself *and* for Peter. He is meekness and majesty, glory and humility personified! These are the excellencies of our beautiful Lord and Savior. Doesn't your heart just fill up with warmth and love as you behold Him? This is Whom the Father wants us to lean in to and listen to. And as we do, we are transformed to be like Him, from glory to glory.

Jesus is meekness and majesty, glory and humility
personified! As we behold Him, we are transformed
to be like Him, from glory to glory.

What about Voices of Judgment?

And how did the other two disciples, James and John, fare? If you read Luke's account of the transfiguration in chapter 9, you'll find that it is followed by our Lord Jesus not being welcomed by the people of a Samaritan village. When James and John saw how the Samaritans rejected Jesus and didn't treat Him with respect, they spoke up and said, "Lord, do You want us to command fire to come down from heaven and consume them, just as Elijah did?" (Luke 9:54).

All three disciples had heard the Father say, "Hear My beloved Son," yet we find Peter looking to Moses, and now we see James and John looking to Elijah as the example to follow. What did Jesus say to their suggestion to call down fire as judgment on the people? Jesus said, "You do not know what manner of spirit you are of. The Son of Man is not come to destroy men's lives but to save them" (Luke 9:55–56).

The spirit of Elijah is a spirit of judgment. Jesus told the two brothers very plainly that in saying what they did, they were not of the spirit of grace. What we see here is that as quickly as Peter returned to hearing the voice of Moses, James and John returned to hearing the voice of Elijah. My dear reader, this is not the heart of the Father. We have to be wise in order not to put our Lord on the same level as the law and the prophets.

There are many today still fighting for the voices of Moses and Elijah—the law and the prophets—not fully understanding that in the new covenant, it is all about hearing the voice of the resurrected Son of God. We are to hear the words of our Lord, Who is today seated at the right hand of God, having completed perfectly His work at the cross, where He took upon Himself the punishment for all our sins once and for all.

The law of Moses demands, while the spirit of Elijah executes judgment, calling down fire on those who fail to meet the law's demands. But I want you to see how our Lord Jesus has fulfilled both (see Matt. 5:17). He did not come to destroy the law or the prophets, but to fulfill them. At the cross He met all the righteous requirements of the law on our behalf and took upon Himself all the fiery judgment of God for our sins. His perfect sacrifice has fully satisfied God and silenced the law and the prophets. Today we hear *Him*!

Jesus' perfect sacrifice has fully satisfied God and silenced the law and the prophets. Today we hear Him*!*

Neither the Law nor the Prophets Hold the Answer

Why does the Father want us to hear only the Lord Jesus? Why are we to focus on Jesus and grow in the knowledge of His grace? Because neither the law nor the prophets hold the answer to our deepest cry for intimacy and peace with God, and to enjoyment of His presence and power in every area of our lives. If you look at Scripture, you will see that while Moses and Elijah did mighty exploits, both great men of God still failed in the end.

Toward the end of his life, Moses hit the rock twice in disobedience, yelled at the people, spoke unadvisedly out of anger and impatience, and wound up not being allowed to enter the promised land. That's how his ministry ended. Why were the consequences of Moses' actions so severe? Because he misrepresented God. In his anger he represented God as angry and judgmental toward His people, when God actually loved and cared for them. This tells us that as preachers of God's Word, we need to be very accurate in how we represent God.

What about Elijah? Despite amazing victories and evidence of the power of God in his ministry, in his last days, Elijah thought Jezebel was greater than God and fled from her. His ministry ended in depression and discouragement (see 1 Kings 19), with his mantle going to Elisha.

In comparison, where the law and the prophets failed, our Lord Jesus succeeded. Look at this beautiful prophecy of the Messiah in Isaiah 42:1, 3–4:

> *Behold! My Servant whom I uphold,*
> *My Elect One in whom My soul delights!...*
> *A bruised reed He will not break,*
> *And smoking flax He will not quench;*
> *He will bring forth justice for truth.*
> *He will not fail nor be discouraged.*

Whereas Moses failed and Elijah became discouraged, the Scriptures tell us that our Lord Jesus, the altogether lovely One, "will not fail nor be discouraged." Whereas Moses was impatient, our Lord Jesus was patient with Peter, and He is patient with you and me today especially when we make mistakes and fail. And whereas Moses failed to bring God's people into the promised land, our Lord Jesus finished the work His Father sent Him to do and has ushered us into all of God's blessings and promises (see Eph. 1:3, 2 Cor. 1:20). Whereas Elijah became discouraged, Jesus was not discouraged by the Samaritans' rejection of Him. He is your rock and your fortress when you are feeling discouraged. All the greatest men of God in the Old Testament put together cannot compare with our beautiful Lord Jesus Christ!

This is God's beloved Son and today He says to you, "Arise. Stand in My righteousness and be lifted up from defeat." In the same way that our Lord Jesus could touch a man with leprosy and make him whole, He can touch any area of deformity, weakness, or shame in your life and transform it into wholeness and strength by His grace. This has been the experience of so many who have written in to tell me their stories of amazing breakthroughs after they began listening to the gospel of grace and allowing the Lord Jesus to lift them up and out of every pit they were in.

God's beloved Son says to you, "Arise. Stand in My righteousness and be lifted up from defeat."

The Power of Hearing Him

Let me encourage you with one such testimony from Javier, a precious brother who lives in Illinois:

> *I grew up as a pastor's kid and was baptized at eight years old. Yet from the age of fifteen right up to when I was twenty-eight, I was involved in heavy drinking, experimenting with different kinds of drugs, and taking antidepressants to cope with my life.*
>
> *I got married at the age of twenty-five. After three years, my wife finally told me she couldn't handle my lifestyle choices anymore, and was taking our brand-new baby girl to live with*

her mother because I was destroying my own life and the lives of those around me. It was then that I cried out to God for help.

Right at that moment, I happened to turn on the television and while channel surfing, I stopped when I heard this man of God telling me that God loves me. I also heard that nò matter what I've done, God has forgiven me and will never stop loving me. Since that day, I have recorded and watched your Destined to Reign *broadcasts twice a day.*

Within two years, by the grace of God, I stopped drinking and doing drugs. I also stopped taking antidepressants and did not suffer any side effects. On top of this, I received the baptism of the Holy Spirit after watching you teach on the topic and within two weeks, began to pray in the Spirit. I've also seen my spiritual life take off.

My wife saw the change in my life and chose not to leave me for good. We have just celebrated our tenth wedding anniversary in July and we now have two beautiful girls, aged seven and five.

After five years of meditation, study, and focusing only on the message of the finished work of Jesus at the cross, I started a grace-based ministry. We began to introduce the gospel of grace to nursing homes and started our own services on Saturdays.

I want you to know that learning about the gospel of grace through your ministry has transformed a depressed drunk and drug addict into a healthy, loving pastor who takes the message of grace everywhere. Praise be to Jesus Christ, the author and finisher of our faith!

My dear reader, whatever you may be facing today, I want to encourage you to heed the words the Father spoke on the Mount of

Transfiguration: *"This is My beloved Son. Hear Him."* He is no longer demanding from you. Christ has come. He has fulfilled all that the law commands and all that the prophets have spoken (see Matt. 5:17). *Grace has come! Hear HIM.*

Take time today to hear the Lord Jesus through anointed preaching and teaching that point you to His finished work that makes you perfectly righteous before the Father. Hear Him reveal His perfect love for you through His Word. As you hear Him and let His words of grace go deep into your heart, you can't help but be transformed from the inside out to walk in lasting breakthroughs and liberty.

CHAPTER 12

A REVOLUTION OF RELATIONSHIP

The grace revolution is all about Jesus. There is no revolution of grace without the cross. What our beloved Lord Jesus accomplished at Calvary has made all the difference. The cross put an end to the old covenant and kick-started the new covenant of grace. What began on a hill in Jerusalem is now a revolution that has spread to the ends of the earth. Today the gospel of grace is preached with power, boldness, and authority like never before.

It's been almost two decades since the Lord first spoke to me about preaching the gospel of grace. He said to me, "If you don't preach grace radically, lives will not be radically blessed and radically transformed." These words He spoke to me while I was on vacation with Wendy in the Swiss Alps are forever etched in my heart.

They have defined my life, my ministry, and my church. As the Lord has promised, we are seeing so many precious lives gloriously transformed by the bold preaching of the gospel of grace. Instead of running away from God, people are falling in love with Jesus all over again. Instead of living in the bondage of sin, precious people are being liberated from the chains of addiction. And instead of living with perpetual guilt, condemnation, and judgment, people are living with greater joy, peace, and assurance of their righteousness in Christ.

This is what the grace revolution is all about! It is a revolution of God's amazing love. A revolution of favor, a revolution of restoration, and a revolution of people's lives transformed by a powerful encounter with our Lord Jesus.

Separation versus Intimacy

The grace revolution is a revolution of relationship. The old covenant of law was about rules, religion, and regulations. The new covenant of grace is all about relationship. The old covenant of law created separation between God and His people; the new covenant of grace brings intimacy between God and His children.

The old covenant of law created separation between God and His people. The new covenant of grace brings intimacy between God and His children.

Let me take you to see what really happened when the law was given at the foot of Mount Sinai. Before God's people had even heard the Ten Commandments, they proclaimed, "All that the LORD has spoken we will do" (Exod. 19:8). This statement reflects man's pride and self-confidence. This is not an indictment against the children of Israel, but against all men who boast they can keep all of God's laws. When people say that they can keep God's laws even before they have heard what those laws are, that is putting confidence in the flesh. That is pride.

So at the foot of Mount Sinai, when man boasted in his own self-sufficiency that he would keep God's laws, God's tone immediately changed. The Lord said to Moses on Mount Sinai, "You shall set bounds for the people around, saying, 'Take heed to yourselves that you do not go up to the mountain or touch its base. Whoever touches the mountain shall surely be put to death. Not a hand shall touch him, but he shall surely be stoned or shot with an arrow; whether man or beast, he shall not live'" (Exod. 19:12–13).

My dear friend, that's the law of the old covenant. Just take a moment and imagine you are at the foot of Mount Sinai. See it as it is described in the Word of God: "Now Mount Sinai was completely in smoke, because the LORD descended upon it in fire. Its smoke ascended like the smoke of a furnace, and the whole mountain quaked greatly" (Exod. 19:18). This is the setting where the Ten Commandments were given.

It was a terrifying place to be at. Don't take my word for it; read for yourself. This is all documented for us in the book of Exodus. "Now all the people witnessed the thundering, the lightning flashes, the sound of the trumpet, and the mountain smoking; and when the people saw it, they trembled and stood afar off. Then they said to Moses, 'You speak with us, and we will hear; but let not God speak with us, lest we die'" (Exod. 20:18–19).

The old covenant of the law was a covenant that was void of relationship. It was a covenant of distance and separation from God. The people, seized by fear, didn't want God to speak to them. That was (and still is) the effect of the law.

When God's people presumed on their own righteousness (reflecting the pride in every person's heart, making them believe they can actually do all that God demands), God unleashed upon them His righteous standards and immediately a division and distance came between perfectly righteous God and hopelessly sinful man. The law certainly wasn't God's best for His people. But since they boasted that they could keep it, God gave it to them for 1,500 years (until Christ came) to show them that they couldn't and that a covenant based on grace was superior.

From that point on, God's people grew afraid of Him and pulled away from any relationship with Him, asking Moses to communicate with Him on their behalf. That's the context of the giving of the old covenant of the law. It was not founded upon a relationship but on separation from God.

God Honors You as You Honor His Son

Unfortunately, there are people today who believe that we are still under the old covenant and that man is made righteous by the keeping of the Ten Commandments. They preach from Mount Sinai and their preaching is full of the thundering, lightning flashes, smoke, fire, and rumblings of Mount Sinai. Have you heard them before? I believe many of them are sincere, well-intentioned, and honest people. But one can be sincere, well-intentioned, and honest but still sincerely wrong.

I believe our teaching of God's Word cannot be evaluated purely by virtue of sincerity; it needs to be evaluated on the basis of our treatment of the person of our Lord Jesus Christ. I believe with all my heart that God honors you according to how you honor His Son.

God honors you according to how you honor His Son.

Exalt the name of Jesus and you will be exalted. Promote the person of Jesus and you will be promoted. Elevate the work of Jesus and you will be elevated. Preaching that man is made righteous by his keeping of the Ten Commandments in reality negates and shows we do not value, or have no understanding of, what our Lord Jesus' sacrifice accomplished for us at Calvary.

Exalt the name of Jesus and you will be exalted. Promote the person of Jesus and you will be promoted. Elevate the work of Jesus and you will be elevated.

The Word of God tells us that "if you are trying to make yourselves right with God by keeping the law, you have been cut off from Christ! You have fallen away from God's grace" (Gal. 5:4 NLT). In another translation it says, "Christ is become of no effect unto you, whosoever of you are justified by the law; ye are fallen from grace" (KJV).

I don't know about you, but as for me, my family, and my church, we don't want Christ to become of no effect to us. When our loved ones are sick, we want all of Christ's healing power to be of effect to us! Amen.

Don't fall from grace and attempt to make yourself right with God by the law. Stop rejecting, fighting, and shoving away God's grace. I pray that even as you are reading this, you are allowing His love, grace, and power to lift you up from every defeat you are experiencing.

My friend, God loves you more deeply than you realize. He values, treasures, and loves you. It is time to let go of your own works and allow the grace of our Lord Jesus Christ to completely revolutionize your life from the inside out.

When Christ is of full effect in your life, that breakthrough you have been believing for shall come to pass swiftly in the name of Jesus.

That destructive addiction you have been battling for years will come crumbling down and no longer have a grip on your life. That health condition you have been trying to beat shall be no more, and I pray for you that you receive supernatural healing right now in your body.

I declare that by His stripes, you are completely healed in the name of Jesus. Cancer and all terminal diseases have no hold over the body of the person reading this right now. I speak health, healing, longevity, and wholeness in Jesus' mighty name. May your youth be renewed like the eagle's, and may you be satisfied with the promise of long life and good days in Jesus' name. Amen and Amen!

As I was writing this, God's spirit of faith to believe with you for your healing and health just arose in me. We have a miracle-working God and He can go above and beyond anything the doctors might have said about your condition, so let's lean in to His love, His grace, and His peace. May His healing power be of full effect in your body, in Jesus' name!

I can't wait to hear from you about what God has done in you, so be sure to write to me at www.josephprince.com/testimony. I look forward to rejoicing and praising the Lord with you.

Are You on the Right Mountain?

If you want true liberty and stability in life, it's important you build your life on the right foundation. Everything proceeds from the right foundation. Build your life on the wrong foundation and you will find yourself easily shaken when the storms of life hit. But build your life on the right foundation and you will be like the man who built his house on the rock—unshakable and rock-solid in the face of adversities.

If you build your foundation on Mount Sinai, you are building on a foundation that breeds fear and insecurity in your relationship with God. In the end you are building on a foundation that feeds your sense of separation from God. How then are you going to find the confidence to go to Him and expect to find the hope and help you need from Him?

There are many still camped on the old mountain of Sinai, preaching the law and thinking that this is what will bring people closer to God and give them confidence in their Christian walk. Unfortunately, the opposite happens. The children of Israel were filled with fear at the smoke, the darkness, the quaking, and the lightning when the law was given at Mount Sinai, and couldn't wait to flee from God. The same thing happens in the hearts of people when they hear about and see only a God of condemnation, judgment, and wrath. Instead of running *to* God, they run *from* Him. Instead of experiencing intimacy with the Lord that gives them strength and changes them from the inside out, they experience separation and distance that drive them deeper into destructive behaviors with no hope of freedom.

My dear reader, I want to announce to you today that God has moved mountains. He is no more on Mount Sinai. Because of the cross of Jesus, where His wrath for all our sins was poured out, God has moved to Mount Zion, the mountain of grace, the place of reconciliation, relationship, and closeness with His people.

God has moved to Mount Zion, the mountain of grace,
the place of reconciliation, relationship, and closeness
with His people.

In the Psalms alone, you will find many Scriptures about how God loves and has chosen Zion, and will bless those on Zion:

For the Lord *has chosen Zion; He has desired it for His dwelling place: "This is My resting place forever; here I will dwell, for I have desired it. I will abundantly bless her provision; I will satisfy her poor with bread. I will also clothe her priests with salvation, and her saints shall shout aloud for joy."*

—*Psalm 132:13–16*

The Lord *loves the gates of Zion more than all the dwellings of Jacob.*

—*Psalm 87:2*

But [the Lord] chose the tribe of Judah, Mount Zion which He loved.

—*Psalm 78:68*

Sing the praises of the Lord*, enthroned in Zion.*

—*Psalm 9:11* niv

"Yet I have set My King on My holy hill of Zion."

—*Psalm 2:6*

They that trust in the Lord *shall be as mount Zion, which cannot be removed, but abideth for ever.*

—*Psalm 125:1* kjv

Look at the last Scripture. It is Mount Zion, and not Mount Sinai, that cannot be removed. It remains forever! What does this mean? If you establish your life on Mount Zion, you will enjoy stability. If your blessings and breakthroughs come from Mount Zion, they will last!

In the New Testament, it is clear which mountain we are supposed to have both feet planted firmly on:

> *For you have not come to the mountain [Mount Sinai] that may be touched and that burned with fire, and to blackness and darkness and tempest.... But you have come to Mount Zion and to the city of the living God, the heavenly Jerusalem, to an innumerable company of angels, to the general assembly and church of the firstborn who are registered in heaven, to God the Judge of all, to the spirits of just men made perfect.*
>
> —*Hebrews 12:18, 22–23*

According to this Scripture, Mount Sinai is a place of "blackness and darkness and tempest." In contrast, what do you find on Mount Zion? You find the city of the living God, an innumerable company of angels, and the church. The living God sits enthroned on Mount Zion, not Mount Sinai.

---

*The living God sits enthroned on Mount Zion,
not Mount Sinai.*

Do you want angels to watch over you and your family? Come to Mount Zion, where you'll find an uncountable number of angels! Do you want to experience what church life is supposed to be like? Then come to Mount Zion, where God as "the Judge of all" judges you righteous and perfect in Christ our Lord!

Why can God judge us righteous and perfect on Mount Zion? It is only because of the sacrifice and finished work of His Son, Jesus. The Hebrew word for Zion is *Tsiyown*, which means "parched place."[1] A parched place is a place that has been made dry or burned by intense heat. Can you see how Mount Zion speaks of Mount Calvary, the place where Jesus, the sacrificial Lamb of God, was burned by God's fiery indignation against all our sins? Mount Zion typifies the finished work of our Lord Jesus at the cross.

The thunder and lightning—tangible symbols of God's judgment—at the giving of the law on Mount Sinai fell on our Lord Jesus at the cross. A divine exchange took place there. He was burned and parched so that we can have the well of living waters in us, springing up into everlasting life (see John 4:14). He was punished so that we can be blessed (see Gal. 3:13–14). He was made sin so that we can be made righteous (see 2 Cor. 5:21). He was made poor so that we can be abundantly provided for (see 2 Cor. 8:9). Beloved, the reason you and I can stand righteous before God on Mount Zion and enjoy every blessing of redemption is that we are standing in the finished work of Christ! Hallelujah!

The reason you and I can stand righteous before God on Mount Zion and enjoy every blessing of redemption is that we are standing in the finished work of Christ!

You've Been Brought Near to God

Did you know that it was on Mount Zion in Jerusalem that the church was born? When the day of Pentecost had fully come, the Spirit of God came like a rushing mighty wind, and filled the 120 disciples in the Upper Room (see Acts 2:2–4). The Spirit of God could not wait to inhabit the believers who had been justified by the blood of Jesus.

Can you imagine God living inside you? How much closer can you get to God? You are so near, you are of one spirit with God (see 1 Cor. 6:17) because our Lord Jesus first came near and gave His life for you. That is what the finished work of our Lord Jesus has accomplished for you!

Let me say this again: the grace revolution is a revolution of relationship. The testimonies my ministry constantly receives have, besides various amazing breakthroughs, one constant: people are falling deeply in love with Jesus. Intimacy with God is being restored. Religion has become relationship. "Have to"s have become "want to"s. People are experiencing new life and an intimacy with God they never had before. Those who were once far off have drawn near to God, and in that place of nearness, their needs are more than met.

The grace revolution is a revolution of relationship.

My dear reader, this can be your reality, your ending to the struggles and dryness you are facing right now. It all begins when you value the person of Jesus and what He has accomplished for you to experience closeness with God.

What happens when you stay in this place of nearness to God?

You dwell in the place of abundance, in the land of Goshen. *Goshen* literally means "drawing near"[2] to God. In the Old Testament story of Joseph, when the land was in famine, Joseph said to his brothers, "Hurry and go up to my father, and say to him, 'Thus says your son Joseph: "God has made me lord of all Egypt; come down to me, do not tarry. You shall dwell in the land of Goshen, and *you shall be near to me*, you and your children, your children's children, your flocks and your herds, and all that you have. *There I will provide for you*, lest you and your household, and all that you have, come to poverty; for there are still five years of famine"'" (Gen. 45:9–11, emphasis mine).

My friend, the world we live in today is fraught with famine, economic uncertainty, corruption, and all kinds of evil and tragedies. People are more afraid than ever to travel by air or sea. Many people are living stressed, anxious lives just due to the chaos they see all around them. As Scripture says, the world will get darker, and it is (see Isa. 60:2).

But in the midst of all this darkness and uncertainty, I want you to know that there is a Goshen you and your family can take refuge in. It's a blessed place where God says, "You shall be *near* to me, you and your children, and your children's children. There *I will provide for you!*"

In the midst of darkness and uncertainty, there is a blessed place where God says, "You shall be near *to me, you and your children, and your children's children. There* I *will provide for you!"*

That's what the grace revolution does for you. It is a revolution of restored relationship. It brings you near to God. To be established on Mount Zion is to have an intimacy with God you never dreamed possible. And in that intimacy, barrenness gives way to fruitfulness. Lack is replaced by abundance. Sadness and sickness with joy and life. Fear with love. Confusion and insecurity with peace and assurance. Defeat with victory. Breakdowns with breakthroughs. And aimlessness with divine destiny!

The grace revolution brings you near to God.

Intimacy with Jesus Produces Good Fruit

Adeline from the United Kingdom wrote to me with her praise report that bears out what I have just discussed. She shares,

> When I came across your broadcast almost two years ago, I was at the end of myself and as you've said, I was both "wandering" and "wondering" what had happened to my relationship with the Lord.
>
> I was serving in church but I felt spiritually dry and I was getting weary and tired. My marriage wasn't doing well. In fact, my relatives were advising me to get out of the relationship because they were concerned about how my children were being affected by the tensions and strains in our marriage.
>
> It was my husband who first saw your broadcast on television and told me about you. Out of curiosity, I watched and I thank God that I did because before that, I'd cried out to God and told Him that I could not live the way I was living anymore. God heard my cries and He has answered me way above what I'd asked or imagined!

Law demands but grace supplies, supplies, and supplies! As I watched and I listened, I fell in love with Jesus all over again. How can I not when Jesus is being unveiled every time the Word is taught? I feel like a sheep that has been led to feed in fresh green pastures, and to rest and drink beside still and restful waters.

For the first time since I came to know Jesus when I was eleven years old, I am experiencing "prosperity" like I've never seen before. Firstly, He caused my soul to prosper. Then, like a ripple effect, my marriage began to prosper because instead of calling time-out, I fell in love with my husband all over again. The feeling was mutual as my husband had also been impacted by the message of grace that he was hearing, and our marriage got born again!

Even my children are being blessed when they listen to your messages and they now enjoy a peace at home that was not there before. My six-year-old would even quote you on Romans 6:14, saying that "sin shall not have dominion over us because we are not married to Mr. Law but Mr. Grace!"

Serving the Lord in church has also taken on a different dimension because I now serve out of and because of the abundance of His grace. Because of the revelation I've received of who I am in Christ, I am also better able to perform my duties as a nurse to care for patients with critical conditions instead of dreading them. I now want to care for them because I am in a position to make a difference to their condition.

It's been an AMAZING time, discovering what grace is! God truly gives us restful increase and this has been a year of unceasing fruitfulness for me and my family. It's the gospel of grace, and God is using you to bring His love, His abundant life to His body.

I can't have enough of this gospel, for this good news that is SO GOOD that it can't be anything but true. All whom I have shared with are encouraged to hear His Word through your ministry and are experiencing a gospel revolution. Thank you, Pastor Prince! GOD IS GOOD!

Hearing the message of grace brought Adeline to the land of Goshen, where she "fell in love with Jesus all over again" and had her marriage restored. Out of that intimacy with God, she also experienced restful increase and unceasing fruitfulness for herself and her family as His grace just kept supplying their every need. She is also now a carrier of His spirit of grace and love in her work as a nurse, and is making a tangible difference in the lives of her patients. Praise the Lord!

Made Eternally Righteous by Faith

Beloved, how do you stay planted on Zion and in the place of nearness and intimacy with the Lord? It is by being established in your righteous standing in Christ Jesus. Our Lord Jesus died on the cross and rose again on the third day to give us an everlasting righteousness that is anchored by faith in Him (see Rom. 4:5). Now that is the gospel of Jesus Christ!

How do you stay planted on Zion and in the place of nearness and intimacy with the Lord? It is by being established in your righteous standing in Christ Jesus.

Please understand that I have nothing against the Ten Commandments. I just have a problem with those who are saying that you need to keep the Ten Commandments in order to be made righteous, because by that standard, no one can! No man can keep the Ten Commandments perfectly inwardly and outwardly. And according to Scripture, if you break just one law, you are guilty of breaking the whole law (see James 2:10). The Ten Commandments are holy, just, and good, but they cannot make you holy, just, and good! We can't be justified by the law. We can be justified only by faith in the Lord Jesus.

Name me one person who has been made righteous by the Ten Commandments. Even the person who is vehemently telling you that you are made right in your relationship with the Lord by keeping the Ten Commandments has failed to do so and will continue to fail in thought, word, and deed. Read what the apostle Paul said in Galatians closely:

> We know that a person is made right with God by faith in Jesus Christ, not by obeying the law. And we have believed in Christ Jesus, so that we might be made right with God because of our faith in Christ, not because we have obeyed the law. For no one will ever be made right with God by obeying the law.
>
> —*Galatians 2:16* NLT

Read the last line again: "For no one will ever be made right with God by obeying the law." Now is the apostle Paul against God's law and against the Ten Commandments? Of course not!

In the same way, we are in favor of the law for the reason for which God gave the law. God gave the law to bring man to the end of himself and to begin to see a need for the saving grace of a Savior. No man can be justified and made righteous by the law.

Righteousness under law is earned by works, righteousness under grace is received by faith through grace. You are made righteous today by your faith in our Lord Jesus Christ. The moment you received Jesus as your personal Lord and Savior you were made eternally righteous without any works.

But Pastor Prince, how can I be made righteous without any works?

That's why, my dear reader, it is a grace revolution! Jesus has overthrown the system where man had to earn God's righteousness, and put us under one where God provides His very own righteousness through His Son. Grace is the undeserved, unearned, and unmerited favor of God. You received everlasting righteousness from God as a free gift by faith through grace the second you believed in our Lord Jesus.

Jesus has overthrown the system where man had to earn God's righteousness, and put us under one where God provides His very own righteousness through His Son.

Under law, righteousness is a work. Under grace, righteousness is a free gift apart from works. Salvation, righteousness, and eternal life are all priceless. Man can never perform enough good works to merit, earn, and deserve them. They had to be given by God as a gift! And boy did He give. He gave up His beloved Son on the cross, so that you and I today can be called the sons and daughters of God.

The Chasm Has Been Bridged

As a son or daughter in God's family, you can enjoy intimate fellowship with God, Who is your heavenly Father. What the law could not do—make us children of God—God did by sending His Son, Jesus Christ. He wanted us close to Him, so close that He can dwell in us and we in Him. It is all about intimacy and relationship.

The law given from Mount Sinai put a great chasm of separation and distance between God and us. It drew a line in the sand, a line that man could not cross in his efforts to draw close to God. But that division has been broken because of Jesus. The chasm has been bridged. His sacrifice has torn the veil separating us from God.

Jesus is the reason we can cross from Mount Sinai to Mount Zion. Now we can draw near to the Father, to His throne of grace, with boldness and confidence. Jew or Gentile, because of the blood of Christ, we have both been brought near to God (see Eph. 2:17–18).

Jesus is the reason we can draw near to the Father, to His throne of grace, with boldness and confidence.

My dear friend, today you can have the intimacy you've always longed for with God. You can enjoy fruitfulness instead of dead works when you live in the realm of His love for you, and not out of a sense of religious obligation. If you've been beaten down by negative circumstances, a long-term condition, or an addiction you can't seem to break, you can be a prisoner of hope and receive His gift of righteousness afresh to reign over it (see Zech. 9:12, Rom. 5:17).

You can have a fresh start in your career even when you have seen your dreams shattered, because you know that in the place of nearness, God loves you, hears you, and will restore to you. You can live free of fear, terror, and oppression as you become more and more established in His righteousness day by day (Isa. 54:14). I pray that as you grow in your revelation of how Jesus has brought you to a place of closeness with God, you will walk in liberty. May you have victory over everything that is holding you back from fulfilling all that our Father has in store for your blessed future in Him.

CHAPTER 13

HAVING A HEART FOR JESUS

Bethany was one place that our Lord Jesus loved to frequent. He was very comfortable in Bethany, where He could be among His closest friends, Martha, Mary, and Lazarus. Bethany was a home away from home for our Lord. There His friends loved Him, honored Him, and truly valued His presence. On His part, He cherished their company dearly, and always felt comfortable and relaxed with them. It was also in Bethany that our Lord ascended into heaven (see Luke 24:50–51).

Six days before He gave Himself up to be crucified, He gathered His friends together in Bethany, which was about two miles away from Jerusalem. They had prepared a feast in His honor, but their reunion was overshadowed by the looming Passover, which was less than a week away. His friends understood to some degree what the Lord intended to do, and their hearts were heavy because they cared deeply for Him.

As our Lord Jesus was eating, Mary brought out a jar of spikenard, a very costly fragrant oil. So costly, in fact, that it was worth a whole year's wages. But it wasn't the hours she had toiled to earn the oil that Mary thought about as she cradled the jar in her hands.

It was Jesus. It was her Lord.

She had come prepared to worship Jesus and her heart overflowed with a love that could not be expressed in words as she drew near to Him. Gratitude and adoration welled up inside her as she knelt quietly beside Him. Not sparing a drop of her exquisite tribute, she anointed the Lord's feet and wiped them with her hair. And the entire house was filled with the opulent fragrance of her worship of our Lord Jesus Christ.

Upon witnessing this lavish and extravagant gesture, one of Jesus' disciples, Judas Iscariot, lashed out indignantly. In sharp criticism of Mary, he demanded, "Why was this fragrant oil not sold for three hundred denarii and given to the poor?" (John 12:1–5).

Did you notice that with only one glance at the jar of precious spikenard, Judas was able to come up with a precise evaluation of its commercial worth? This man had an acumen for business and knew instantly that this perfume was worth three hundred denarii. The sad reality is this: Judas could tell the value of the oil straightaway, but he couldn't see the value of our Lord Jesus.

Unveiling the Value of Jesus

Many people in the world today know the value of real estate, the value of commodities, and the value of publicly traded companies in the stock market, but they don't know the value of Jesus.

I am so glad that you appreciate the value of our Lord Jesus, which is why you are taking time to read this book that is all about the person of Jesus. The grace revolution is all about unveiling the value of Jesus. When you know the value of Jesus, Who He is, what He has done, and what He is still doing in your life today, you will experience a grace revolution in your life. You will begin to live above every defeat when you have a personal encounter with the Lord Jesus.

When you know the value of Jesus, Who He is and what He
has done for you, you will begin to live above every defeat.

People can argue about doctrine, about law and grace, about the confession of sin, about your eternal security, and about different Bible interpretations. But at the end of the day, let me teach you how to test every doctrine, teaching, and scriptural interpretation.

Ask yourself—how is our Lord Jesus valued in this teaching? Does it make you want to worship, praise, and glorify the Lord Jesus with your life? Or does it put more value on you and what you have to perform? Does it cause you to be centered on and occupied with the person of Jesus? Or does it cause you to be centered on and occupied with yourself and whether you have failed or succeeded?

Pastor Prince, are you saying that performance is unimportant?

Absolutely not! I am sharing with you that the key to performance comes by the power of His love, grace, and unmerited favor in your life! You will be able to truly perform when you know you are perfectly loved.

Look at children who are bold, confident, and secure. They come from families that are full of love and affirmation. Families that free them to succeed. These children are not afraid to fail and they stand out in the crowd because they dare to be different for the glory of our Lord Jesus Christ. They dare to say no to the influences of the world. They are not ashamed when their peers mock their Christian values. At the same time, in an environment of love, grace, and affirmation, the child's parents are also able to discipline, correct, and guide the child in learning to make good decisions for himself without crushing his spirit.

Corrected Because We Are Loved

Some people have the erroneous idea that when you are under grace, there is no correction and every and anything goes. This cannot be further from the truth. Is there correction under grace?

Just ask any of my pastors and they will tell you, "Of course there is!" But the correction is always saturated with love, grace, and wisdom. Is there discipline under grace? Of course there is! All effective discipline and correction is communicated with an abundance of grace, patience, and love.

There are those who argue that if we are indeed always highly favored by the Lord, then there is be no need for Him to correct and to discipline us. My dear friend, let me help you understand it from the perspective of a parent. When my kids do something wrong, Wendy and I certainly correct and discipline them. But in our hearts they are always loved and favored by us even when they have failed and even while being corrected by us.

Why? Simply because they are our children! No matter how they perform, we will always love them and they will always be favored in our hearts. How highly favored they are to us is a matter of their identity, not their performance. It is based on *who* they are and *whose* they are, not what they have or have not done.

In the same way, our state of being loved and favored by our Father in heaven is a result of our identity as the sons and daughters of God through the finished work of Jesus Christ. We can call God our Father and God can call us His children because of what Jesus has done on the cross on our behalf!

As we grow in the grace and knowledge of our Lord Jesus Christ,

He will correct, discipline, and guide us. But it is vital for you to know that our Lord will *never* correct us with tragic accidents, sicknesses, and diseases. The Bible says, "For the LORD corrects those he loves, just as a father corrects a child in whom he delights" (Prov. 3:12 NLT). In other words, the Lord corrects those whom He highly favors, just as an earthly father would correct a child he loves.

Would a father correct a child in whom he delights by inflicting pain and suffering on that child? Of course not! In the same way, our heavenly Father corrects us not by inflicting pain and suffering but with His Word (see 2 Tim. 3:16). Correction may come through the preaching of His Word, or through godly leaders whom He surrounds you with in a local church, leaders who love you and who care enough to speak into your life.

The truth is, when people know that their heavenly Father loves them, they can receive correction and discipline with gratitude and humility. That is why it is so important for every child of God to experience the grace revolution—to become established in His perfect love and anchored in His unconditional grace toward them. Grace imparts to us the power to perform and to live a life above defeat. Grace is the key to holiness.

When people know that their heavenly Father loves them,
they can receive correction and discipline with gratitude
and humility.

It is vital that we keep on receiving teaching that is full of the abundance of God's grace and the gift of righteousness. When you keep receiving teachings on the person of Jesus, you will end up reigning over every defeat, sin, addiction, fear, doubt, and challenge in your life! Value our Lord Jesus accurately in your life and you will be unstoppable.

Why This "Waste"?

Let's go back to what Judas said when he saw Mary worshiping our Lord Jesus with the costly spikenard. He thought it was a waste and said that had the oil been sold, the money could have been used for the poor.

Does that sound familiar to you?

Have you ever been told that reading the Bible is a waste of time? That serving and being engaged in your local church is a waste of time? That bringing your tithes to your church is a waste of money? My dear reader, there will always be such accusatory voices in the world. Why? Because these voices do not understand the value of our Lord Jesus. Much like Judas.

Judas certainly did not understand the value of Jesus. Some time after he had berated Mary for wasting the perfume on Jesus instead of selling the oil and giving the proceeds to the poor, Judas went to the chief priests in Jerusalem and asked for a price for him to deliver Jesus to them. They offered him thirty pieces of silver and instantly he agreed without negotiating for more. Judas probably thought that the amount was more than fair and that it was a good deal for him. Just for a paltry sum of thirty pieces of silver, he was willing to betray Jesus to the priests. That tells us precisely how much Judas Iscariot valued our Lord Jesus.

Pastor Prince, how can you say that thirty pieces of silver is a paltry sum? It would be worth a lot of money at today's trading prices.

Well, perhaps you might be able to buy many things today with thirty pieces of silver. But the person of our Lord Jesus?

Priceless.

Mary understood the value of our Lord implicitly. Because she esteemed Jesus so greatly, anointing Him with her most valuable possession was simply an outward representation of just how much she loved, valued, and cherished our Lord Jesus inwardly. What Judas Iscariot saw as waste, Mary saw as worship.

Do you know what the last recorded words of Judas Iscariot were? He took the thirty pieces of silver, threw it at the chief priest, and cried out in despair, "I have betrayed innocent blood." Then he went out and committed suicide by hanging himself on a tree. It was a very sad and tragic end for one who didn't value the person of Jesus.

The truth is, Judas Iscariot did not have to hang himself on that tree; our Lord Jesus was on His way to hang on another tree (the cross) for the sins of the whole world, so that "whoever believes in Him should not perish but have everlasting life" (John 3:16)! Judas Iscariot didn't believe in Jesus. He wasn't born again and he certainly didn't value the work of our Lord Jesus Christ. He rejected the Lord and his guilt drove him to hang himself.

It is sad to see that there are so many people today who are punishing themselves for their own sins! They live in perpetual guilt and condemnation, punishing themselves and subjecting themselves to self-destructive behavior.

To anesthetize the voices of accusation in their own consciences, many become bound to alcohol, drugs, and all kinds of debilitating substance abuse. They end up living in a state of constant fear, anxiety attacks, sleeplessness, and psychosomatic illnesses.

My friend, that is not the abundant life that Jesus came to give us! He came that you might have life and have it more abundantly. I pray that as you read these pages, you will value our Lord Jesus and all that He has sacrificed on the cross for your forgiveness, your deliverance, your redemption, and your freedom!

You can stop punishing yourself today by receiving the truth that

Jesus took all your punishment when He stood in your place at the cross. Our Lord was punished on the cross so that today you can be healed and made completely whole, body, soul, and spirit!

You can stop punishing yourself today by receiving the truth that Jesus took all your punishment when He stood in your place at the cross.

Let me share with you a really precious testimony I received from Garrett, who lives in South Africa. Unable to find a way out of a downward spiral of addictions and despair, Garrett grew to hate himself to the point where he attempted suicide. Be blessed as you read how his encounter with Jesus and His amazing grace completely turned his life around:

> *I struggled with depression and despair for years, which led me down a path of self-destruction. During that time, I lost so much in my life—even the people I loved left me. Lost and confused, I moved from place to place, trying to make a better life for myself, but nothing ever worked out.*
>
> *I married out of vanity, not for love, but out of the marriage came a son whom I love more than life itself. However, due to my unhappiness and bad decision-making, I found myself in a world of drug addiction and alcohol abuse. As a result I lost my job, my wife, and my beloved son.*
>
> *I had to travel from Ireland to South Africa to see my son. I managed to find a job, but the drugs, alcohol, and despair were stronger than my ability to put things back together. I was a slave to my situation.*

Living alone, feeling lonely, and hating what I had become, my mind turned to suicide, but I also failed in that attempt. Then I met a lady named Linda who helped me find my feet, and I slowly moved forward, enduring life and my addictions.

I would cry to God for help, but I didn't really think that He would help me, or know if He even existed. Nonetheless, I kept looking up and asking.

My relationship with Linda went very badly and it seemed as if we were going to go our separate ways. I thought to myself, "There is no effect in believing in God." So I asked again, "God, what do You want from me? What is it that I have to do? Where are You? Am I being punished for the way I am... do You really exist?"

I came home to an empty house that night. I sat on the couch, turned on the television to watch the news, but the volume was too high. I pressed a button to turn the volume down, but instead of changing the volume, the television stations started to scroll down, and I came to your TV broadcast. Now, I am not one for listening to Christian television, so I immediately tried to change the channel back to my news channel, but the channel got stuck.

Pastor Prince, at that very instant, you looked into the camera and said, "Perhaps there is somebody here in this service, or watching this on television. Your life is right now being tossed by certain winds. Maybe it is a wind of financial turbulence, maybe it is a storm of sickness that has come into your life. Whatever the winds are, whatever the storm is, I am here to tell you, in the midst of the storm, look out for Jesus."

I felt like I was being hit by a freight train. I stopped in my tracks and I was freaked out because just a few minutes ago

I was screaming at God for answers. I was certain that God was pointing me somewhere that moment. My body started to tingle and the light in the room started to get brighter. Even though I am not one for having "religious" moments, I was positive that I was having a moment with Christ. That was how real it was, and totally unexpected.

Your sermon changed my world! I had no idea that God could love a person like me after all I had done. The next day, I went out and bought one of your books. I finished it in two days and after reading it, I felt a hunger that I never experienced before, an understanding that I had never grasped. My eyes were opened and I wanted more.

Through your teachings, I am now able to understand the Word of God like never before. I am applying the Word in my life. I am now free! Free to be loved by God because of the finished work of our Lord Jesus Christ. I am free to hope, free to receive, and free to come to Jesus even when I fail.

Pastor Prince, as a result of the knowledge of Jesus and His amazing grace, I now have no drug addictions, no alcohol dependence, and my relationships are better than ever. My son from my first marriage is prospering. My life of unhappiness and despair is gone. My job is prospering. My heart has changed, my family has expanded (God has blessed Linda and myself with twins—a son and a daughter), and I know our future is secure in Jesus Christ, all because of the message of grace. Hallelujah!

God's grace in my situation has even overflowed into the lives of my friends, who are now also saved and prospering, thanks to the amazing grace of our Lord Jesus Christ, and your grace-filled books. I am now full of the Holy Spirit and reigning in life.

Thank you, Pastor Prince! Thank You, Jesus!

What a beautiful testimony and testament to the love and mercy of our Lord Jesus! Garrett, thank you for sharing and encouraging so many with your testimony.

Beloved, perhaps, like Garrett, you've been bogged down in the mire of loneliness, discouragement, and self-destruction for what seems like forever. Don't waste another day in this dark and self-destructive place. Instead worship the One—our Lord and Savior, Jesus Christ—Who gave up everything and allowed Himself to be spat at, utterly humiliated, brutally beaten, and pierced with heavy nails at the cross for your redemption.

Worship Him, and allow the fragrance of His love and His grace to flood every area of your life. Allow the perfume of His sacrifice to permeate and heal every hurt, every disappointment, and every insecurity. He has already paid the price for you to be whole. He has already paid the price for you to be restored. He has already paid the price for you to come boldly and freely before His throne of grace. Oh, how He loves you! He loves you! He loves you!

Hearts Revealed

I started this chapter by sharing what happened in Bethany because I believe the Holy Spirit wants to show us the hearts of the different people there. Bethany was the same town where Jesus had raised Lazarus, who had been dead for four days, back to life. Do you know what happened after Jesus performed this astounding miracle?

John 11:53 records that from that day on, the chief priests and the Pharisees plotted to put Jesus to death. That was the response of the religious leaders of that day—they wanted to kill Jesus—the One Who opened blind eyes, unstopped deaf ears, cleansed those with leprosy, and raised the dead! Why? And what does this tell you about what was in their hearts?

In order to be a chief priest or a Pharisee, one needed to be a student of the Word of God from a young age, and to know the Torah from front to back. Yet the religious leaders, who were zealous for the law and knew all about the Torah, were the very people who plotted to kill Jesus.

Now lean in and listen closely to what I am about to say. They had *head* knowledge, but they did not have a heart for the person of Jesus. They had all this Bible knowledge, but they did not have the Author of the Bible in their hearts.

I am sure you have seen how in a marriage, husbands and wives can use Bible verses to condemn one another. Now, please don't do that— please don't use your Bible knowledge to make people feel lousy about themselves! That is what the Pharisees did.

They would quote from the Old Testament to tear people down instead of saving them. They wanted to stone the woman caught in adultery, quoting from the law of Moses, but Jesus saved her by inviting the one who had no sin to cast the first stone. Beginning with the eldest Pharisee, they dropped their murderous rocks and departed. Whenever you find people using the Bible to condemn and to crush those who have failed and who are in need of a Savior, your spiritual antenna needs to be on high alert.

Head versus Heart Knowledge

It is possible for people today to accumulate a lot of head knowledge on *this* theology and *that* theology, and yet not have any heart knowledge that burns with love and passion for our Lord Jesus Christ. It is possible to enrich your mind or to study about this interpretation and that interpretation of the Scriptures, and still have a heart that is stone-cold when it comes to an intimate and personal relationship with Jesus.

Now, don't misunderstand me—I am not saying that you should not acquire Bible knowledge. If you have followed my ministry for some time, you know that I love studying and digging out treasures from the Word of God. I am saying that we need to study the Bible not simply to accumulate head knowledge, but to have a revelation of Jesus.

We need to study the Bible not simply to accumulate head knowledge, but to have a revelation of Jesus.

To have a heart of love for Jesus, you must know the Bible. In fact, true scriptural knowledge about Jesus will lead you to have a heart for Jesus. Don't be like the Pharisees, who had Bible knowledge, but no love for our Lord Jesus. Don't miss the Author when you are reading His Word.

When you study the Bible, study to *feed* on the person of Jesus. Feed on His beauty, His grace, His majesty, and His immense and sacrificial love for you. We read the Word to feed on Christ.

Oh, how I love the phrase, "to feed on Christ." He is the bread of life, and the more you feed on Him in the Word, the more you will be strengthened and nourished with His health, life, and wisdom for every area of your life. When you see Jesus in the Word, you will know how to esteem and value Him. Jesus becomes real food for your soul and He gives you strength for your service.

Real holiness comes from beholding Jesus. As you behold our Lord, you are transformed from the inside out, from glory to glory. When you value Jesus, your heart's desire is just to glorify Him in everything that you think, say, and do. When you have a heart for Jesus, everything in your life—whether it is your marriage, your parenting, or your career—will fall into place as you receive His finished work!

Real holiness comes from beholding Jesus. As you behold our Lord, you are transformed from the inside out, from glory to glory.

What John recorded about Mary's anointing of Jesus' feet also reveals a lot about what was on Judas Iscariot's heart. When Judas said, "Why was this fragrant oil not sold for three hundred denarii and given to the poor?" the Word of God reveals to us that "This he said, not that he cared for the poor, but because he was a thief, and had the money box; and he used to take what was put in it" (John 12:5–6). Judas's heart was for the money, not for the Lord and certainly not for the poor. Judas had plenty of heart for money, but no heart for our Lord Jesus.

My dear friend, God has no problem with you having money; He just doesn't want money *to have you*. Money is a good servant but a bad master. Use money to love people; do not love money and use people.

The Word of God tells us that "the love of money is the root of all evil" (1 Tim. 6:10 KJV). Notice that *money* itself is not the root of evil. It is the *love of money* that is highly destructive. Something is very strange if you come alive only when you hear about money and the only thing you study in the Bible is about money.

No, my friend, God wants you to be abundantly supplied so that you are more than able to provide for your family, to build His church, to help the poor, and to worship the Lord as Mary did. However, let your heart be all about Jesus, and not about accumulating, gathering, and grabbing!

Let your heart be all about Jesus, and not about accumulating, gathering, and grabbing!

The Heart of Worship

In the account in John 12, another heart that is revealed to us is Mary's beautiful heart of love and worship for the Lord. She poured out and gave her very best to the Lord.

Whatever you do for Jesus out of love for Him cannot be hidden. People will "smell" it. You will carry the fragrance of Christ all about you, and it's a fragrance of victory, not defeat! And have you noticed that whatever you give to Jesus is never forgotten? What you hold in your hand may be temporal. But the moment you put it into Jesus' hands, it becomes eternal.

Look at what Jesus said about Mary when He defended her against Judas's accusation that she had wasted the very costly spikenard on Jesus. Jesus said, "Let her alone, she has kept this for the day of My burial" (John 12:7). Mary prepared Jesus for His burial, but only for the moment, because He would rise from the dead. But in these words, Jesus enveloped her forever in the sweet incense of His praise of her. Today we are still talking about and honoring what Mary did for our Lord two thousand years ago. Talk about your good works having an effect for generations to come!

Have a Bullock-Size Revelation of Jesus

In closing, let me share something powerful with you. In the Old Testament, the burnt offering came in three sizes—literally big, medium, and small (see Lev. 1:1–17). The rich would bring an expensive bullock; the middle-income a lamb; and the poor a pair of easy-to-obtain pigeons or turtledoves.

Now, while the offerings differed in size, in terms of value to God, they were all equal and acceptable to Him, because they all reminded Him of the one final and perfect sacrifice of His beloved Son. So whether it was a bullock, lamb, or pair of turtledoves, they were all accepted and killed, and their blood was shed to make atonement for the offerers' sins.

What's the significance of all this? The three animal sacrifices are actually typologies of our appreciation of Jesus and His finished work today. For instance, many believers have a lamb-size revelation of Jesus. They know that Jesus is the Lamb of God Who has washed away their past sins with His blood.

Then there are some Christians who have only a pigeon-size revelation of Jesus. They see Him as the Son of God Who came down from heaven to die for man's sins. And finally there are believers who have a bullock-size revelation of Jesus and His cleansing blood. As the bullock was the most expensive of the three sacrifices, these believers are spiritually rich because they have a large and deep revelation of Jesus, His blood, and how it has cleansed them of all their sins.

In the same way that all the three sacrifices were acceptable to the Lord, we as believers are all accepted in His sight, no matter what our revelation and how we value Jesus. But God wants you to grow from having a pigeon-size revelation of His Son to having a bullock-size appreciation of Him.

Why is this so important? Because everything starts from the inside out. That inward spiritual wealth will translate into outward benefits of peace, stability, joy, provision, and victory. Back then, the wealthier you were, the bigger the size of your offering. Today, the larger your revelation of Jesus, the more spiritually wealthy you are!

My dear reader, when you esteem Jesus, when you worship Him and give unto Him, it brings lasting transformation not only in your life. As we have seen with Mary, it also has an effect for generations and generations to come.

Your time spent in studying the person of Jesus and worshiping Him will come back to you. You will experience a quality of life beyond your wildest imagination when the Lord Jesus is at the center of it all. And that is why the grace revolution is all about having a heart for Jesus!

CHAPTER 14

FULLY POSSESS THE FINISHED WORK

As we close the key that is all about valuing the person of Jesus, I want to let you in on something that our Lord Jesus really values. I believe that the Lord finds it very important that you be a part of a local church. While it is fantastic that you are receiving the gospel of grace through television, teaching resources, online materials, or even from this book, I want to encourage you to also be engaged in a local church in your community. Everything I teach about the gospel of grace functions best in the context of a local church where there is fellowship, accountability, and wise counsel. The local church is not man's idea, it is God's idea, and indeed, there is something powerful about gathering together in an assembly of believers as part of the body of Christ.

Have you noticed that when you meet a fellow believer, there is always an affinity toward him or her? You may not really know this person, but in the spirit there is a connection. I am talking about the fellowship of true believers. I am talking about *possessors* of Christianity, not *professors* of Christianity. The New Testament contains many warnings concerning professors of Christianity, people who verbally profess to be or call themselves Christians, but in actuality have never invited Jesus to be their personal Lord and Savior.

You may know of some people who had attended church for some time, then broke away and started to live a sinful lifestyle with no desire to repent and no interest in listening to the counsel of the church's leadership. Some of them may even have gone on to embrace another belief system. When such things happen, people often wonder, *How can these people be believers of Jesus Christ? Have these people lost their salvation?* I submit to you that in some extreme cases, these people might not have accepted Christ into their hearts in the first place. It is not a case of believers losing their salvation; the reality is these people may never have been saved in the first place. It is important we recognize that there are people who outwardly profess to be Christians but who have never received the Lord as their Savior and been born again.

The Difference between Possessing and Professing

Let me show you a verse that has been mistakenly used to refer to believers. The verse I'm talking about is 2 Peter 2:22, which says, "'A dog returns to his own vomit,' and, 'a sow, having washed, to her wallowing in the mire.'" This verse is often quoted when a "Christian" is seen to have backslidden, turned away from the Lord, and is in danger of losing his salvation.

Now, I submit to you that this verse does not refer to believers at all. Notice that when the verse says, "A dog returns to his own vomit," it is talking about a dog, not a sheep (which refers to believers). There is no inward transformation that came from the power of God's grace. In the same way it is a sow (not a sheep) wallowing in the mire. Hence 2 Peter 2:22 refers to people who have never had the born-again experience of receiving Jesus as their Lord and Savior. In other words, these people are not true believers; they are *professors* and not *possessors* of Christianity.

When a person is born again, he is made a new creation in Christ Jesus. The old has passed and the new has come. He is no longer a dog or sow, but a new creation in Christ Jesus. A sheep can fall and fail, but it will never want to wallow in vomit and mud. Sin—like vomit and mud—is contrary to the new nature a new creation has in Christ. I believe true believers in Christ are looking for freedom *from* sin. They genuinely hate being entangled and bound in sin that is destructive. That is why when we focus our energies on preaching the gospel of Jesus Christ, lives are transformed by the power of His grace. When people discover their true identity in Christ, they will experience the power to reign over every sin. That is why the Bible declares that "sin shall not have dominion over you, for you are not under law but under grace" (Rom. 6:14). True grace always produces true holiness. Right believing always leads to right living.

When we focus our energies on preaching the gospel of Jesus Christ, lives are transformed by the power of His grace.

But Pastor Prince, this person has been in church for a long time and was even in a position of leadership.

Well, all I can say is that going to church doesn't make you a believer, any more than going to a garage makes you a car. That is why we have to be aware that there are people who are professors and not possessors of Christianity.

What You Need to Know to Be Secure

Well, what about 2 Peter 2:20? Doesn't this Scripture say that these people have "the knowledge of the Lord"?

That's a good question. Let's take a closer look at 2 Peter 2:20, which says, "For if, after they have escaped the pollutions of the world through the knowledge of the Lord and Savior Jesus Christ, they are again entangled in them and overcome, the latter end is worse for them than the beginning."

Now, before we dive into this, let me bring up another Scripture, found in the book of Hebrews, that will be useful for our discussion:

> *For it is impossible for those who were once enlightened, and have tasted the heavenly gift, and have become partakers of the Holy Spirit, and have tasted the good word of God and the powers of the age to come, if they fall away, to renew them again to repentance, since they crucify again for themselves the Son of God, and put Him to an open shame.*
> *—Hebrews 6:4–6*

My dear reader, as we saw in the previous chapter, it is completely possible to have head knowledge of the Bible and the Lord Jesus, and still reject Him and not value Him as our personal Savior. We looked at the best example of this—Judas Iscariot. He outwardly experienced the favor, protection, and power of the Lord and escaped the pollutions of the world by being associated with our Lord Jesus. He was physically with Jesus and the disciples day and night. He witnessed and even partook of the miracles of Jesus, from the feeding of the five thousand to the raising of Lazarus. He witnessed the healings of the blind, lame, and demon-possessed (see Matt. 4:24). And yet never once did he acknowledge Jesus as his personal Lord and Savior. He is an example of someone described in Hebrews 6:4–6—one who was once enlightened (he knew who Jesus was), tasted the heavenly gift, partook of the Holy Spirit (even performed miracles by the power of the Holy Spirit upon him, see Matt.10:1–4), and tasted the good Word of God, yet never believed Jesus as his Lord and Savior. His was an outright rejection of Jesus. And as the Scriptures describe, Judas Iscariot suffered an ignoble end (see Acts 1:16–20). It was a sad end for someone who had once enjoyed such physical proximity to Jesus.

Judas Iscariot was one of twelve men who had the privilege of being appointed by Jesus as His disciples. He was one of only twelve men who were Jesus' closest companions during His earthly ministry. Yet he used his free choice to reject Jesus. So you see, the Scriptures we are discussing refer to *professors* of Christianity who, like Judas Iscariot, were never genuine believers. So it is important that these Scriptures (2 Pet. 2:20, Heb. 6:4–6) should never be used to threaten and bring fear to true believers, scaring them with the lie that they can easily lose their salvation and eternal security in Christ.

Some people point to Judas as an example of a Christian who lost his salvation. But that makes no sense because Judas was never a *born-again Christian*, any more than any of the other disciples were. How could they be when our Lord Jesus had not yet died and the church had not yet been birthed? They might have been disciples, but they were not born-again believers. They had the Spirit *upon* them to perform miracles, but they did not have the Spirit *in* them permanently. So Judas wasn't a Christian who lost his salvation—he never had it to begin with! Don't let anyone use Judas to scare you into thinking that as a born-again believer, you can lose your salvation.

My friend, if you have received the Lord Jesus into your life, I want you to know this beyond the shadow of any doubt: you are born again, you have received the gift of *eternal* life, your salvation is as secure as the promises in God's Word, and you are safe in the Father's hand (see John 10:28–30)!

If you have received the Lord Jesus into your life, your salvation is as secure as the promises in God's Word, and you are safe in the Father's hand!

What Is the Will of the Father?

Another Scripture that is commonly used to threaten believers and cause them to erroneously believe that they can lose their salvation is found in the Gospel of Matthew. In this gospel Jesus is recorded as saying:

> *"Not everyone who says to Me, 'Lord, Lord,' shall enter the kingdom of heaven, but he who does the will of My Father in heaven. Many will say to Me in that day, 'Lord, Lord, have we not prophesied in Your name, cast out demons in Your name, and done many wonders in Your name?' And then I will declare to them, 'I never knew you; depart from Me, you who practice lawlessness!'"*
>
> *—Matthew 7:21–23*

Notice that our Lord Jesus said, "I *never knew* you." Now, how can this be applied to believers who have been born again and who have a relationship with the Lord? It is clearly referring to people who never had a personal relationship with the Lord. That is why Jesus could say to the latter group, "I never knew you." Again it is clear that this passage is to be used as a warning only to professors of the Christian faith, not to those who have genuinely accepted Jesus as their Lord.

Oh, but Pastor Prince, doesn't the first part say that only those who do the will of the Father will enter the kingdom of heaven? This means that if you are not doing the will of the Father, you can lose your salvation.

Dear reader, it is important to let the Bible interpret the Bible. If you study the Bible, you will see that the will of the Father is that you believe in the One Whom He has sent and receive eternal life. Jesus said, "For this is the will of My Father, that everyone who beholds the Son and believes in Him will have eternal life, and I Myself will raise him up on the last day" (John 6:40 NASB). And in John 6:29 (NLT) He tells us plainly, "This is the only work God wants from you: Believe in the one he has sent." That is the gospel. That is doing the will of the Father.

Jesus also said, "Behold, I have come to do Your will, O God" (Heb. 10:9). What was that will that Jesus had to fulfill? It was to die for our sins and to bring us into His new covenant of grace. The same verse tells us, "He takes away the first [old covenant] that He may establish the second [new covenant]."

So what Jesus was saying in Matthew 7 is this: "Not all who call Me 'Lord, Lord' in that day are saved, but only those who fulfill My Father's will, which is to believe in Me." He is not saying that the moment you make a mistake in thought or deed, He denies you and you have lost your salvation.

Always Secure in Your Father's Hand

Why am I sharing all this with you? It is so you will be established in our Lord Jesus, and not be easily swayed and tossed and turned by every wind of doctrine (see Eph. 4:14). You are His precious child and your heavenly Father wants you to have a strong foundation built on your secure salvation in Christ. Instead of being confused by obscure passages in the Bible, I want to encourage you to be anchored on certain and clear passages like this one found in John 10:

> *"My sheep hear My voice, and I know them, and they follow Me. And I give them eternal life, and they shall never perish; neither shall anyone snatch them out of My hand. My Father, who has given them to Me, is greater than all; and no one is able to snatch them out of My Father's hand. I and My Father are one."*
> *—John 10:27–30 (emphasis mine)*

Now, doesn't simply reading this promise in God's Word impart to you confidence, assurance, and security in your salvation in Christ? Let me draw your attention to the word "never." This is going to bless you. The word "never" here is translated from the Greek particle *ou me*, which is a double negative, strongly emphasizing the meaning of "never, certainly not, not at all, by no means."[1] In other words, once you are saved, you will never, by no means, ever perish!

Unfortunately, there are people today who won't hesitate to cast doubt on a believer's salvation. I have seen a minister do that and even say that he wasn't sure if he himself was saved and would make it to heaven. That, my friend, is dangerous talk that does not accurately value the finished work of Jesus Christ on the cross. It actually makes light of what our Lord Jesus suffered at Calvary for our salvation, forgiveness, and redemption.

I don't know what Bible such people are reading, but my Bible tells me in no uncertain terms that "if you confess with your mouth the Lord Jesus and believe in your heart that God has raised Him from the dead, you will be saved" (Rom. 10:9). My Bible tells me that "no one is able to snatch them out of My Father's hand" (John 10:29). My Bible tells me, "For God so loved the world that He gave His only begotten Son, that whoever believes in Him should not perish but have everlasting life. For God did not send His Son into the world to condemn the world, but that the world through Him might be saved" (John 3:16–17). That's what my Bible says!

The Safety Net under You

My dear friend, if you don't feel assured of your salvation in Christ, it will affect how you live life as a Christian. Are you familiar with what happened during the construction of the Golden Gate Bridge in San Francisco? Building this magnificent suspension bridge (costing approximately $35 million)[2] in the 1930s was a colossal task fraught with many dangers. At the top of the list was the possibility of workers plunging to their deaths in the deep, icy water below. In fact, the workers *expected* death, because it was a well-known fact that in their industry, there was at least one death for every million dollars spent.[3]

Because of this, Joseph Strauss, the project's chief structural engineer, made sure rigorous safety measures were enforced and practiced. He insisted on investing in and installing an enormous safety net below the bridge. Costing $130,000 (a massive expense during the Depression era), the vast net was wider and longer than the bridge. The moment it was installed, something happened to the workers. They gained the confidence to move freely and quickly across slippery steel structures. The safety net not only boosted their morale, it also sped up the construction process. One of the workers, Lefty Underkoffler, said in an interview, "There's no doubt the work went faster because of the net."[4]

Now, let me ask you a question. Did the presence of the safety net make the workers careless and irresponsible? Did it make them spend all their time trying out dangerous stunts when they should have been working? Of course not. On the contrary, they became more motivated and efficient in going about their work. It is the same in our Christian walk. When we have the assurance of salvation and know that nothing can pluck us out of our Father's hand, it gives us confidence and strength to look to the Lord, run the race better, and go from glory to glory.

When we know that nothing can pluck us out of our Father's hand, it gives us confidence and strength to look to the Lord, run the race better, and go from glory to glory.

Assurance and confidence in your salvation through all that our Lord Jesus has done is vital. Imagine if our children believed that we would disown them at the drop of a hat. Imagine if they had no assurance and confidence in our love for them. I think they would grow up warped! As parents you and I don't find every opportunity to inject doubt, fear, and insecurity into our relationships with our children. If we earthly parents don't do that with our children, how much more so our Father, Who loves us with an everlasting love?

What Brings Real Transformation

Some people say, "Oh, Pastor Prince, if you preach like this, people will live licentiously with no regard for God."

Really? Do you really believe that? Do you really believe that when you tell your children that you will always love them, and that no matter what they do, they will be your children and nothing will ever change your love for them, your children will leave your house and say, "Yippee! Now I can do anything I want because my parents have said that they will always love me and never disown me"?

I believe otherwise. I believe that children who know they are loved become secure and do better in life. It is the same with Christians who are secure in the Father's love. Instead of conforming to the influences of the world, they will be transformed by the renewing of their minds with the power of God's amazing grace. I believe with all my heart that born-again believers established in His grace want to live lives that glorify His holy name. They are not looking for ways to break their wives' hearts, abandon their children, and run off with their secretaries! That is not the result of being established in God's grace.

If you know someone who is living like that, let me be the first pastor to tell you that this person is not living under grace. God's grace produces faithful husbands, loving wives, and children who honor their parents. God's grace produces strong marriages and healthy families that are anchored in a local church. Why? Because grace isn't a teaching, doctrine, or formula. Grace is a person and His name is Jesus!

That is why I like to use the phrase, "the person of Jesus." Grace is personified in our Lord Jesus. You can relate to Him as a person. You can talk to Him, hang out with Him, share with Him your struggles and your challenges, and have really good, honest, and deep conversations with Him. Once you see our Lord Jesus as a person, and you see all His beauty, glory, grace, love, and forgiveness, there is no way you would want to live a lifestyle that does not glorify His holy name. When you value Jesus in your life, you value His glory.

When you value Jesus in your life, you value His glory.

I want to invite you to meditate on this powerful Scripture:

> *For the grace of God that brings salvation has appeared to all*
> *men, teaching us that, denying ungodliness and worldly lusts,*
> *we should live soberly, righteously, and godly in the present*
> *age, looking for the blessed hope and glorious appearing of our*
> *great God and Savior Jesus Christ, who gave Himself for us,*
> *that He might redeem us from every lawless deed and purify*
> *for Himself His own special people, zealous for good works.*
> *—Titus 2:11–14*

Now that's the result of being under grace and that is what it means to be a part of the grace revolution! As we behold the person of Jesus, grace teaches us to deny ungodliness and worldly lusts, and we become a people zealous for the glory of our Lord Jesus in our lives and "zealous for good works"!

As we behold the person of Jesus, He teaches us to
deny ungodliness and worldly lusts.

Be Rooted in a Local Church

Let's come back to what I mentioned earlier about the importance of being rooted and involved in a local church. As we saw in the previous verse, people transformed by the gospel of grace are zealous for good works. First let me establish that you don't have to serve as a volunteer in a local church to be favored and loved by the Lord. I tell all the people who volunteer in my church to serve out of rest. It is not an obligation but a privilege to serve in our Father's house. And we serve not as servants with a slavish mentality, but as sons and daughters with the spirit of sonship.

When you value the person of Jesus, you value what He values. Our Lord greatly values the local church. His Word tells us, "And let us consider one another in order to stir up love and good works, not forsaking the assembling of ourselves together, as is the manner of some, but exhorting one another, and so much the more as you see the Day approaching" (Heb. 10:24–25). The grace revolution is not an isolated experience. It is best experienced in the context of a local church where there is fellowship with true possessors of our Lord Jesus Christ.

Delighting the Father

Ephesians 1:6 tells us that by "the glory of His grace...He made us accepted in the Beloved." It is by His unearned, undeserved, and unmerited favor that we have been made accepted in the Beloved, Jesus. This is true for every believer. If you are a believer, then by God's grace, you are accepted in the Beloved. The Greek word for "accepted" here is *charitoo*, which means "highly favored."[5] Our Father in heaven wants you to know that you are *charitoo*, that is, highly favored in the Beloved. Joseph Henry Thayer, a well-known American Bible scholar, goes on to expound that *charitoo* also means "to compass with favor."[6] In other words, we are *surrounded* with favor. This is our position in Christ: highly favored and surrounded by favor by the glory of His grace!

This is our position in Christ: highly favored and surrounded by favor!

Now let me show you another Scripture, which says, "Where-fore we labor, that...we may be accepted of him" (2 Cor. 5:9 KJV). We have just established that by God's grace, we are accepted in the Beloved without labor. So what does this Scripture mean? The word "accepted" here is not the Greek word *charitoo*. It is another Greek word, *euarestos*, which means "well pleasing."[7] Hence the New King James translation says, "Therefore we make it our aim...to be well pleasing to Him."

Now, *euarestos* is not about your position in Christ. *Euarestos* (in 2 Cor. 5:9) refers to something that you do that brings your Father in heaven great delight and joy. In Christ the Beloved we are already highly favored, but there are things we can do to glorify and be extra pleasing to our Father in heaven. Let me illustrate my point: Our children Jessica and Justin are always highly favored in Wendy's and my hearts. There is nothing they can ever do to change that position. It is a position anchored on their identity as our children. Yet there are times when they do something special for us that brings us great delight and touches our hearts. In those moments not only are they highly favored, they are also extra well pleasing to us. Do they have to do those special things to earn our love? Absolutely not! They are already loved and highly favored in our hearts. In fact, their desire to do something special for us stems from their having confidence in our love for them. They desire to please us because they know just how much we already love them.

It is the same in our relationship with our heavenly Father. When we know how much we are loved and are established in His grace, we want to do good works to bring delight to Him. The apostle Paul, who was zealous for the gospel and good works, said, "But by the grace of God I am what I am, and His grace toward me was not in vain; but I labored more abundantly than they all, yet not I, but the grace of

God which was with me" (1 Cor. 15:10). Paul, who had a revelation of God's grace, didn't become a lazy, passive Christian. On the contrary, he worked harder than all the other apostles for the gospel's sake, and he attributed all his ministry success to God's grace in his life. That, my friend, is *euarestos* (well-pleasing good works) in action.

> *When we know how much we are loved and are established in God's grace, we want to do good works to bring delight to Him.*

Everything we do today must flow from the lavish supply of God's grace. Our giving has to be out of His grace. Our serving has to be out of His grace. When His grace is our delight, we can't help but labor more abundantly and bring delight to our Father's heart. This was the experience of Jayden, who lives in the Philippines. Where he once struggled to please God, discovering how beloved and highly favored he is in Christ has turned him into a joyful and unstoppable evangelist of the goodness and grace of God:

> *I used to be so conscious of myself and my performance. Even though I was a longtime Christian and Bible school graduate, I felt that holiness was beyond my reach. I tried to earn God's favor through my daily routine of praying and reading the Bible. Any failures to go through this routine would make me feel defeated, lousy, and guilty.*
>
> *However, when I started watching your sermons and reading your teaching resources, I started to look at God and myself in a new way. Praise God for opening my eyes! He gave me the truth and set me free from the law through your materials!*

Now, I am Jesus-conscious and know that I am God's beloved. I've been healed from arthritis, which had plagued me for years. The pain used to be so severe that I could not even hold a pen. I am now also at a healthy weight. Instead of weighing a mere 114 pounds, I now weigh 141 pounds. I am totally healed! Hallelujah! When my friends ask me, "What did you do?" I simply say, "I discovered and I believed right about God's grace for me."

When I think of God's grace—how Jesus has overpaid my debt—my tears fall unconsciously. Grace has driven addictions, condemnation, guilt, sin, and bondage to the law out of my life. Pastor Prince, your message of grace has made such a big impact on my life that I can't help but share this message of God's love with my friends. I tell them how this message has brought not bondage but freedom to my life.

Today, I pray for the church to be filled with grace-conscious people who will impact the world. There's going to be a grace revolution and we are going to preach it! God bless you and your family.

Everything we do today must flow from the lavish supply of God's grace. Our giving has to be out of His grace.

My dear friend, this is the grace revolution that we have been talking about in this book! It is a revolution that begins from the inside and flows to the outside. When a believer is established in just how *charitoo*—beloved, highly favored—he is in Christ, his outward response is *euarestos* (well-pleasing) actions. He can't help it—he is just inwardly motivated to do things that glorify the Lord and bring Him great delight.

Those who have been transformed by the gospel of grace from the inside out and who have a revelation of how *charitoo*—how deeply loved, highly favored, and greatly blessed—they are in Christ have a desire to be *euarestos* (well pleasing) to God in their daily lives. Not only are they set free from the bondage of legalism and sin, they also desire to bring great glory, honor, and delight to their Father in heaven with good works.

Anchored in the Father's Love

The Bible tells us, "Children, obey your parents in all things, for this is well pleasing to the Lord" (Col. 3:20). The words "well pleasing" here is *euarestos*. Children, when you obey your parents, it is well pleasing to the Lord. You will never lose your position in Christ, but your obedience to His Word brings great delight to Him. My daughter, Jessica, will never lose her position of being highly favored by me. She will never lose that place of closeness with me. Even when she does wrong, or makes a mistake, she will never, never, *never* lose that place of closeness with me. In fact, that's the time she needs me the most.

Religious teachings tell you that when you make a mistake, God is disappointed and angry with you. Do such teachings make you want to draw near to your Father in heaven, or to run further away from Him? There are people who can't believe that we are always loved and highly favored by the Father. They question, "When we fail, isn't God disappointed with us? Won't He withdraw His love from us?"

My dear friend, when the father saw the prodigal son coming home, before his son could utter one syllable to confess his mistake, the father ran to his son with all his might, embraced him, clothed him, put a ring on his finger, gave him new shoes, and threw the biggest party in town to celebrate his return. Does that sound like a father who was disappointed and withholding his love from his son?

Now take a moment to think about this. If the prodigal son had thought that his father was hard, harsh, judgmental, angry, and disappointed with him, would he have considered heading home? Of course not! According to the law of Moses, the father had the legal right to have the prodigal son stoned to death (see Deut. 21:18–21). If the son had thought that his father was judgmental and sure to punish him with the law of Moses, he would never have considered returning home. In fact, he would have run in the opposite direction!

God wants every person to run to Him, not away from Him. That, I believe, is why God is causing this grace revolution to sweep across the world. Come on, let's tell the world about the loving, caring, smiling Father Who runs to those who have failed. Let's tell the world to stop running away from Him and to run TO Him because He is waiting. Waiting to embrace them. Waiting to restore to them all that they have lost and more. Waiting to unreservedly and unconditionally lavish His love on them. He is not angry or disappointed with them, and He is not holding their mistakes against them (see 2 Cor. 5:19). A thousand times no! His loving heart has been yearning for their return. Let's tell the world that now is the time for them to come home to the Father's love!

PART FOUR

SPEAK THE
LANGUAGE OF FAITH

CHAPTER 15

LOVE LIFE AND SEE GOOD DAYS

In this chapter I want you to see that your words are powerful. What you speak over yourself can change your life. Allow me to draw your attention to a weighty and important Scripture in the New Testament, in which the apostle Peter quotes from a psalm of David, saying, "For 'He who would love life and see good days, let him refrain his tongue from evil, and his lips from speaking deceit'" (1 Pet. 3:10).

God's Word is so beautifully clear. If you desire to love life and see good days, all you need to do is to refrain your tongue from speaking evil. It sounds simple. In fact, you may even contend that it is *too* simple. How many of us truly believe that our tongues wield so much influence and power over our future and even our day-to-day living?

Our tongues wield so much influence and power over our future and even our day-to-day living.

The tongue seems minute and insignificant compared to the rest of our body. How can such a little organ, which doesn't have any skeletal support, have such a direct and pronounced effect on our future? Yet the Bible reminds us not to despise the tongue simply because it is small, and compares it to the rudder of a fully rigged sea vessel to help us appreciate the power of our words: "Look also at ships: although they are so large and are driven by fierce winds, they are turned by a very small rudder wherever the pilot desires. Even so the tongue is a little member and boasts great things" (James 3:4–5). In the book of Proverbs, Solomon also declares, "Death and life are in the power of the tongue, and those who love it will eat its fruit" (Prov. 18:21). It is evident that God does not want you to underestimate the power of your words!

God wants you to see and experience many good days. Ephesians 6:13 says, "Therefore take up the whole armor of God, that you may be able to withstand in the evil day." Notice that the Bible talks about an evil *day*—singular, but good *days*—plural! We all know what an evil day is. It's a day when anything that can go wrong goes wrong. You wake up in the morning and have a horrible headache. Your child is down with a bad cold, your car won't start, and you make a big mistake at work. Been there before? And an evil day isn't necessarily a twenty-four-hour day; it can also be a difficult and challenging season. But I have good news for you—it doesn't have to be a protracted season. It's one evil day versus many good days, Amen! Let's believe God together for many good days! The only thing that God wants us to remember in order to see many good days is to refrain our tongues from speaking evil. That's how powerful our words are.

The only thing that God wants us to remember in order to see many good days is to refrain our tongues from speaking evil.

The Grace Revolution in Action

Now let's take a step back to examine the scriptural context of 1 Peter 3:10:

> *Finally, all of you be of one mind, having compassion for one another; love as brothers, be tenderhearted, be courteous; not returning evil for evil or reviling for reviling, but on the contrary blessing, knowing that you were called to this, that you may inherit a blessing. For "He who would love life and see good days, let him refrain his tongue from evil, and his lips from speaking deceit."*
>
> *1 Peter 3:8–10*

Notice that Peter quoted the verse in the context of our relationships with people. As you have been transformed by the gospel of grace, God also wants to transform your relationships with people. These people would be your spouse, kids, parents, relatives, friends, colleagues, employers, and business associates, and any other person you come in contact with!

We are people called to be a blessing everywhere we go. That's the grace revolution in action.

I believe that people who have been touched by the grace of God are carriers of His Spirit of humility and graciousness. We are not people who render evil for evil, reviling for reviling. We are people called to be a blessing everywhere we go. That's the grace revolution in action.

Our Lord Jesus first transforms your relationship with God from the inside out, and that grace that you have experienced overflows into all your earthly relationships like a mighty tidal wave.

Use Your Words to Bless, Restore, and Heal

Let me show you something very interesting. The original Greek word for "a blessing" in 1 Peter 3:9 is *eulogeo*, which means "to speak well of,"[1] and is where we get the English word "eulogy." That is the key to speaking a blessing! Every time you speak well of something, you are blessing that thing and being a blessing!

So speak well of your marriage, your children, your family, and your friends. That's how you bless and become a blessing everywhere you go. Bless your body too, by speaking well of it—don't keep saying it's getting old! Speak well also of your relationship with the Lord. Call yourself the beloved of the Lord. Declare His protection, favor, and righteousness over you and your loved ones and begin to experience His blessings like never before. Every time you speak His blessings over your life, you are taking possession of your blessed place in Christ.

---

*Speak well of your marriage, your children, your family,
and your friends. That's how you bless and become a
blessing everywhere you go.*

Our Lord believed in the power and authority of His Word. He spoke to the demons and they departed. He spoke to the fig tree and it died. He spoke to the winds and waves and they stilled. He spoke to sick bodies and they were healed. Most of us use our "sophisticated" intellect and logic, and we think we are "too smart" to speak to trees, storms, and diseases. Some may even say, "Pastor Prince, all this speaking to inanimate objects and diseases seems very *foolish* to me." Well, you know what? The Bible tells us that "God has chosen the foolish things of the world to put to shame the wise" (1 Cor. 1:27). I would rather be foolish and healthy in Christ, than be really "smart" and dying of a disease. Amen! As for me and my house, we will follow the Lord's way.

Our Lord believed in the power and authority of His Word. He spoke to the demons and they departed. He spoke to the winds and waves and they stilled. He spoke to sick bodies and they were healed.

Jesus taught His disciples to speak to their mountains (see Mark 11:23). You feel a pain in your body? Speak to the pain and say, "Pain, go in Jesus' name." If your hair is falling out, speak to it and say, "Hair, be fruitful and multiply in Jesus' name." Start somewhere! If you have a pimple on your nose, start there and say, "Pimple, be removed in Jesus' name!"

Pastor Prince, you mean God cares about my hair and my pimples?

My friend, God cares for you. And that means He cares about what you care about. His Word encourages you to cast "*all* your care upon Him, for He cares for you" (1 Pet. 5:7, emphasis mine). Another Scripture tells you, "Don't worry about anything; instead, pray about everything. Tell God what you need, and thank him for all he has done. Then you will experience God's peace, which exceeds anything we can understand. His peace will guard your hearts and minds as you live in Christ Jesus" (Phil. 4:6–7 NLT).

Change Your Words and Change Your Life

Do you know what the opposite of speaking well is? It is to curse. When our Lord cursed the fig tree, what did He say? Did He say, "I curse you, fig tree"? No, He simply said, "Let no one eat fruit from you ever again" (Mark 11:14). And the next day, when they passed by the fig tree again, Peter said, "Rabbi, look! The fig tree which You *cursed* has withered away" (Mark 11:21, emphasis mine).

Jesus never used the word *curse* when He spoke to the fig tree, but He also did not correct Peter for using the word *cursed*. Why? Because Peter was right. Even though Jesus did not use the word *curse*, the negative words spoken were tantamount to a curse. Oh, I hope you got that! Many times people don't realize that they are unintentionally cursing themselves and the people around them with the constant flow of negative words that they speak about themselves and others. Words of defeat, anger, bitterness, and complaint are toxic. Change your words, and change your life. Flush out the negative words in your life with the words of God's grace, love, and power!

Words of defeat, anger, bitterness, and complaint are toxic. Change your words, and change your life.

We can learn another truth from our Lord's cursing of the fig tree. When He spoke to the fig tree, nothing immediately visible happened to the tree. In other words, it did not wither away instantly. It was only when they came back the next day that His disciples noticed the fig tree had died. This was because when our Lord spoke to the fig tree, it first dried up at its very roots before death reached the leaves. So don't be discouraged when you speak to your challenge and nothing seems to be happening. Believe that you are speaking directly to the root of the problem and that the outward manifestation of your faith is on its way!

I received this wonderful testimony from Lorraine, who resides in Darby, England. It shows you the power of praying or speaking, and how change begins from the very first day you speak:

> *My son and his wife have been married for ten years, and were trying desperately for a baby with no success. Six years ago, they began undergoing in vitro fertilization (IVF) treatments and have had at least seven unsuccessful treatments.*
>
> *Last March, my sister gave me a copy of your devotional and the entry for March 19 was about pleading the blood of the Lamb of God over all that is ours and our families'. The verse in the devotional was Exodus 12:13—"And when I see the blood, I will pass over you; and the plague shall not be on you to destroy you when I strike the land of Egypt." And you shared that what the nine plagues could not do, the blood did.*
>
> *I was thrilled when I read this. So I prayed for my son and my daughter-in-law, pleading the blood of Jesus over their situation, and I was just so excited because I knew that something had happened in the spirit.*
>
> *My son and his wife have been living abroad for the past four years, and every Sunday morning, they would call home. A few weeks after I prayed, my son called to say that his wife was pregnant. I told him that I wasn't surprised, as I had prayed for both of them recently. So what six years of medical treatment could not do, the blood of Jesus did! We all celebrated and were so thrilled that she was pregnant after all these years.*

A few Sundays later, our son called to say that she was exactly eight weeks pregnant. And it was exactly eight weeks from the day I prayed. Hallelujah!

Isn't this an amazing testimony? Whatever you may be believing God for, I want to encourage you to open your mouth to speak His Word. Pray to your Abba and proclaim the blood of our Lord Jesus over your situation! The presence of blood means that there has already been a death. It signifies that a payment has already been made. Today you and I, believers of our Lord Jesus Christ, can stand upon the unshakable foundation of God's promises because there has already been a death! The Lamb of God was sacrificed at Calvary and His blood is on the doorposts of our lives. So no plague, no death, no punishment, no harm, no danger, no evil can come near our dwelling, because the full payment for our sins has already been made by our Lord Jesus. What wonderful assurance and peace we can have today—all because of the complete and efficacious work of Jesus!

Whatever you may be believing God for, open your mouth to speak His Word in that area.

The New versus the Old

Let's take a moment to examine what the apostle Paul says about the power of speaking in the new covenant of grace:

For Christ is the end of the law for righteousness to everyone who believes. For Moses writes about the righteousness which is of the law, "The man who does those things shall live by them." But the righteousness of faith speaks.... "The word is near you, in your mouth and in your heart" (that is, the word of faith which we preach): that if you confess with your mouth the Lord Jesus and believe in your heart that God has raised Him from the dead, you will be saved. For with the heart one believes unto righteousness, and with the mouth confession is made unto salvation.

—Romans 10:4–6, 8–10

In this passage you see the comparison and contrast between the old and new covenants. Christ is the end of the law. The Greek word for "end" here is *telos*, which means "termination, the limit at which a thing ceases to be."[2] In other words, Christ is the termination and conclusion of the old covenant of the law. Christ is the termination of the old covenant that is based on man's good works to achieve righteousness. Christ also marks the beginning of the new covenant of grace, where man is made righteous by believing. See the differences that the apostle Paul skillfully laid out for us? New covenant versus old covenant. Faith versus works. The gift of righteousness versus righteousness by works. Believing versus working. Speaking versus doing.

It is vital for you to recognize the differences between the two covenants. They cannot be mixed together. Today God deals with us according to the new covenant. Some people mistakenly believe that because I preach about the new covenant, I have something against the old covenant laws. The truth is, I have the utmost respect for God's sacred laws. And I have never said that there was something wrong with the law. But the issue here is covenant. Which one is in place today and how are we made righteous today? That is the question! Are we made righteous by our works through keeping the law? Or are we made righteous by grace through believing in our Lord Jesus Christ? The answer is crystal-clear. Christ is the end of the law and we are made righteous today by believing in our Lord Jesus Christ.

Christ is the end of the law. We are made righteous today by believing in our Lord Jesus Christ.

You see, the new covenant is all about right *believing*, whereas the old covenant was all about right *doing*. The new covenant is all about the power of *speaking* well, whereas the old covenant was about the power of *working* well. I believe in the power of right believing. When a person believes right, he will live right. When a person believes that he is made righteous by the blood of Jesus Christ, he will be inwardly transformed to live right, and the spirit of godliness will be evident in his life.

He won't only be outwardly fulfilling the letter of the law. A person can keep the law outwardly for fear of punishment, but his heart can still be full of idolatry, covetousness, and adulterous thoughts. That is not what the grace revolution is about. The grace revolution is about inside-out transformation. It is about a heart emancipated by grace. A person transformed by grace not only keeps the law of God outwardly, but his heart is full of Jesus. He overflows with generosity, he is passionate for his spouse, and he is zealous for good works and the glory of his Savior, Jesus Christ. See the difference? It's like night and day.

Your words are powerful. The Bible says that the word of faith is near you, "in your mouth and in your heart" (Rom. 10:8). Notice that it is first in your mouth, and then it drops into your heart. When you speak words of faith, what you speak will finally drop into your heart, and what is in your heart will lead you. The law is characterized by *doing*; faith is characterized here by *speaking*. So when you are sick, speak well over yourself, declaring, "Lord Jesus, I thank You that by Your stripes I am healed."

Faith Is Released by Speaking

It is important that under the new covenant you are not working for your own righteousness in order to be healed and blessed. Moses says this of the righteousness that is by the law: "The man who does those things shall live by them" (Rom. 10:5). The focus is on *doing*. What about the righteousness that is of the new covenant? According to Romans 10:6, "the righteousness of faith speaks." The focus is on *speaking*. Therefore speak! Open your mouth and speak! Faith (believing) is released by speaking.

The righteousness of the law doeth, but the righteousness of faith speaketh (see Rom. 10:5–6 KJV). You and I are made in the image of God, Who, when things were very dark at the beginning of creation, didn't say, "Wow, it is so terribly dark here!" If God had said that, it would have gotten even darker! No, God spoke forth what He wanted to see. He wanted to see light and He said, " 'Let there be light'; and there was light. And God saw the light, that it was good" (Gen. 1:3–4). God saw good *after* He spoke it. Do you want to love life and see good days? Then start speaking it before you even see it.

Do you want to love life and see good days? Then start speaking it before you even see it.

When God saw the darkness, He didn't speak about the darkness. He did not speak what He saw. No, He spoke what He wanted to see. When Abram was still childless, God changed his name to Abraham, which means "father of many nations" (see Gen. 17:5). When the man with the withered hand met our Lord Jesus, Jesus spoke the word, asking the man to stretch out his hand, and the man was completely healed (see Matt. 12:10–13). Similarly, when our Lord met the man who had had an infirmity for thirty-eight years, He said to him, "Rise, take up your bed and walk." And the Bible records for us that "immediately the man was made well, took up his bed, and walked" (see John 5:5–9).

With physical eyes, man saw Abram as barren, the man with the withered hand as an invalid, and the man by the pool of Bethesda as a hopeless case. But our Lord saw and spoke differently! We serve a God "who gives life to the dead and calls those things which do not exist as though they did" (Rom. 4:17). I love the King James translation, which says our God is a God "who quickeneth the dead, and calleth those things which be not as though they were." He quickened the dead and brought nonexistent things into existence with His spoken words!

Speak What You Want to See

In the new covenant, God wants us to come back to believing and speaking. I am not denying that the darkness, barrenness, sickness, or infirmity that you may be faced with is there. I am asking you to speak by faith what you want to see. While God saw the darkness, instead of speaking what He saw, He spoke what He wanted to see. So the question you must ask yourself is this: What do you want to see in your life? What do you want to see in your body, your marriage, your children, your family, your household, and your place of employment? Listen carefully: I am not asking you what you *currently see*. I am asking you what you *want to see*.

It is unfortunate that the enemy has been successful in deceiving many people into speaking negatively, often with bitterness and unforgiveness, over their own lives and the lives of those around them. Some years ago a pastor who has been used mightily by the Lord in healing miracles shared something very thought-provoking with me. He noticed that people who had been completely healed were susceptible to developing the same disease again when they harbored bitterness and anger against another person in their hearts.

There is a proverb that says, "A calm and undisturbed mind and heart are the life and health of the body, but envy, jealousy, and wrath are like rottenness of the bones" (Prov. 14:30 AMP). Holding bitterness against someone is like you drinking lethal poison and expecting the other person to die. It is just not worth it, my dear reader. You are killing yourself slowly. I am not saying that the injustice inflicted upon you by this person is acceptable or insignificant. What I am saying is that today you can choose life and let go of that anger in your heart. Release that person, and most importantly, release yourself. Bless that person. Choose to love life and see many good days.

But Pastor Prince, you don't understand. He doesn't deserve my forgiveness!

Precisely. Forgiveness is for those who don't deserve it. That's what grace is all about. Remember what the Word says: don't return evil for evil, reviling for reviling (see 1 Pet. 3:9). Instead, have a spirit of grace and bless those who curse you. Bless them and set yourself free to love life and see many good days. Amen!

Have a spirit of grace and bless those who curse you.
Bless them and set yourself free to love life and see many
good days.

The sad reality is that the enemy has successfully programmed death into the human language. We hear casual expressions in our daily conversations like, "That dress is to *die* for," or "I am *dying* for that piece of cheesecake." Come on, let's change our vocabulary and saturate it with life. Instead of dying, let's be living for something!

I like the salutation Jews use when they propose a toast. They say, "*L'chaim,*" which means, "To life!"[3] Don't be preoccupied with what is dark and deathly; let's celebrate the abundant life that our Lord came to bring us! *The power of life and death is in the tongue, and those who love it will eat its fruit.* Love life and see good days. Start by refraining your lips from speaking evil and begin filling your mouth with the good news of all the wonderful things our Lord has done and will continue to do in your life. When you change your words, you will change your life. *L'chaim!*

CHAPTER 16

THE POWER OF IDENTITY

I read the story of a businessman in New York City who was rushing to board a subway train on his way to work one wintry morning. From the corner of his eye, he saw a beggar with a cup of pencils in his hands sitting on the platform. Without thinking too much about it, he quickly grabbed some money from his wallet and dropped the notes into the beggar's collection plate before boarding the train.

Just before the train doors closed, the businessman jumped back out onto the platform and took several pencils from the beggar's cup. He apologized to the beggar, explaining that in his haste, he had neglected to pick up the pencils he had purchased. "After all," he said, smiling, "you are a businessman just like me. You have merchandise to sell and it's fairly priced." After that the businessman boarded the next train and went about his day.

At a social event several months later, a well-dressed salesman approached this businessman and introduced himself. "You probably don't remember me and I don't know your name," he said, "but I will never forget you. You are the man who gave me back my self-respect. I was a 'beggar' selling pencils until you came along and told me that I was a businessman."[1]

I share this story to highlight to you the power of identity. The businessman gave this beggar a renewed sense of meaning and identity by simply speaking over him and calling forth a latent potential that was in him. By calling this beggar a businessman, he awakened in him a renewed sense of worth, value, and importance. The words gave the beggar a new perspective. And they gave him a new belief and vision that propelled him to walk away from the lie that a beggar was all he could be.

A Case of Mistaken Identity

We can draw many parallels in this story for believers of our Lord Jesus. I believe that many who are struggling with sin, addictions, and destructive bondages don't have the revelation of their new covenant identity in Christ. When you see a believer struggling with sin, it is often a case of mistaken identity. The best way to help him is to point him back to his righteousness in Christ, as the apostle Paul did to those in the Corinthian church who had fallen into sin. Paul didn't point these believers back to the law of Moses. All he did was remind them of who they truly were.

> *When you see a believer struggling with sin, it is often a case of mistaken identity. The best way to help him is to point him back to his righteousness in Christ.*

The Bible records the apostle telling them, "*Know ye not* that your bodies are the members of Christ?...*know ye not* that your body is the temple of the Holy Ghost which is in you, which ye have of God, and ye are not your own? For ye are bought with a price: therefore glorify God in your body, and in your spirit, which are God's"

(1 Cor. 6:15, 19–20 KJV, emphasis mine). Paul knew that if they were reminded of their righteous identity in Christ, they would repent. They would return to grace and turn away from their sins when they were reminded of their value according to the heavy price Christ had paid on the cross to ransom them.

I encourage you to use Apostle Paul's method to encourage and lift up believers who you know are struggling with sin. Point them back to their identity in Christ. They probably do not know, or have forgotten, how they have been made the righteousness of God through Jesus' blood. Because of this, like the beggar in the story, they are living a life of defeat. They are living far below the high place God has called them to. Believers in Christ are called to be the head and not the tail, to be above and not beneath, to reign over sin and not be defeated by sin!

Righteous in Christ

I want to share with you this moving praise report from Melissa, a lady from Texas. I believe that you will be greatly blessed and inspired by the journey that she has taken to discover her true identity in Christ:

> *From a young age, I had always felt I was worthless. My mother, who was constantly fighting with my father when I was growing up, kept telling me I was a nobody just like my dad, and that just like my dad, I would amount to nothing. This feeling of worthlessness stayed with me and became stronger when I was molested as a child. I blamed myself for it happening—that it happened to me because I really was worthless and a nobody.*

Growing up without having the love of my father, I became desperate to find and hold on to what I thought was love. I ended up having many relationships and partners. I was so afraid to let them go. I felt like I needed them to be there because I was so afraid to be alone.

All these things eventually led to my living a destructive lifestyle of sin in which I was deeply unhappy. I knew it was destroying me from the inside, but I didn't know how to stop it. I felt confused, lost, and empty all the time. I didn't think of going to God and church because people I knew would tell me, "You're going to go to hell because of your choices and how you're living. God's angry with you. He's disgusted with you and He's not going to bless you."

Because this was what I constantly heard, this was what I believed about God, and thought there was no way I could come to Him. Thankfully, I came across your television program late one night when I was channel surfing. I saw this Asian preacher on TV preaching and actually wanted to pass it up when something inside me said, "Just listen to what he is talking about."

I'm so glad I did because you were talking about the finished work of Jesus at the cross, how Jesus loves us, and how much He loves me just as I am. I found that I couldn't stop listening to the sermon. It was the start of my discovering how God gave His best—His Son, Jesus—for me, so that I could have a relationship with Him as my Daddy God and come into His presence without fear or shame.

At the end of the sermon, you invited us to pray and ask God into our lives if we'd never done it before. I prayed that prayer and told God, "I need You and I need Your help. I don't know how to change what I've become but I know that You'll help me. Only You can help me get out of this lifestyle, the drugs, the alcohol, and having so many different partners. There's a relationship I need to get out of right now but I don't know how to. I'm so unhappy. There has to be more to life than the kind of life I'm living."

As I was praying, I felt Jesus' love just overwhelm me, and all the bitterness, confusion, unhappiness, and pain in my life just melted, as you like to say, "like butter." I can't explain it. The dull ache, the frustration, and the gnawing emptiness all just left, and for the first time, a joy I couldn't explain came in.

The very next day, God opened doors for me to get out of the bad relationship I was in—effortlessly and without bitterness on both sides. Since that time, so many amazing things and blessings have happened. My relationship with my mother has been restored. Through experiencing Jesus' love for me, I've been able to forgive my mother for the times I'd felt hurt and rejected by her, and I've come to genuinely love her. I've also been able to forgive other family members who had told me I was worthless and who didn't want to have anything to do with me.

Everything is so different now. Today, I wake up and say, *"Thank You, Jesus, for Your supply of grace to me. Thank You for all Your blessings. Thank You that You've already done everything for me. You will keep me on the path You want me to go."*

I know that Jesus loves me and that He has great plans for me. I see His favor in my life. My bosses tell me, "You're doing such a good job and you're always smiling." People I meet tell me, "You look younger than your age." I tell them all that it's Christ in me.

Now, when I get a little frightened about things or situations in my life, I remember to cast all my cares to God. I plug into my iPod and listen to your sermons. Even though they are sermons I've heard before, I'll still get something new out of them. I'll see the beauty and love of Jesus all over again and feel His rest and peace wash over me. And when I make a mistake, I just say, "Jesus, thank You that You still love me even when I make a mistake. I am still forgiven—my past, present, and future sins are forgiven." That gives me strength to get past that mistake and move on.

Even when I make a wrong turn, He always finds a way to bring me back. And whenever I'm in a negative situation, Jesus tells me the outcome is going to be good because He's there and He's working on it.

Sometimes, thoughts of my past would come back but I've learned to say, "I'm a new creation. I'm the righteousness of God in Christ. It's not about what I've done but what Jesus has done." Amazingly, the temptations that held me in the past have all lost their hold. It feels like I'd never lived a destructive lifestyle before. Today, my life testifies that Daddy God loves and saves. More importantly, the change has been effortless— it's all by the grace of Jesus. It's had nothing to do with my willpower but the divine power of Christ at work in me. Thank you, Pastor Prince, for unveiling Jesus' beauty and love for me. I feel so loved by Him and I'm so grateful for His finished work at the cross!

Melissa, thank you for taking the time to share the precious journey you have taken with our Lord Jesus. It really blessed me to hear how you have discovered your righteous identity in Christ, and how this has led you to experience so many breakthroughs in your life. I am so proud of you and so excited for all the good things that our Father in heaven has in store for your future. I have no doubt that your testimony will inspire many people to discover the power of their righteous identity in Christ!

What Are You Hearing?

My dear reader, I believe that you too have been greatly blessed and encouraged by Melissa's praise report. Some of you may be able to identify with her about the people around her who kept telling her that she was a nobody and that she would amount to nothing. Those are the lies that the enemy wants you to believe. He will keep telling you those lies and surround you with people who will reinforce those lies in your mind until you believe that you are truly a worthless nobody. Why? Because when you start to have even the slightest belief that these people could be right, you will start behaving as if you are a valueless and worthless nobody. That is the negative power of wrong believing.

Unfortunately, that was exactly what happened to Melissa. When she began to entertain those lies of worthlessness, it drew her rapidly down a slippery slope of defeat. As she candidly describes, "All these things eventually led to my living a destructive lifestyle of sin in which I was deeply unhappy. I knew it was destroying me from the inside, but I didn't know how to stop it."

Many people harbor the misconception that those who are constantly partying, drinking, getting high, and sleeping around are having the time of their lives. Hollywood and the secular media have deified and glamorized the party lifestyle as cool and carefree.

They have sold the lie that the YOLO life—the you-only-live-once, consequence-free existence—is awesome. But if you peel back the curtains, you will see just how deeply unhappy and depressed these people entangled in a sinful lifestyle are. Our teenagers and youths are being bombarded with these images on their social media channels, in movies, and on television shows, where sinful lifestyles are not only tolerated but celebrated. This is what our kids are faced with daily in school and on their mobile devices.

How have many churches responded? By saying, "We have to go back to the Ten Commandments! We have to preach more on the law of Moses, on repentance, and on character." But do you know what this generation hears when the churches say that? Melissa gives us a pretty good sense of what young people actually hear and what it made her believe: "I didn't think of going to God and church because people I knew would tell me, 'You're going to go to hell because of your choices and how you're living. God's angry with you. He's disgusted with you and He's not going to bless you.' Because this was what I constantly heard, this was what I believed about God, and thought there was no way I could come to Him."

Is it any wonder some churches are losing the next generation? What Melissa has described is unfortunately what young people hear about their Father in heaven. They hear about an angry and capricious God Who is just looking for an opportunity to club them with a big stick and send them to an eternal furnace of fiery damnation. The church proudly proclaims, "We love the sinner but hate the sin." But in reality, all that those struggling with sinful lifestyles hear is, "WE HATE THE SIN," and they stay away from the church because they understandably equate that with, "WE HATE YOU." That, my friend, is simply not the gospel.

The gospel is our beloved Lord Jesus reaching out to the woman at the well who had had five husbands and was cohabiting with another man out of wedlock. The gospel is our Lord Jesus rescuing the woman caught in adultery from the religious mob that wanted to exercise its legal right to brutally bludgeon her to death with rocks. When you observe our Lord Jesus, He was always comfortable with those who were tangled up in sin, so much so that the religious leaders mocked Him and called Him a friend of sinners (see Matt. 11:19). He was undeterred by His critics, and just one encounter with His love and grace caused sinners to be transformed forever from the inside out.

My dear friend, that's the grace revolution that we have been talking about throughout this book. Our Lord never endorsed people's sinful lifestyles; He simply awakened them to His deep and personal love for them, and once they experienced His love, they had the power to walk out of the prison of sin, addiction, and bondage. Grace opens the prison doors for those trapped in sin. The woman at the well became an evangelist in her city and many came to know Jesus because of her. The woman caught in adultery walked away with the gift of no condemnation and the power to sin no more. The religious actively shunned the sinner; Jesus actively pursued the sinner.

Grace opens the prison doors for those trapped in sin.

Speak Your Righteousness in Christ without Doubt

I love the powerful Scripture in the book of Romans that says, "For what the law could not do in that it was weak through the flesh, God did by sending His own Son" (Rom. 8:3). The answer, my friend, is found not in the law, but in the Son. The law was given by a servant,

Moses; grace came through the Son, Jesus. The grace revolution begins with a person and His name is Jesus. When you have Jesus as your Lord and Savior, you have everything. You have, most importantly, a new and righteous identity in Christ.

When you have Jesus as your Lord and Savior, you have a new and righteous identity in Him.

We learned in the previous chapter that the law is about doing, whereas the righteousness of faith speaks. I wrote this chapter because I want to encourage you to have a daily consciousness of your righteousness in Christ by speaking and confessing your righteousness out loud. Now that you have made it through so many chapters of this book, I believe that you know you are righteous in Christ, and that righteousness is a gift you cannot earn. While knowing this is fantastic, I want you to take a step further with me today and begin to practice confessing your righteousness in Christ daily.

Throughout the day, whether you are driving to work, shopping for groceries, or preparing a meal for your family, just say quietly under your breath, "I am the righteousness of God in Christ. All the promises, blessings, and protection that belong to the righteous are mine" (see Prov. 10:6). This is the word in season for you, and I want to challenge you to cultivate a robust revelation of your righteous identity in Christ by repeatedly confessing your righteousness in Christ. If you listen closely to what Melissa shared in her testimony, that is what she continually did to experience lasting breakthroughs in her life.

Quite often a person experiences a breakthrough but that breakthrough doesn't last. Why? Because after some time, they forget the scriptural revelation they received that gave them the breakthrough in the first place. Many believers don't realize this, but revelations can be stolen and forgotten. That's what happened to the Corinthian church and Paul had to step in to remind them of their righteous identity in Christ.

This is also why it is so essential for you to be part of a local church where you can keep on hearing and hearing messages that are full of the person of Jesus, and be surrounded by Christ-centered leaders and friends who will always point you back to the Lord. The grace revolution is not just about momentary breakthroughs; it is about experiencing permanent breakthroughs.

It is so essential for you to be part of a local church where you can keep on hearing messages that are full of the person of Jesus, and be surrounded by Christ-centered leaders and friends who will always point you to the Lord.

One of the most powerful and practical ways for you to experience such breakthroughs is to keep speaking forth your righteous identity in Christ. Listen to how Melissa practiced this and experienced lasting breakthroughs in her life: "Sometimes, thoughts of my past would come back but I've learned to say, 'I'm a new creation. I'm the righteousness of God in Christ. It's not about what I've done but what Jesus has done.' Amazingly, the temptations that held me in the past have all lost their hold. It feels like I'd never lived a destructive lifestyle before. Today, my life testifies that Daddy God loves and saves. More importantly, the change has been effortless—it's all by the grace of Jesus. It's had nothing to do with my willpower but the divine power of Christ at work in me." Wow, this is so good, Melissa! When you hear her share, all you hear is our Lord Jesus and how it is all about what He has done. Amen! All praise, honor, and glory belong to our Lord Jesus—to Him and Him alone!

My dear friend, when you are stressed out and a thousand things are screaming for your attention, say quietly under your breath, "I am the righteousness of God in Christ." When you read some horrible news in the morning papers and your heart is gripped with fear for your loved ones, just say quietly under your breath, "I am the righteousness of God in Christ." And when you are feeling the strong temptation to indulge in a secret addiction that nobody knows about, now you know what to do: say quietly under your breath, "I am the righteousness of God in Christ."

Your victory is directly related to how conscious you are of your righteous identity in Christ. If you truly desire to see more breakthroughs in your life and experience the power to live above defeat, speak! Speak out, speak up, and speak without doubt. And I promise you that you will start living more stress-free, more fearlessly, more boldly, and more victoriously than ever before!

CHAPTER 17

RELEASE THE POWER TO REIGN

She had given up all hope that she would one day have a child. But everything changed when she stood before the faithful prophet Elisha.

Elisha had asked his servant Gehazi to find out what he could do for this woman who had been a gracious and generous supporter of his ministry. Gehazi told the prophet that she had no son and her husband was old. Upon hearing this, Elisha quickly called for her. And as she stood in the doorway, before she could even cross the threshold to enter the upper room that she and her husband had constructed for Elisha, he looked at her and said, "About this time next year you shall embrace a son."

Surprised by the prophet's words, the woman forgot all decorum and blurted, "No, my lord. Man of God, do not lie to your maidservant!" But sure enough, she soon conceived, and a year later held her miracle child, just as Elisha had prophesied.

The boy grew up with a precocious talent for all things outdoorsy. He loved climbing and swinging from the trees in their backyard. He brought such gaiety to the household and had such a contagious laugh that even the reapers in the field loved having the boy around as they labored. But one morning, while accompanying his father, who was working with the harvesters, the young boy suddenly cried out that his head was hurting. Thinking that the boy had simply been out in the heat of the blazing sun for too long, the father instructed a servant to carry him home, where his mother held him on her lap.

Then the unthinkable happened. As his mother gently stroked his head, the boy fell unconscious and died at about noontime. The woman was deeply distressed by the sudden and inexplicable turn of events, but she did not tell anyone what had happened. Instead she carried her little boy to the upper room and laid him on the prophet Elisha's bed. She then asked her husband for a donkey so that she could hurry to the man of God and come back.

Perturbed by her sudden desire to look for Elisha when it wasn't a day of any religious significance, her husband asked, "Why are you going to him today?"

Fighting back all her tears and emotions, she simply replied, "It is well."

As she approached Elisha's home on Mount Carmel, the prophet saw her in the distance and sent Gehazi to run to her and ask her, "Is it well with you? Is it well with your husband? Is it well with the child?"

Once again, she said, "It is well." But the moment she came before Elisha, she fell at his feet. Elisha followed her back to her home, prayed to the Lord, and supernaturally raised her precious boy back to life (see 2 Kings 4:8–37).

Say "It Is Well"

What a powerful account in the Bible. I believe we can all learn something from the woman's response to probably the toughest challenge she had ever faced in her life. She held back the turmoil in her heart over the death of her child and spoke contrary to her natural circumstances. Outwardly everything was not well. Yet she kept saying to herself and the people around her, "It is well. It is well. It is well." She didn't speak what she saw; she spoke what she wanted to see. She kept her eyes and her faith on God, and believed with all her heart that in God, all things were well and all things would work out for her good.

My friend, you may be going through some adversity in your life even as you are reading this. Be encouraged by this story of the Shunammite woman and start speaking well over your current challenge. Refrain your lips from speaking evil. Declare, "It is well, in Jesus' name." Many times the simplest prayers are the most powerful prayers. If you have suffered a great loss, or are going through a very challenging season in your life, please know that I am by no means belittling or dismissing what you are going through. I have personally suffered the loss of a loved one and I know how unbearable the pain can be. But I humbly encourage you to strengthen yourself in the Lord and declare, "It is well. It is well. It is well."

Start speaking well over your current challenge. Declare, "It is well, in Jesus' name."

Horatio Spafford penned the beautiful and renowned hymn *It Is Well with My Soul* during the most traumatic and turbulent time in his life. In 1873 he wanted to travel to England with his family, but decided to send them ahead, as he had business matters to attend to. As his wife and four young daughters sailed across the Atlantic, their ship collided with another vessel in a horrific accident and over two hundred people, including all of Spafford's daughters, died. En route to be reunited with his devastated wife, who had survived, Horatio worshiped the Lord. As his ship passed close to where his daughters had died, the words of this hymn flowed from within him: "It is well (it is well), with my soul (with my soul), it is well, it is well, with my soul."[1]

Speak Forth Your Authority in Christ

Many people think that God has full control over the world today and so pin the blame on Him for disasters, tragic accidents, and sicknesses. Some people become atheists because they say they can't worship a capricious God Who would allow children to suffer terminal diseases. Sadly, what they don't understand is that there is a devil who is very real, active, and destructive in this world. God is *not* the author of calamities and diseases. Our Lord Jesus came that we might have life and have it more abundantly! But the devil is a thief. He comes to steal, to kill, and to destroy (see John 10:10).

Our Lord Jesus came that we might have life and have it more abundantly!

The world we live in today is a fallen world. God gave Adam and Eve dominion over this world, but the moment Adam and Eve bit into the forbidden fruit, sin and death corrupted it. Adam and Eve ceded control of this world to the devil. Satan is called "the prince of the power of the air" in Ephesians 2:2, "the god of this age" in 2 Corinthians 4:4, and "the ruler of this world" in John 12:31.

Now, this *does not mean* that Satan rules the world completely and has unlimited power in the world. Please pay absolute and close attention to this. I don't want you to miss this. It is very important that you know and understand that believers of the Lord Jesus Christ are no longer under the dominion of Satan's power and influence in this world. In Christ, we may be *in* this world, but we are not *of* this world (see John 17:11, 14). We belong to a higher power and His name is Jesus. The Bible also tells us, "He who is in you is greater than he who is in the world" (1 John 4:4).

In Christ, we may be in *this world, but we are not* of *this world. We belong to a higher power and His name is Jesus.*

That is why we can stand firm, stand strong, and stand proud upon the promises of God, and speak, "It is well" over every area of our lives. We are *His*! We are not like sheep without a shepherd. All the blessings, promises, and protection that belong to the righteous "are Yes, and in Him Amen" (see 2 Cor. 1:20). We need only receive them by grace through faith. They are not received through our works, so no man can boast, but purely through faith in His unmerited favor (see Eph. 2:8–9).

Just take the promise in Proverbs 11:21 (KJV) that says, "The seed of the righteous shall be delivered." This means that your sons and daughters shall be kept safe and protected in Jesus' name. There may be times when you hear about a disaster and your heart breaks for the families going through the horror. At the same time, fear can begin to work its way into your heart. Perhaps you begin to be anxious about the safety of your children. Our children are so mobile these days. They are traveling all around the world on exchange programs and meeting new people all the time through their friends and through social media channels.

When fear grips your heart, that is the best time to claim this promise in God's Word. Just say, "Lord, I thank You that I am the righteousness of God in Christ, and You promised in Your Word that the seed of the righteous shall be delivered." And don't stop at your family. You can use your authority as a believer to pray for those who are suffering!

When Doubts Arise

My dear friend, if you are not established in the gospel of grace, all kinds of teachings that you have received will begin to put doubt in your heart:

> *Are you sure you have done enough to be considered the righteousness of God?*
> *Are you holy enough for God to protect you and your children?*
> *Have you done enough, given enough, served enough?*
> *Have you been completely obedient and done all that God has asked you to do?*
> *Is your heart 100 percent devoted to the Lord?*

Do these questions sound familiar to you? My dear reader, when you are not anchored on the person of our Lord Jesus Christ and His finished work, all these questions will make you self-focused, self-absorbed, self-conscious, and self-occupied. And self-occupation is the complete opposite of true holiness, which is about being completely occupied with our Lord.

Self-occupation is the complete opposite of true holiness, which is about being completely occupied with our Lord.

When someone tells you that you have to obey more in order to be made righteous, they are essentially making righteousness a work, when in truth, new covenant righteousness is a gift received by faith. So today, because you are a believer, I encourage you to say, "By faith I have been made righteous and the seed of the righteous shall be delivered." Furthermore, Psalm 112:2 (KJV) declares this of the believer: "His seed shall be mighty upon earth: the generation of the upright shall be blessed." Amen!

I want to encourage you to take the gospel of grace seriously. There is a real enemy and his aim is to deceive you into thinking you have to work for your righteousness, so he can keep you constantly feeling inadequate and disqualified. But the truth is this: the blood of our Lord Jesus has qualified you!

Today God's Word, God's power, and God's protection over you are far stronger than anything the enemy can throw at you. The devil is the ruler of this world, but don't forget what God's Word proclaims over you: "He Who lives in you is greater (mightier) than he who is in the world" (1 John 4:4 AMP). You are so utterly cleansed by the blood of our Lord Jesus that today the Holy Spirit, God's own Spirit, lives in you. And He Who is in you is *greater* than any demon, any adversity, and any bondage. Amen!

The Power of Receiving

For almost twenty years now, I have been preaching the gospel of grace and teaching believers around the world to confess their righteousness in Christ. If you have been following my ministry, you know that one of my favorite verses is Romans 5:17: "Much more those who receive abundance of grace and of the gift of righteousness will reign in life through the One, Jesus Christ."

Unfortunately, there are people who mock what the Word of God says, thinking that it is too simplistic. Essentially, they make light of receiving and they see receiving as weak and insubstantial. They think, "Is that all a Christian does? Just receive God's grace?" Their focus is on doing, on duty, on what is man's responsibility. My dear reader, don't ever underestimate the power of receiving. Man's greatest doing—his greatest duty and greatest responsibility—is to humble himself to receive from the Lord Jesus!

Don't ever underestimate the power of receiving.
Man's greatest doing—his greatest duty and greatest
responsibility—is to humble himself to receive from
the Lord Jesus!

Look at what Mary did—she sat at our Lord's feet and just pulled, drew, and received from her Savior. But Martha came along and complained to Jesus, saying, "Lord, do You not care that my sister has left me to serve alone? Therefore tell her to help me" (Luke 10:40). What was Martha consumed with? Duty, responsibility, serving, and doing!

I believe that the Martha-type of believers we have today, who are constantly complaining against believers like Mary, are precious, beloved, and deeply sincere. But they can be so committed to their duties that they forget the person it's all about. Martha was zealous about serving the Lord, but she ended up being hopping mad with her sister, and even chided the Lord. Mary looked beyond the exterior and saw a fullness in the Lord to draw from. Martha, on the other hand, saw Him in the natural, as needing her ministry. Which sister do you think made the Lord feel like God? Whom was the Lord more pleased with?

Can you see how Martha completely missed the point of all her service? Martha was like a horse wearing leather blinkers—she was utterly consumed by her duty and missed the divine deity, the Lord Jesus Himself, Who was sitting right in her living room! And listen to our Lord's response (I believe that He said this tenderly and with a loving smile): "Martha, Martha, thou art careful and troubled about many things: But *one thing is needful*: and Mary hath chosen that good part, which shall not be taken away from her" (Luke 10:41–42 kjv, emphasis mine). I believe that when Martha heard that, she had a revelation immediately. Instead of buzzing around and fuming at the Lord and her sister, she put down her pots and pans, removed her apron, and sat with her sister to receive from the Lord. Never underestimate the power of receiving from our Lord.

The more you receive the abundance of grace and gift of righteousness, the more you will reign, the more you will perform, the more you will be responsible, the more you will glorify the Lord, and the more you will fulfill your call, duty, and destiny. Because Mary did the one thing needful and focused on receiving from the Lord, she ended up performing the right service for Him. We read in John 12:1–8 that she anointed the Lord with costly fragrant oil for His burial. All the other women who wanted to anoint Him for His burial were too late on resurrection morning (see Luke 24:1–3). Mary was able to do the right thing at the right time because she kept her heart centered on receiving from the Lord. So keep receiving from Jesus. Every day receive His Word, His grace, and His gift of righteousness. And keep confessing your righteousness in Him—it will result in your doing the right thing at the right time.

The more you receive the abundance of grace and gift of righteousness, the more you will reign, glorify the Lord, and fulfill your call, duty, and destiny.

The Problem of Having a Wrong Identity

But Pastor Prince, how can I confess righteousness when I know that my life is not perfect? Shouldn't I be confessing my sins?

That's a great question. First let me make it absolutely clear that I have no problem with confessing sins. I practice the confession of sins because when you know you are *already* loved and forgiven by your Father in heaven, you can stand in the throne room of His grace with boldness and talk to Him openly about your failings.

A businessman who knows that all his debts have been paid has no problem opening up his ledger and seeing all the red that once marked his debts. Why? Because those debts are no longer on his conscience. Those debts don't frighten him anymore. In the same way, when you know that you have the forgiveness of sins and that the payment of our Lord Jesus' blood has perfectly washed you clean, you can openly confess your sins. You can talk to your Father about your failings and mistakes with no sin debt on your conscience. Instead of running away and avoiding Him when you have failed, having full assurance in your heart of your forgiveness and righteousness in Christ brings you closer to Him.

The problem starts when people think they have to confess *all* their sins *in order to be forgiven*. This is an impossible standard to live by. How many people can successfully confess all their sins every day? The answer is none, because no one can. And what man cannot do, God did with the precious blood of His beloved only Son. Again, please understand that I am not against your confessing your sins and having honest conversations with God about your failings and mistakes. But if you are confessing your sins *in order to be forgiven*, you are putting yourself on a never-ending treadmill.

As long as you are still in this world, there will always be some sin and temptation in your life, whether in thought or deed. Thinking that you have to confess your sins in order to be forgiven will, in fact, cause you to be sin-conscious. This sin-consciousness will make you more susceptible to temptations—"Might as well go all the way"—because you are constantly feeling like a dirty sinner. But if you are forgiveness-conscious and Christ-conscious, you will live like the confident, righteous, and victorious believer that you already are in Christ. The question is one of identity. The first leads to a life of defeat, the second to a life of victory.

If you are forgiveness-conscious and Christ-conscious, you will live like the confident, righteous, and victorious believer that you already are in Christ.

Judicial versus Parental Forgiveness

Let me now deal with a teaching that attempts to segment God's forgiveness. This teaching argues that there is a difference between "judicial forgiveness" and "parental forgiveness." Judicial forgiveness refers to God's forgiveness of all our sins because of the penalty that Jesus paid on our behalf on the cross. On the other hand, while all our sins are forgiven *judicially*, we are out of fellowship with God when we commit a sin—until we confess that sin to receive *parental* forgiveness. The end result of believing this teaching is similar to what I have described earlier.

If you go by this teaching, you will always feel you are lacking in parental forgiveness, simply because there will always be sins (in thought or deed) you have not confessed. And if you live by this doctrine, you can't conveniently pick and choose which sins you need or want to confess (see chapter 5). The bottom line is that you won't have full assurance of your forgiveness in Christ. You will always be sin-conscious and doubt your forgiveness, and both your conscience and the devil will exploit this.

So are you forgiven or are you not? Which is it? The Bible isn't uncertain with something as critical as your forgiveness of sins, but deals with it with great clarity. Where do we see this? In Acts 13:38–39, the apostle Paul clearly declares, "Through this Man is preached to you the forgiveness of sins; and by Him everyone who believes is justified from all things from which you could not be justified by the law of Moses."

Can the forgiveness of sins be made any clearer? The apostle Paul preached the forgiveness of sins with no apology, no qualifications, and no distinction between judicial and parental forgiveness. So be careful of these man-made distinctions that are not in God's Word. Forgiveness is forgiveness; there are no subdivisions. You are either forgiven or you are not, and how much you enjoy your forgiveness depends on what you believe about our Lord Jesus and what He has done on the cross.

Scripture is crystal-clear regarding our complete forgiveness in Christ. Yet there are some who feel the need to whisper to Apostle Paul, "Be careful, Paul, you can't preach forgiveness like this—you need to qualify what you are saying. There is no telling who is listening to you and how they will live." To these critics of the ministry of our Lord Jesus Christ and the power of His forgiveness, Paul lovingly but firmly gives the warning in the next two verses, saying, "Beware therefore, lest what has been spoken in the prophets come upon you: 'Behold, you despisers, marvel and perish! For I work a work in your days, a work which you will by no means believe, though one were to declare it to you' " (Acts 13:40–41).

The prophets already foresaw that there would be despisers of the gospel of grace—those who would hear it, but dismiss it as being "too good to be true." Paul warned and reminded those who heard him not to be numbered among those despisers.

Grace Is the Work of God

When the disciples of our Lord began preaching the gospel of grace in the book of Acts, the high priest and other temple leaders were furious. They brought the disciples in for further questioning (after they had been supernaturally led out of prison) and heard what they had to say. The religious leaders got even angrier after that and plotted to kill them. At this meeting in Acts 5, a Pharisee named Gamaliel, a teacher of the law held in respect by all the people, stood up.

Gamaliel was a leading authority on Jewish laws. He was so revered that even the apostle Paul, when defending himself and presenting his credentials later in another meeting (in Acts 22), mentioned Gamaliel. Paul said of Gamaliel, "As his student, I was carefully trained in our Jewish laws and customs. I became very zealous to honor God in everything I did, just like all of you today" (Acts 22:3 NLT).

Now, although Gamaliel didn't have an understanding of the gospel of grace, he stood up and spoke with great wisdom at the earlier meeting, saying, "Men of Israel, take heed to yourselves what you intend to do regarding these men. . . . I say to you, keep away from these men and let them alone; for if this plan or this work is of men, it will come to nothing; but if it is of God, you cannot overthrow it—lest you even be found to fight against God" (Acts 5:35, 38–39).

I have a lot of respect for Gamaliel's wisdom. He did not have a revelation of the person of Jesus, the gospel of grace, and forgiveness of sins through Christ, but he was also not going to be found standing in the way of or fighting against what God might have been doing. He advised the other religious leaders to let time test the disciples' ministry and to let their ministry be validated by its fruit and by God Himself, even if the leaders themselves did not fully understand it.

Understanding "Parental Forgiveness" Biblically

If you are still confused and wondering about the concept of "parental forgiveness," let me share with you what the Bible says. In fact, you need look no further than Jesus' parable of the prodigal son. When the father saw his son coming toward home from afar, what did the father do? Did the father shout to him, "First confess your sins, my son, then you'll be welcomed home"? Remember, the son had insulted his father when he demanded his inheritance, left home, and then promptly squandered all his inheritance on riotous living. Eventually, when he couldn't possibly sink any lower, he decided to return to his father's house.

This story is really about a father forgiving his son, and I want you to pay attention to what Jesus says because He is talking about His own heavenly Father here. The father saw the son from afar and did this: he pulled up his long robes and started running toward his son. Notice that the father ran to his son before the son confessed any sin. The father then met his son and embraced him. Again, which happened first? Did the son confess his sins first, or did the father embrace him first? The father's embrace came first! That's not all. After the father had embraced his son, he kissed him. The son, who had had to work in a pigpen just before his return, probably smelled like a pig—the pits for a Jew. Yet the father rained kisses on his son. Did you notice that up to this point, there is no record of the son's making a single confession of sin?

The prodigal son does eventually say, "Father, I've sinned against heaven and in your sight" (Luke 15:21), but that is after the father ran to him, embraced him, and kissed him. So we know it is not the son's confession that produced the hugs and kisses of the father. Now answer this question: is this parental or judicial forgiveness? Remember, the father here is a picture of our heavenly Father. So Jesus' parable is showing us clearly what real, biblical, parental forgiveness is and looks like. This is what the Father wants us to understand about His forgiveness. There is no *judicial*, as opposed to *parental*, forgiveness with God. You are simply and really forgiven because of His Son.

There is no judicial, *as opposed to* parental, *forgiveness with God. You are simply and really forgiven because of His Son.*

Let me point you to another verse that the Lord gave me, to give you full assurance of your forgiveness:

> I write to you, little children, because your sins are forgiven you for His name's sake.
>
> —*1 John 2:12*

Notice how 1 John 2:12 opens up with, "I write to you, *little children*" (emphasis mine). "Little children" denotes the "parental" aspect of the forgiveness that God gives. So what does God the Father want us to understand about "parental forgiveness"? That our sins are forgiven because of Jesus. And as mentioned in chapter 4, the original Greek word for "are forgiven" is in the Greek perfect tense, which means this forgiveness is a definite action completed in the past with its effect continuing into the present.

The Word of God makes this clear in no uncertain terms: you have been and you continue to be forgiven. Amen! Because of this, in your darkest moments, and even when you have failed, you can say with boldness and confidence, "I *am* the righteousness of God in Christ. I *have* forgiveness of sins, and God loves me and is for me. It is well with my soul!"

The Word of God makes this clear in no uncertain terms: you
have been and you continue to be forgiven in Christ.

The Righteousness of Faith Speaks

My dear reader, the righteousness of faith speaks! The Bible exhorts us by saying, "Let the weak say, 'I am strong'" (Joel 3:10). Faith always speaks what it wants to see, not what it currently sees. Faith is "the substance of things hoped for, the evidence of things not seen" (Heb. 11:1). So when you are weak, you say by faith, "I am strong in the strength of the Lord. I can do all things through Christ who strengthens me" (see Phil. 4:13). When there is sickness in your body, you say by faith, "By His stripes I am healed" (see 1 Pet. 2:24). When there is lack in your life, you say by faith, "My God provides for all my needs according to His riches in glory by Christ Jesus" (see Phil. 4:19).

And when you have sinned, what do you say? That's the time to say by faith, "I am the righteousness of God in Christ Jesus" (see 2 Cor. 5:21). That's the time to declare and reinforce your righteous identity in Christ. Those who receive the gift of righteousness receive the power to reign over sin (see Rom. 5:17)!

There are people who think that all the gospel of grace does is liberate people from guilt and condemnation. That is certainly true, yet I receive many more testimonies from people who were liberated from *destructive sins, addictions,* and *bondages* when they began to understand the gospel of grace and actively confess by faith their righteousness in Christ. Here is one from Jimmy, a young man who resides in New York:

> *For more than fifteen years, I struggled with pornography. As someone who is trained in martial arts, I can safely say that I possess great self-discipline. Yet I still could not free myself from this addiction.*
>
> *Not too long ago, I began to hear your sermons on grace and began to apply them in my life. I began to confess that I am righteous before God because of Jesus' finished work.*
>
> *At first, my desire to indulge in my addiction seemed to increase and I wondered if I would ever be free. But I decided to continue confessing that I am righteous because of what Jesus has done for me.*
>
> *Within a few weeks, those habits began to cease on their own! I began to effortlessly see victory in this area, and I no longer concentrated on "not sinning" but on Jesus' finished work!*
>
> *What willpower, self-discipline, techniques, and methods could not do, God's grace did! I am free and am a living testimony that the GRACE OF GOD IS THE KEY TO OVERCOMING SIN! Praise Jesus!*

What an amazing testimony! Fifteen years of pornography addiction that could not be removed no matter what he did just left effortlessly when Jimmy began to believe and confess his righteousness in Christ. And just like Jimmy, many others today are overcoming sin in their lives by awaking to righteousness. They are learning to lay hold of this gift that they have through Christ and to speak it boldly.

I think it is rather ironic that there are people who have criticized ministries for their "overemphasis" on God's abundant grace, thinking that this is dangerous and will lead to licentious and sinful living. Well, what is the result of a ministry that is constantly preaching our Lord Jesus and what He says about the abundance of grace? We keep receiving praise report after praise report from people who have been set free from different addictions, including pornography, smoking, drinking, and using drugs, and from other destructive bondages.

Isn't this the holiness that we as ministers of God are all desirous to see in God's precious people? Instead of debating and arguing, I believe that ministers should be united in lifting up the name of our Lord Jesus and His finished work. We should be helping God's people discover their righteous identity in Christ so that they can start experiencing the power to live above defeat. This is what the grace revolution is all about.

PART FIVE

RECEIVE HIS ABUNDANT RESTORATION

CHAPTER 18

RECEIVE GOD'S MUCH-MORE RESTORATION

It has been almost fifteen years since I had the dream in which I heard the Lord saying to me, "The grace revolution is here." That was way back in 2001. I still remember thinking, "Yes, Lord, I know it is coming." Then He said, "No, it is *here.*" And He added, "I will set up shepherds over My flock and they will feed them. *And My flock will fear no more, nor be discouraged, nor be lacking.*"

As I heard the Lord speaking in the dream, I knew He was quoting from Jeremiah 23:4. Then He gave me an impartation in my spirit and unveiled to me that the message to be preached—the *now word* for the grace revolution—was also found in Jeremiah 23.

In the grace revolution, God Himself is setting up shepherds who will preach the gospel of grace with authority and impart to the hearers security, certainty, assurance, and confidence so they will no longer be oppressed by fear or discouragement! If you have lost many years living in doubt, fear, and depression, God is restoring those lost years to you in the grace revolution. So as we kick off the final key of this book, I can't wait to show you how the Lord is going to bring about restoration in every area of your life.

---

*In the grace revolution, God Himself is setting up shepherds
who will preach the gospel of grace with authority and impart
to the hearers security, certainty, assurance, and confidence.*

God's Principle of Restoration

When the Lord restores, what He gives is always greater in quantity or quality than what was lost. Whatever the enemy has stolen from you, we are going to believe the Lord for a 120 percent restoration. Why 120 percent? Because it is based on the principle of restitution in the trespass offering found in Leviticus 5 and 6. Leviticus 6 says,

> *Because he has sinned and is guilty... he shall restore what he has stolen, or the thing which he has extorted, or what was delivered to him for safekeeping, or the lost thing which he found, or all that about which he has sworn falsely. He shall restore its full value, add one-fifth more to it, and give it to whomever it belongs, on the day of his trespass offering.*
>
> *—Leviticus 6:4–5*

Here we see God detailing what a person must do to provide restitution (or restoration) to someone he has injured. Notice this law states that he "shall restore its full value, add one-fifth more to it, and give it to whomever it belongs." The full value of whatever was lost, defrauded, or stolen, plus one-fifth, is 120 percent of the original value. Now, this principle of restoration was under the law of Moses. How much more, then, can we expect restoration under the new covenant of grace—"a far better covenant with God, based on better promises" (Heb. 8:6 NLT). This is why we are going to trust God for a 120 percent—and more—restoration!

Notice also that the person brings his restitution on the day of his trespass offering. The trespass offering is a picture of what Jesus did for us at the cross. He became our substitute and was judged in our place for every trespass we committed so that we can freely receive every blessing of God, including the blessing of restoration. My dear friend, if you have accepted Christ as your trespass offering, God's much-more restoration is coming your way. If the enemy has stolen from you or defrauded you of the best years of your life, then in that very area in which you have suffered loss, God is going to give you much more than you had before. He is going to restore to you the years the locusts have eaten—and in greater measure than you can imagine. Your best days are ahead of you!

Your best days are ahead of you!

Restoring All that the Locusts Have Eaten

Joel 2:25–26 contains this beautiful promise that I want you to read for yourself:

> *"So I will restore to you the years that the swarming locust*
> *has eaten,*
> *The crawling locust,*
> *The consuming locust,*
> *And the chewing locust....*
> *You shall eat in plenty and be satisfied,*

And praise the name of the LORD *your God,*
Who has dealt wondrously with you;
And My people shall never be put to shame."

The most precious thing that our Lord Jesus can restore to you is the lost years of your life. All the years that the locusts have eaten, God can supernaturally restore to you. Every minute spent in fear, worry, doubt, guilt, condemnation, addiction, and sin adds up to wasted years that have been stolen from you. But I have good news for you today. Because of what our Lord Jesus has done for us on the cross, you can believe for total and complete restoration, for God to redeem ALL the time that has been lost and wasted!

Because of what our Lord Jesus has done for us on
the cross, you can believe for total and complete
restoration, for God to redeem ALL the time that has
been lost and wasted!

Let me share this phenomenal testimony of God's restoration from a brother by the name of Clarence, who resides in West Virginia:

I was a drug addict for ten years, injecting opiates into my veins every day. Even though I knew that the addiction was destroying me, I did not want to stop what I was doing.

But two years ago, my heavenly Daddy delivered me from the addiction by placing me in a halfway house. I was stuck there, unable to leave, and unable to get anyone to pick me up. And God not only removed my drug addiction, but my smoking addiction at the same time!

While I was in the halfway house, I listened to many grace preachers but always ended up with a feeling of weight on my shoulders. My mother had been telling me to listen to Joseph Prince, but I resisted it initially, wondering how a man from Singapore could have anything to say about God's grace. Boy, was I wrong. Singapore sent a missionary to America! Praise the Lord!

Through Joseph Prince's messages, I found rest in understanding Jesus' finished work at the cross. I also learned that condemnation kills and that on the cross, Christ had absorbed all my condemnation. Once I saw that, I saw the next crucial thing—that GOD IS MY DAD, and that means all good things are mine in Christ Jesus!

Today, I am running a successful art business that has grown by leaps and bounds. I now own a home with my wife and she also has a growing business. In addition, my relationship with my daughter from my previous marriage has also been restored. I was not allowed to see her for the past ten years but now, she has been staying with me over the weekends!

It is truly overwhelming to think of how fast my Dad has restored all the wasted years! Not only has He restored my life, but He has also restored my heart and mind toward Him. What a contrast to the years when I was still a drug addict, homeless, and eating scraps off plates at the houses of drug dealers!

Set Free to Experience Restoration of Lost Days

The grace revolution is a revolution of restoration. All the years this precious brother had lost to his addiction were restored to him when he embraced the grace of our Lord. In the same way, all the years lost wandering in the parched wilderness of legalism, Christian religion, and the ways of the old covenant can be restored to you. You don't have to live bound by the shackles of legalism. Our Lord Jesus said,

> *"If you abide in My word, you are My disciples indeed. And you shall know the truth, and the truth shall make you free.... Therefore if the Son makes you free, you shall be free indeed."*
> —*John 8:31–32, 36*

You don't have to live bound by the shackles of legalism.

What is "the truth" that has the power to set us free? Remember, our Lord was speaking to the Jewish people, so "the truth that they *shall* know" could not have been the old covenant of the law, which the Jewish people were already well versed in, as they had studied it from a young age. Knowing and attempting to keep the law to earn their righteousness had not given them the freedom they sought. It had, in fact, become for them an impossibly heavy yoke to bear.

To understand what "the truth" is, I want to bring you to Acts 15, where the Jerusalem Council had convened to debate which of the old covenant laws should be imposed on Gentile believers. Look at what Peter said:

> *"So God, who knows the heart, acknowledged them by giving them the Holy Spirit, just as He did to us, and made no distinction between us and them,* purifying their hearts by faith. *Now therefore, why do you test God by* putting a yoke on the neck of the disciples which neither our fathers nor we were

able to bear? *But we believe that through the grace of the Lord Jesus Christ we shall be saved in the same manner as they."*
　　　　　　　　　　　　　　　—Acts 15:8–11 (emphasis mine)

There are so many things we can glean from this passage. Let's start by looking at what Peter was referring to when he spoke about God giving the Holy Spirit to the Gentile believers in the same way that He had given the Holy Spirit to the Jewish believers. Peter was referring to his preaching to Cornelius's household and how the Holy Spirit fell upon *all* the Gentiles there who heard him as he was speaking these words: "To Him all the prophets witness that, through His name, *whoever believes in Him will receive remission of sins"* (see Acts 10:43–44, emphasis mine). Notice at what point the Holy Spirit fell—when Peter said that those who *believe* in Jesus will receive forgiveness of sins. When the Gentiles there simply put their *faith* in the Lord Jesus for the forgiveness of their sins, they were filled with the Holy Spirit!

The Jewish believers who were present with Peter then were astonished to see the gift of the Holy Spirit being poured out on the Gentiles for the first time. They saw how even Gentiles could receive the Holy Spirit in the same way they did (see Acts 10:45–46). It was an unprecedented, unthinkable phenomenon for the Jews of the early church to witness, since under Old Testament laws, Gentiles were considered unclean (see Acts 10:28).

In Acts 11, when Peter was later criticized by Jewish believers for having entered the home of Gentiles and preached to them, he shared with them his vision in which a voice from heaven had told him, "What God has cleansed you must not call common." And when he told them how the Holy Spirit had fallen on the Gentiles "as upon us at the beginning" (see Acts 11:9, 15), the Jewish believers acknowledged that God had also granted to the Gentiles "repentance unto life" (see Acts 11:18 KJV). Notice that although Peter himself didn't use the word *repentance* in his preaching at Cornelius's house, what happened there was nonetheless seen as God's granting them repentance unto life!

Having Our Hearts Purified by Faith

This brings me to my next point. At the Jerusalem Council, what did Peter say about *how* the hearts of the Gentile believers were purified? By their confession of sins or by faith?

By faith (see Acts 15:9)!

The Gentiles heard the forgiveness of sins being preached by Peter, *believed* the good news, and had their hearts *purified by faith*. Not by works, but by faith in Christ. Their hearts were purified by their *believing right*—believing that those who believed in the Lord would receive the remission of sins and be made the righteousness of God. Can you see that?

How are we made righteous today? How are our hearts purified today? By faith in our Lord's finished work at the cross!

How are we made righteous today? How are our hearts purified today? By faith in our Lord's finished work at the cross!

In the Sermon on the Mount, Jesus said, "Blessed are the pure in heart, for they shall see God" (Matt. 5:8). Now you are equipped to answer this question: *who* are the pure in heart? Those whose hearts have been purified by faith. Amen! This is how we use Scripture to interpret Scripture. So don't let someone impose on you his own opinion about how a person can be pure in heart. People can inject all kinds of their own beliefs and tell you that in order to have a pure heart, you need to do this and that. And you will end up thinking that if you fail to keep to their list of dos and don'ts, your heart will not be pure. Can you see how dangerous man's opinions can be? Just like that, precious believers can come under great fear that if they aren't doing something hard enough to continually keep their hearts pure, they will lose their salvation and end up not seeing the Lord.

Restoration Begins with Rest

I really struggled with Matthew 5:8 when I was a young believer. This was before the Lord opened my eyes to the gospel of grace. I sincerely wanted to have a pure heart before the Lord, and based on the teachings I had heard, I believed that I had to keep my heart pure by continually confessing my sins throughout the day. So I kept trying to confess all my sins, but the harder I tried, the more oppressed I felt. It felt as though I could never confess my sins enough to keep my heart pure. But praise the Lord for revealing to me that according to the authority of His Word (and not the uncertainty of human tradition), our hearts are purified *by faith* in our Lord Jesus. Hallelujah!

Now let's go back to what the apostle Peter was saying. He told the Jerusalem Council, "[God] made no distinction between us and them, purifying their hearts by faith. Now therefore, why do you test God by putting a yoke on the neck of the disciples which neither our fathers nor we were able to bear?" (Acts 15:9–10). I submit to you that the "yoke" that Peter described as unbearable and impossible to keep is the old covenant law. Some people will argue that the yoke here refers only to the ceremonial law of circumcision, but does that make sense to you?

Jewish males were circumcised on the eighth day after their birth—a time when they would not have been conscious of the law. Why would Apostle Peter describe circumcision as something that they and their fathers could not bear when it was something that was practiced on infants? Clearly the ritual law of circumcision was not the yoke he was referring to. The yoke that he was referring to was the yoke of the law. It was heavy, unbearable, and, when preached by our Lord, an impossible standard for any man to keep. That's why the Lord told all the Jewish people who were under the heavy yoke of the law,

> *"Come to Me, all you who labor and are heavy laden, and I will give you rest. Take My yoke upon you and learn from Me, for I am gentle and lowly in heart, and you will find rest for your souls. For My yoke is easy and My burden is light."*
> —*Matthew 11:28–30*

That, my friend, is the gospel of grace! Stop trying to be justified through the law of Moses. You are justified by faith. The Lord Jesus says to you, "Come to Me, and I will give you *rest.*" Notice that the word *restoration* begins with REST. As you rest in His grace and finished work, you will receive your restoration!

As you rest in the Lord's grace and finished work, you will receive your restoration!

Understanding the Times

The Bible makes it so clear that we are justified by faith. So why is it that so many people continue to be bound by the crushing demands of the law of Moses? I believe that it is because they don't fully understand what our Lord Jesus paid for on the cross of Calvary. They don't understand what the new covenant is all about. I'm about to delve into something that could seem somewhat profound if you are hearing it for the first time. But stay with me. I believe that you will be greatly blessed when your eyes are opened to the truths I'm about to share!

When our Lord stood in the synagogue in Nazareth, He was handed the book of Isaiah and He found the place where the following was written:

> *"The Spirit of the LORD is upon Me, because He has anointed Me to preach the gospel to the poor; He has sent Me to heal the brokenhearted, to proclaim liberty to the captives and recovery of sight to the blind, to set at liberty those who are oppressed; to proclaim the acceptable year of the LORD."*
> —*Luke 4:18–19*

Now pay close attention to what our Lord did next. The Bible records this: "Then He closed the book, and gave it back to the attendant and sat down.... And He began to say to them, 'Today this Scripture is fulfilled in your hearing'" (Luke 4:20–21).

Many people have missed what our Lord did. He *closed the book.* Why is this significant? My dear reader, if you don't understand why our Lord closed the book, you will struggle to understand God's

Word. There are even respected Bible scholars and learned theologians who fail to fully grasp why our Lord closed the book. As a result they don't have a holistic understanding of the gospel of grace.

The apostle Paul would be able to identify intimately with such ministers. Before his encounter with the Lord on the road to Damascus, he too had the veil of the law over his eyes and couldn't see and appreciate God's grace. With all sincerity he persecuted those who believed in the gospel of grace. In fact, Paul was so zealous that the Bible records he "made havoc of the church, entering every house, and dragging off men and women, committing them to prison" (Acts 8:3).

Having personally experienced such blindness, Paul described the condition in 2 Corinthians 3:14–15: "But their minds were blinded. For until this day the same veil remains unlifted in the reading of the Old Testament, because the veil is taken away in Christ. But even to this day, when Moses is read, a veil lies on their heart." But once the veil was removed from Paul's heart, God entrusted to him the gospel of grace. That's right, God turned the most notorious and zealous Pharisee of Pharisees into His biggest champion and evangelist for the gospel of grace. So don't be surprised if one day, you see the most notorious critic of the gospel of grace become the biggest evangelist for the grace revolution!

Let's come back to the question I asked: Why did our Lord close the book of Isaiah after He had read the portion that we quoted earlier? To understand this, you have to look at the Scripture He was quoting from in fuller context:

> *To proclaim the acceptable year of the* Lord,
> *And the day of vengeance of our God....*
>
> —*Isaiah 61:2*

Notice that a comma separates "the acceptable year of the LORD" and "the day of vengeance of our God." And it is right at this comma that our Lord closed the book of Isaiah. He didn't go on to read the part about the day of God's vengeance. Why? Because our Lord, Who was standing in Nazareth as He read those Scriptures, had come to proclaim the acceptable year of our Lord—remember what He said next: "Today this Scripture is fulfilled in your hearing." Our Lord Jesus was teaching us to rightly divide the Word of God.

The Age of Grace

The age that we live in today is the age of grace. We are under the dispensation of grace. The "acceptable year" is not a calendar year from January to December. It speaks of the dispensation, time, and season that we are in. We are not in the age of "the day of vengeance." That day will come, and our Lord will return to deliver Israel from total destruction and judge the earth.

The age that we live in today is the age of grace. We are not in the age of "the day of vengeance."

The Greek word for "acceptable" here is *dektos*. According to the Greek scholar Thayer, *dektos* is "that most blessed time when salvation and the free favors of God profusely abound."[1] Praise be to God, we are still in this *dektos* season. We are still in the acceptable year under the dispensation of grace. Our preaching and understanding of God's Word must be according to the dispensation we live in.

If I were living in the time of the Old Testament, I would be a preacher and advocate of the Ten Commandments and all the rituals of the tabernacle. But I am not living in that time, and neither are you. We are living in "the acceptable year," the *dektos* year of our Lord, which has spanned two thousand years. Isn't it amazing that God's Word is so rich that a comma represents a divide of two thousand years? So when you study God's Word, you have to read the context, understand whom the Scripture is written to, and, as we have just seen, *rightly divide the Word*, as our Lord Jesus did in Nazareth.

There are people who accuse those who preach grace of picking and choosing Scriptures that fit into their messages. Hang on a second—are you saying that our Lord Jesus was picking and choosing Scriptures when He read from the book of Isaiah? I didn't think so. The Word of God is very consistent and precise. And like a surgeon wielding his scalpel, those who are teaching God's Word need to be skillful and rightly divide God's Word. We just witnessed how precise our Lord is. Once He proclaimed the *dektos* year, He shut the book. Is our Lord ignoring the context of those Scriptures? Absolutely not. In fact, He saw the bigger context in terms of dispensation and declared that at that precise moment, Isaiah's prophecy was being fulfilled. The age of grace had come.

Unfortunately, there are many who are getting the larger context of the dispensations and covenants all jumbled up. They mix the dispensation of the law with grace, and confuse the old covenant with the new covenant. The result is a confusing theology. They preach grace and they also preach the law. They preach new covenant truths, but they also preach old covenant truths. They preach righteousness by faith, but they also preach righteousness by works. They preach that all your sins are forgiven, but then qualify that your sins aren't forgiven if you don't confess them. They take Scriptures that are specifically meant for Israel and apply them directly to the church today. They preach an unconditionally loving Father, but also an angry, frustrated, and disappointed God. What they think is "balance" is really mixture—and it results in confusion for all who hear them.

Learn to Rightly Divide the Word

My dear reader, God is not a schizophrenic God. God is the same yesterday, today, and forever. There isn't one God of the Old Testament and another God of the New Testament. There is only *one* God. But He relates to us according to the age, dispensation, and covenant that we are in. You can't simply take something that was recorded and spoken during the dispensation of the law of the old covenant, and apply it to new covenant believers today.

Likewise, you cannot take what was recorded and spoken *before* the cross of Jesus and apply it to new covenant believers today. Can you learn and draw principles from those Scriptures? Absolutely, for "all Scripture is given by inspiration of God, and is profitable for doctrine, for reproof, for correction, for instruction in righteousness, that the man of God may be complete, thoroughly equipped for every good work" (2 Tim. 3:16–17). You can draw guiding principles from all Scriptures, but you need to be discerning and to rightly divide the Word. As the apostle Paul said to his young apprentice, Timothy, "Be diligent to present yourself approved to God, a worker who does not need to be ashamed, *rightly dividing* the word of truth" (2 Tim. 2:15, emphasis mine).

When you learn to rightly divide God's Word, I believe you will

begin to see His grace, His love, and His security flood every area of
your life. Let me share with you a precious testimony of restoration
that Valerie, a lady from Illinois, sent to us:

> *I became a believer almost twenty years ago and my life
> changed tremendously. Despite being saved, I felt that some-
> thing was still wrong because I was repeatedly diagnosed with
> cancer—four times in all.*
>
> *After my last relapse of cancer, I watched Pastor Joseph
> Prince on television and ordered his materials. The first thing I
> remember learning was that all of my sins have been forgiven!
> Before that, I was taught of the need to repent and receive for-
> giveness from God whenever I sinned. I also learned that God
> was not looking at my performance to accept me, love me, or
> bless me, but at Jesus' finished work on the cross. What a deep
> blessing these truths were to my heart, body, and soul!*
>
> *I became a partner with the ministry and today, I have all
> of Pastor Prince's teachings and I meditate on them all the
> time. Now, my walk with the Lord is amazing! I no longer
> feel condemned or guilty and I am no longer walking in fear!
> I also have a revelation of Christ's love for me and I have an
> intimate relationship with Him.*
>
> *With God's help, my finances have also improved. I am
> fifty-six years of age and I now have my first home! On top
> of all this, I am cancer-free, have witnessed salvations in my
> family, and am enjoying better relationships with my family
> members.*
>
> *I can't express in words how much Pastor Prince's ministry
> has blessed my life. It is forever changed! My eyes have been*

opened to GOD'S GRACE and I will never go back to my old beliefs and ways of thinking.

Valerie, thank you for sharing your powerful faith journey!

Isn't it amazing that as Valerie began to learn how to rightly divide God's Word, she began to experience God's abundant restoration in quite literally every area of her life, that included an intimate relationship with Him, restoration of physical health, and blessed family relationships? This is such an encouragement to my team and to me because preaching the gospel of grace is all about helping and lifting up God's precious people. I am deeply humbled and grateful to be a part of this grace revolution that is transforming one life, one marriage, and one family at a time across the entire world. All honor, glory, and praise to our Lord Jesus Christ!

CHAPTER 19

LIVE WITH FULL ASSURANCE OF FAITH

In the previous chapter, I talked a little about how the Lord showed me that the "now word" for the grace revolution is found in Jeremiah 23:4, where the Lord says, "I will set up *shepherds* over them who will *feed* them; and they shall fear no more, nor be dismayed, nor shall they be lacking" (emphasis mine). God is setting up shepherds who will care for, nourish, and *feed* His sheep, not beat, threaten, and intimidate them.

God is setting up shepherds who will care for, nourish, and feed His sheep, not beat, threaten, and intimidate them.

This is happening all over the world today, from Australia to America, from Asia to Europe, and from Africa to the Middle East. Shepherds are rising up and proclaiming the gospel of grace with great boldness and we are seeing lives transformed by the power of our Lord Jesus Christ. Notice that the verse talks about "shepherds," plural, who will bring about sweeping changes across the world. It's not about one ministry or church. Our Lord Jesus has raised and will continue to raise many shepherds. This is the grace revolution that began with our Lord Jesus and all that He accomplished for us at Calvary!

These are the exciting days of grace we live in. Under the grace dispensation, we are living in the season of *dektos*, defined as "that most blessed time when salvation and the free favors of God profusely abound."[1] My desire for you as you come to the closing chapters of this book is that you experience the profusely abundant favor of God in every area of your life. I pray you will experience the power of living above defeat through His grace and gift of righteousness. The grace revolution is a revolution of restoration of everything the enemy has stolen—your health, your provision, your confidence, even your meaning and purpose in life. Our Father in heaven will restore to you and rebuild you from the inside out.

The grace revolution is a revolution of restoration of everything the enemy has stolen—your health, your provision, your confidence, even your meaning and purpose in life.

Experience Restoration of Healing

As you saturate yourself with the good news of God's Son, Jesus Christ, take a moment to be inspired by this amazing testimony of restoration from Marcus, a precious brother from Houston, Texas. Marcus suffered excruciating pain in his body for twenty years until he had an encounter with our Lord Jesus through the preaching of the gospel of grace:

I injured my back when I was ten years old. My older brother had dared me to do a flip, which I thought would be fun and easy to do. I tried doing the flip, didn't make it, and landed flat on my back. That's when I started to have a serious problem with my back and really bad back pains for the next twenty years.

Shortly after my fall, I noticed that breathing brought on pain in my sides. My mother, who was greatly alarmed, took me to chiropractors, who thought it was only a matter of making adjustments regularly to my spine. Well, after numerous adjustments over the next few years, the pain didn't go away. All the chiropractors and doctors that I saw couldn't tell me what was wrong with my back. The chiropractors kept telling me all I needed was more adjustments while the doctors told me to expect more pain the older I got "because the spine degenerates as you get older." Basically, nobody had answers or a cure for me.

As I grew up, I lived with pain as a constant companion. It was hard to get up and walk around. It was painful to sit up and stand up. Some days, the pain was so intense it hurt even to breathe—every little movement gave me pain. Even on "better" days, I couldn't exercise and driving was hard because I couldn't turn my head or move my body without pain shooting through my body. Sometimes, the pain would take me down for days to weeks at a time.

I hated the fact that I couldn't experience the kind of success I wanted in my family life and career. I knew my wife and two beautiful kids wanted a husband and a dad around to do fun stuff with, but I just couldn't do those things. I couldn't take them to the park and play with them like I wanted to.

Work was also frustrating because often I had to call in sick. I wanted to be able to go to work, to do all I needed to do, and just be successful at my job, but I felt so limited because I had to deal with the pain all the time.

I hated not being able to enjoy my family or my job, but I didn't know how to change things. Medicines weren't working—they only made me nauseous, tired, and drowsy, and gave only very temporary pain relief. Even though I was in church, I wasn't sure God loved me or that He would heal me, because I wasn't perfect. In fact, I was quite sure He would not heal me because I had messed up and hadn't done enough or made enough sacrifices to please Him. Some days, I was so depressed, I even wondered if God was real.

Things pretty much stayed the same until early 2013 when I started to listen to Pastor Prince's television broadcast. From his preaching, I found out that because of what Jesus did for me at the cross, God still loves me and was there for me even when I messed up. That was such a huge comfort and assurance for me that I wanted to hear more, so I started to record every single episode that came on.

A few months later, I tuned in to Pastor Prince's program when I had to call in sick again because of the pain. I lay on the couch and watched him teach on healing. I heard him say again that even when I have failed, God still loves me and He can still heal me. Pastor Prince taught how Jesus was the final sacrifice for us and how only through Jesus Christ, we are righteous, and through Jesus Christ, we are healed. And the more he broke it down using Scriptures, the more I saw that Jesus alone—not what I did—made me eligible for God's healing.

During that broadcast, Pastor Prince asked everybody who had a condition whether in the congregation or at home to stand up while he prayed for them. Before he prayed, he said, "Lift up your hands and pray with me. God is going to touch you." As he was praying, he suddenly stopped and said, "There is a man at home who is suffering pain in the right side of his back." Then, he snapped his fingers and said, "God has healed you."

I'll never forget it because immediately, I felt a warmth, a relaxation in my muscles that I hadn't felt since the accident, and I knew that God had healed me. Right in front of the TV, I started bawling. I couldn't believe it! One moment I couldn't move without pain, and the next moment, I was bending and I could feel the muscles in my back stretching…and there was no pain. The feeling was so indescribable that all I could do was cry for a while, before I called my wife to tell her what had happened.

Since that day, the pain has not come back and everything has changed. I can run around with my kids. We go to the park now and run and play, and I don't come back with any pain, nor does the pain show up the next day. I no longer feel pain when I stand, sit, or breathe, like I used to. I've started exercising and can even run through an obstacle course now. Work has become a joy too—my company has been experiencing success and I know it's because of God's favor bringing in the sales.

It's been amazing and I'm so grateful to Pastor Prince for preaching the truth about God's grace, and I'm so grateful to God for healing me, for showing me He still loves me, and for changing my life so tremendously!

Marcus, I am rejoicing with you and your family at the breakthroughs and restoration that you have experienced. Isn't our Lord wonderful? All glory and praise to our Lord for this powerful healing testimony!

A Revolution of Assurance and Peace

We are living in the days that Jeremiah prophesied about. We have read so many praise reports of God's beloved children experiencing abundant restorations, miraculous healings, and freedom from sin and addiction. And these are just a handful of the many testimonies that have been e-mailed to my ministry office.

Let me draw your attention to what Marcus experienced when he began tuning in to the preaching of the gospel of grace. In just a couple of weeks, he discovered what our Lord Jesus had done for him on the cross and especially His love for him even when he had messed up. Marcus shared that there was "such a huge comfort and assurance" for him. I thought that was a very appropriate choice of words because the grace revolution is a revolution of *assurance* and *peace*.

The grace revolution is a revolution of assurance
and peace.

Romans 10:15 tells us that those who "preach the gospel of peace" are those who bring "glad tidings of good things." When you hear about our Lord and what He has done for you at Calvary, it imparts deep shalom-peace, comfort, and rest to the innermost recesses of your troubled heart. From that position of rest, Marcus received complete and total restoration of his health. The severe back pains that plagued him for twenty years are now totally gone. Hallelujah!

Our heavenly Father wants His beloved children to live with great assurance—assurance of their salvation, assurance of their forgiveness, and assurance of their righteousness in Christ.

Our heavenly Father wants His beloved children to live with great assurance—assurance of their salvation, assurance of their forgiveness, and assurance of their righteousness in Christ. Unfortunately, there are certain sectors in Christianity that believe keeping believers insecure about their salvation and forgiveness will help them to be more holy and zealous for the Lord. They don't realize that what they are doing is actually counterproductive and producing just the opposite effect. Love and insecurity cannot coexist in a healthy relationship. Our Father in heaven wants us to "draw near with a true heart in full assurance of faith" (Heb. 10:22). And the Word of God is intended to impart this full assurance of faith. Just read these Scriptures:

> *"God has given us eternal life, and this life is in His Son. He who has the Son has life; he who does not have the Son of God does not have life. These things I have written to you who believe in the name of the Son of God, that you may know that you have eternal life, and that you may continue to believe in the name of the Son of God."*
>
> —1 John 5:11–13 (emphasis mine)

Read it again.

These words are recorded in the Holy Word so that you may *know* with absolute certainty that you have eternal life as a believer in our Lord Jesus Christ. Faith doesn't deal with conjectures and uncertainties; it deals with the "full assurance of faith"! Today it is my desire that you be established in this assurance of faith. If assurance has been stolen from your heart, I believe that you will experience complete and total restoration as we delve more into the Word of God. Amen!

Live with Full Assurance of Faith

So what is the foundation we can stand on to have the "full assurance of faith" mentioned in Hebrews 10:22? Several truths are laid out for us in Hebrews 10, so let's go slowly and look at what this chapter says one step at a time. To make it easier for you, I'll be outlining three *W*'s that work together to give us the full assurance of faith.

The chapter begins by talking about how the law had only a *shadow* of the good things to come. In other words, the law did not have the real thing. It was only a shadow of the new covenant of grace. All the offerings required under the law—the burnt offering, meal offering, peace offering, sin offering, and trespass offering—were shadows of the substance. The substance is our Lord Jesus Christ—His perfect offering on the cross is the only offering that could take away all our sins once and for all. All the other offerings failed, for "it is not possible that the blood of bulls and goats could take away sins" (Heb. 10:4).

Next let's see what our Lord Jesus said to the Father in verse 9:

> *"Behold, I have come to do Your will, O God." He takes away the first that He may establish the second.*
>
> *—Hebrews 10:9 (emphasis mine)*

We have just seen the first *W*—the *will* of the Father. Now, what was the will of the Father? The Father's will was to send His only begotten Son to take away the first covenant, which is the covenant of law, and to establish the second covenant, which is the covenant of grace. In fact, just two chapters before this, the Bible tells us that God found fault with the first covenant of the law: "For if that first covenant had been faultless, then no place would have been sought for a second" (Heb. 8:7).

Why did God find fault with the first covenant, that of law? The first covenant is filled with "Thou shall not," "Thou shall not," "Thou shall not." If you are able to fulfill all the *not*s, you are blessed. But if you break just one law, then you are guilty of breaking all the laws (see James 2:10). This also means that you cannot pick and choose which laws you want to keep. Under this system, failure is guaranteed. Always remember that under the first covenant, the law *always* disqualifies you.

Under the law the Lord told Moses, "Command the children of Israel that they put out of the camp every *leper*, everyone who *has a discharge*, and whoever becomes *defiled by a corpse*" (Num. 5:2, emphasis mine). Anyone who was "unclean" was rejected and disqualified. But under grace, we see every disqualification reversed! Look at three miracles that are frequently preached from the Gospels. When our Lord finished preaching the Sermon on the Mount, a *man with leprosy* came to Him, asking Him to cleanse him, and He did (see Matt. 8:1–4). Then, in Capernaum, a woman who had had a *discharge* for twelve years touched the hem of His garment and was completely healed (see Mark 5:25–34). Following that He went into Jairus's house, held the hand of Jairus's daughter, who had *died*, and raised her back to life (see Mark 5:35–43).

Isn't this amazing? Our Lord Jesus, the very personification of grace, came and qualified every one of the three types of people disqualified under the law! That's the will of the Father that our Lord was sent to fulfill. In these three instances, we see how He took away the first covenant that He might establish the second—the new and better covenant of grace. And by this will of the Father, "we have been sanctified through the offering of the body of Jesus Christ once for all" (Heb. 10:10). Hallelujah!

Build an Unshakable Foundation

We are doing a line-upon-line teaching of Hebrews 10 and I hope you are enjoying this as much as I am. I love studying God's living Word and building an unshakable foundation for our faith. Hebrews 10:11–12 goes on to say that "every priest" under the old covenant "*stands* ministering *daily* and offering *repeatedly* the same sacrifices, which can never take away sins. But this Man, after He had offered *one sacrifice for sins forever,* sat down at the right hand of God" (emphasis mine). This is the second W—the *work* of the Son.

Our Lord's sacrifice on the cross was one sacrifice for sins forever. It was a perfect and finished work *never* to be repeated again—unlike the continual, imperfect offerings made by the Old Testament priests. When we fail today, we don't need our Lord Jesus to be offered again on the cross. It was one sacrifice for sins forever. Because the work of the Old Testament priests was never finished, they remained standing and ministering daily, offering sacrifice after sacrifice that could never take away sins. Our Lord's work, on the other hand, was so perfect in removing our sins once and for all that He could sit down at the Father's right hand.

Please understand that our Lord Jesus did not sit down because

He was the Son of God. He was always the Son of God. He sat down by virtue of the fact that He had *finished* the job of removing all our sins—"when He had by Himself purged our sins, [He] sat down at the right hand of the Majesty on high" (Heb. 1:3). Because of what our Lord Jesus accomplished on the cross, and because we are believers, *all* our sins—past, present, and future—have been forgiven. If our sins had not been perfectly taken care of, He would not have sat down. Our forgiveness is total, complete, and secure in the perfect, finished work of the Son of God. To question our forgiveness today is to insult the perfect work of the Son. It is to say that Calvary was not enough and we need to do something more to add to what our Lord already did.

As established in the previous chapters, there is no such thing as dividing your forgiveness into "judicial" and "parental" forgiveness. We won't have the confidence to come before the Father with full assurance of faith if we are always wondering if we are truly judicially forgiven and if we have done enough to be parentally forgiven as well. The bottom line is that such a teaching does not esteem the finished work of the Son. Instead it places the onus back on man to ensure that he does enough to hang on to his forgiveness. No, my friend, the work that our Lord did on the cross is a finished work and we do not need to add to it! Let me once again point you to the verse that the Lord gave me to give you full assurance of your forgiveness:

> *I write to you, little children, because your sins are forgiven you for His name's sake.*
>
> *—1 John 2:12*

We've learned that the original Greek word here for "are forgiven" is in the perfect tense, which indicates that this forgiveness is a completed past action with effects continuing into the present. The verse is also addressed to "little children." I believe that the Lord foresaw that there would be people who would teach on "parental forgiveness." It's almost as if God was saying, "You want parental forgiveness? Here you go." And He recorded this in His Word: "*My little children*, your sins are forgiven you."

Washed Once by the Blood, Again and Again by the Word

My dear reader, find your security in the work of the Son. You are forgiven and made righteous in Christ *once and for all* by His blood. You are also progressively being sanctified daily by His Word. Even as you are reading and studying His Word with me today, you are being washed by His Word. I like to say it this way: we are washed once by the blood of Jesus Christ, and again and again by His Word, which sanctifies us daily.

The apostle Paul describes so beautifully how the Lord loves the church:

> *Husbands, love your wives, just as Christ also loved the church and gave Himself for her, that He might sanctify and cleanse her with the washing of water by the word, that He might present her to Himself a glorious church, not having spot or wrinkle or any such thing, but that she should be holy and without blemish.*
>
> *—Ephesians 5:25–27*

Amen! That's why even though you have been completely forgiven by the blood of our Lord Jesus, it is vital you be part of a local church that is preaching the Word of Christ. This will help you to be continually washed by the Word and to grow in the grace and knowledge of our Lord Jesus Christ.

Let me bring you back to our study of Hebrews 10, where it says in verse 14, "For by one offering He has perfected forever those who are being sanctified." You have been forgiven, made righteous, and perfected once and for all by the blood of Jesus. And daily you are being sanctified by the washing of God's Word and the preaching of the gospel of grace. That is why you need to keep listening to the gospel of grace. The preached Word of Christ washes and sanctifies you from all the dirt, dust, and corruption of this world.

Beloved, you cannot be made more righteous or be more forgiven. But as you are washed daily by the Word of Christ, you can become more holy, sanctified, or set apart. You can become less conformed to the sinful patterns of this world, and experience daily renewal in your mind, heart, and spirit.

You cannot be made more righteous or be more forgiven.
But as you are washed daily by the Word of Christ, you
can become more holy, sanctified, or set apart.

As you keep allowing yourself to be washed, the people around you can't help but see the glorious transformation that begins inside you. Good works will flow from you—your graciousness toward people and your liberation from sin will cause your Father in heaven to be glorified. After all, the grace revolution is about inside-out transformation from glory to glory that results in lasting breakthroughs and freedom from every kind of bondage.

Hear the Witness of the Spirit

Let's recap. The first *W* is the *will* of the Father. The second *W* is the *work* of the Son. Now we come to the third and final *W* mentioned in Hebrews 10—the *witness* of the Holy Spirit. As we continue our study, we see the triune God—the Father, the Son, and the Holy Spirit—all involved in giving us assurance of faith.

In terms of the witness of the Holy Spirit, Scripture tells us:

> *But the Holy Spirit also* witnesses *to us.... "Their sins and their lawless deeds I will remember no more."*
> —*Hebrews 10:15, 17 (emphasis mine)*

The Holy Spirit, the third person of the Godhead, dwells in all believers today. He is the Spirit of truth and the Comforter sent to *witness* to you the cornerstone truth that you have been made the righteousness of God in Christ. He witnesses to you that your sins and lawless deeds God will remember *no more*. If you were standing in the courts of heaven, who would you want to have on the witness stand? The most honest man in the world? How about the third person of the Godhead, witnessing that your sins are no more remembered by God? The Holy Spirit was there at Calvary to witness Christ bearing all our sins in His own body. That's why He can be the faithful witness today that our sins and lawless deeds God remembers no more.

My friend, the Bible declares that God will remember your sins no more. Not because He has swept your sins under the carpet. No way; God is a holy God. He is thrice holy and He cannot do that. God cannot have any complicity with sin. It was our Lord Jesus on the cross

Who gave God the righteous foundation to declare that your sins are forgiven and proclaim you righteous.

That's why the Bible does not say that God is *merciful* in making you righteous. It says that God is *righteous* in making you righteous (see 1 John 1:9, Rom. 3:23–26). What Christ did—shedding His blood and dying on the cross—has fully met all the claims of divine holiness in your life. Today God is able to make an ungodly sinner who has placed his faith in Christ fully righteous (see Rom. 4:5), without compromising on His holiness. Such is the wisdom and power of God.

What Christ did—shedding His blood and dying on the cross—has fully met all the claims of divine holiness in your life.

In His grace and wisdom, He has placed us in a covenant where we cannot be made unrighteous. In the old covenant, there was no one who could be justified and made righteous by the law. But in the new covenant, all who believe in our Lord Jesus are made eternally righteous. And we have the Holy Spirit to *witness* to us the *will* of the Father and the *work* of the Son. Doesn't this good news make you want to just lift up your hands, do cartwheels, and worship your Father in heaven?

To be led by the Holy Spirit today is to be constantly reminded that you are righteous in Christ. When you are righteousness-conscious, you will find the Holy Spirit leading you out of destructive habits, thoughts, relationships, and situations. He will remind you of your righteousness, even when you miss the mark and fail. In fact, *that's* the time you need the Holy Spirit's witness to pick you up from where you have fallen.

Instead of allowing you to sink deeper into the pit of sin, the Holy

Spirit pulls you out of it. As Proverbs 24:16 says, even though "a righteous man may fall seven times," he will "rise again." Notice that the verse is not talking about the *ungodly* falling. It is talking about what happens when the *righteous* fall. By the witness of the Holy Spirit, the righteous man knows he is still righteous in Christ. And because of that assurance, he will have the power to rise again. Praise the Lord for the Holy Spirit, Who witnesses to us that we are the righteousness of God in Christ!

Well, Pastor Prince, the Bible says the Holy Spirit convicts us of sin.

My dear reader, that's a horrible misquote from John 16:8! If you want to quote what the Lord said, please quote this entire portion from John 16 in its context: "And when He [the Holy Spirit] has come, He will convict the world of sin, and of righteousness, and of judgment: of sin, because they do not believe in Me; of righteousness, because I go to My Father and you see Me no more; of judgment, because the ruler of this world is judged" (John 16:8–11).

So what did our Lord Jesus actually say? He said that the Holy Spirit will "convict the world of sin." What is this "sin"? And why is the noun *sin* in the singular? Because it refers to the *one* sin of not believing in the Lord Jesus—"of sin, because they do not believe in Me." Before we became born-again believers, all of us responded to the Holy Spirit's conviction of the sin of unbelief in Christ. We responded to an altar call or perhaps prayed with a friend to invite Jesus to be our Lord and Savior. Then Jesus said that the Holy Spirit convicts us believers of our righteousness in Him—"of righteousness, because I go to My Father and you [referring to His disciples, which includes all believers today] see Me no more." You hardly hear this conviction of the Holy Spirit being preached today. Now what about judgment? The Holy Spirit convicts believers that *the devil* is judged—"because the ruler of this world is judged."

So you see again how essential it is to read everything in its context and rightly divide the Word. Truth be told, you don't need the Holy Spirit to convict you of sin; your own conscience and the devil do a good job of that. (And sometimes our spouses and those around us too, if I may add!)

Be Convicted of Your Righteousness

Dear reader, knowing that you have sinned doesn't give you *any power* to get out of that sin. What the Holy Spirit (also known as the Helper) was sent to do is help you out of the clutches of sin. How? The only way out of sin, addiction, bad habits, bondages, and anything that is destroying you is to be convicted in your heart and mind that you are today the righteousness of God in Christ Jesus (see 1 Cor. 15:34). Remember, it is a strong consciousness of your righteous identity in Christ that gives you true freedom.

The only way out of sin and anything that is destroying you is to be convicted in your heart and mind that you are today the righteousness of God in Christ Jesus.

I can show you testimony after testimony of precious brothers and sisters who have broken free from destructive addictions such as those to pornography and smoking. Their testimonies reflect a common theme—they believed and confessed out loud their righteousness in Christ, even in the midst of their failings. Then one day the conviction of the Holy Spirit just clicked inside them, and suddenly they found that they no longer had any desire to sin and were set free from their addictions.

My friend, this conviction of your righteousness is more powerful than knowing the good to do that you do not do, or the bad you don't want to do but keep doing (see Rom. 7:19). The knowledge of good and evil never helped, saved, or transformed anyone. The law is the knowledge of good and evil. It is holy, just, and good, but it doesn't give you the power to do the good and break out of the evil. Only the abundance of grace and the gift of righteousness through Christ can give you the power to do the good you want to do and break free of the evil you don't want to practice.

Only the abundance of grace and the gift of righteousness through Christ can give you the power to do the good you want to do and break free of the evil you don't want to practice.

The woman caught in adultery had full knowledge that she had sinned. She didn't need to be convicted and made aware of her sin. What she needed was the conviction and awareness that even though she had sinned, the Lord still loved her and didn't condemn her (see John 8:11). Because He knew He would pay for her sin at the cross, our Lord was in effect saying to the woman, "Your sins and lawless deeds I remember no more. Now go and sin no more."

Can you see this? It wasn't the knowledge of her sin that gave her the power to sin no more; it was the conviction that our Lord did not condemn her that gave her the power to sin no more. That's the revelation of our righteousness in Christ that needs to be preached from the rooftops of the world in this grace revolution. Can I have a good "Amen"? This is the gospel of grace, my friend, and if you get this, your life will never be the same again!

Draw Near with Full Assurance of Faith

Let's take a look at the three *W*'s that we have covered:

- The *will* of the Father
- The *work* of the Son
- The *witness* of the Holy Spirit

When you are established in these three *W*'s, you will experience the full assurance of faith Hebrews 10:22 talks about: "Let us draw near with *a true heart in full assurance of faith*, having our hearts sprinkled from an evil conscience and our bodies washed with pure water" (emphasis mine). I like how the New Living Translation says it: "let us go right into the presence of God with sincere hearts fully trusting him. For our guilty consciences have been sprinkled with Christ's blood to make us clean, and our bodies have been washed with pure water."

Today, my friend, you have been reminded that you are forgiven once and for all by the blood of our Lord Jesus, and you have also been washed by the pure water of God's living and powerful Word. The grace revolution is a revolution of assurance. It is the end of being insecure, always fearful, and forever wondering if you have done enough for God. Start living every day, beloved and righteous one, with full assurance of faith and boldness to draw near to God. Your restoration begins today!

CHAPTER 20

THE GRACE REVOLUTION IS HERE

We all know the renowned Shepherd's Psalm, Psalm 23, but did you know that Jeremiah 23 is also about shepherds? It begins with the Lord rebuking and correcting pastors and leaders (who are shepherds in God's eyes): "Woe to the shepherds who destroy and scatter the sheep of My pasture!" (Jer. 23:1). You see, God doesn't appreciate pastors and leaders who are destroying and scattering His sheep, instead of loving and nourishing them. The Lord then adds, "You have scattered My flock, driven them away, and not attended to them. Behold, I will attend to you for the evil of your doings" (Jer. 23:2).

Correction in the House of Grace

You have to understand that there is correction in the house of grace. This is something you see in the book of Revelation, where God speaks to the pastors of the seven churches. In chapters 2 and 3, when He corrects the "angel" of each church, the original Greek word used for "angel" is *angelos*, meaning "a messenger; especially an 'angel'; by implication, a pastor."[1] A messenger sent from God can be angelic or human. But since God is addressing the churches, *angelos* here refers to the pastor of the church, who is God's messenger to His flock. If it were referring to an angelic being, that would be "remarkable," since the Lord said, "Remember therefore from where you have fallen" (Rev. 2:5). That would make it a fallen angel, wouldn't it? That cannot be!

So to the pastor of the church of Pergamos, for example, in correcting him, the Lord said, "I have a few things against you, because you have there those who hold the doctrine of Balaam" (Rev. 2:14). Notice when you study these corrections that they pertain to the pastors allowing wrong *doctrine* into their churches, resulting in all kinds of immorality.

Wrong doctrine leads to wrong believing, and wrong believing always leads to wrong living. It has the opposite effect of right believing, which always leads to right living. But when the Lord says, "I will attend to you for the evil of your doings" (Jer. 23:2), or "I will come to you quickly and remove your lampstand from its place—unless you repent" (Rev. 2:5), He is not talking about believers losing their salvation. Unfortunately, this is exactly what some ministers have taught, putting much fear in the hearts of many precious people.

So what is the Lord saying? First you need to understand that these two verses were written to *pastors*, so they are applicable only to pastors. If you are not pastoring a flock, these verses are not for you. Second, when the Lord says, "I will remove your lampstand from its place," He is talking about removing the pastor and his church from their *place of influence*. The Lord is willing to do this because He is highly protective of His sheep, who are His people. He has entrusted them to pastors and it is the pastors' responsibility to preach the Word of God accurately, rightly dividing it and preaching without compromise the gospel of the new covenant of grace.

But even if the Lord removes a pastor from his place of influence or his church, He will ensure that the church's congregation is taken care of. Observe the pastoral language that He uses in Jeremiah 23. He speaks like the Chief Shepherd that He is (see 1 Pet. 5:4). He is the Senior Pastor of senior pastors and He declares, "But I will gather the remnant of My flock out of all countries where I have driven them, and bring them back to their folds; and they shall be fruitful and increase" (Jer. 23:3).

Let's look at another Scripture. In James 3:1 the apostle James says, "Let not many of you become teachers, knowing that we shall receive a stricter judgment." Again, this Scripture is not talking about pastors or leaders losing their salvation. Apostle James is simply saying that those who teach the Word have greater responsibility and accountability. Pastors, ministers, and leaders are expected to preach with accuracy, rightly dividing God's Word.

James is also not discouraging people from being teachers of the Word. Absolutely not. It is a great honor and privilege to preach and teach God's Word. James is just highlighting how sacred this privilege is and how wisely pastors need to steward their teaching ministry. He is exhorting them to not be flippant about doctrine—remember, all the errors in the churches in the book of Revelation are errors that relate to doctrine, resulting in sin and idolatry. Wrong believing leads to wrong living! This is why James exhorts teachers of the Word to be diligent in understanding the gospel of grace, rightly dividing the covenants, and teaching God's flock the true gospel of Jesus Christ without compromise.

"THE LORD OUR RIGHTEOUSNESS"

Let's go back to Jeremiah 23. How do you know if you are under God-appointed leadership? Our Chief Shepherd answers this question in verse 4: "I will set up shepherds over them who will feed them; and they shall *fear no more, nor be dismayed, nor shall they be lacking*" (emphasis mine). Those are the three promised results of being under God-appointed leadership. When pastors and leaders preach the unadulterated gospel of grace, their flocks will fear no more, nor be dismayed, nor lack. Are you experiencing these blessings of God's grace in your life? Or are you still fearful, discouraged, and constantly feeling as if you haven't done enough?

From Jeremiah 23:4 the Lord imparted to me the message to be preached and emphasized in this day and hour of the grace revolution. In the dream that I had over fifteen years ago, He said to me, "This is what you are to feed My people with in this hour," and gave me Jeremiah 23:5–6:

> *"Behold, the days are coming," says the* LORD, *"That I will raise to David a Branch of righteousness; a King shall reign and prosper, and execute judgment and righteousness in the earth. In His days Judah will be saved, and Israel will dwell safely; now this is His name by which He will be called: THE LORD OUR RIGHTEOUSNESS."*

Don't you simply love how even in our modern Bibles, the revelation of the grace revolution—"THE LORD OUR RIGHTEOUSNESS"—is highlighted in full capitalization? In Hebrew it is *Jehovah-Tsidkenu*.[2] It is the Holy Spirit's way of telling us, "Don't miss this. Seeing this will change your life!"

So, my dear reader, you who have pressed on to the very last chapter of this book, what is the message that causes God's people to fear no more, nor be discouraged, nor be in lack? You are absolutely right and blessed are your eyes for you see this truth! It is the revelation that *the Lord is our righteousness*. Not our works, not our efforts, not our perfect obedience to the law of Moses. The Lord wants Himself to be our righteousness. He wants us to take Him as our righteousness. And this righteousness He offers is to be received as a gift by faith. It was paid for with His own blood! When you start to live conscious of the Lord as your righteousness, you will begin to live righteously. From the inside out, genuine good works, obedience, holiness, and love will flow unabated out of an authentic relationship with your Father in heaven.

What is the message that causes God's people to fear no more, nor be discouraged, nor be in lack? It is the revelation that the Lord is our righteousness.

Can Division Happen When the Gospel Is Preached?

THE LORD OUR RIGHTEOUSNESS. That's the message of the grace revolution! There is a division today in Christianity between those who believe in the Lord as their righteousness and those who believe that they have to be their own righteousness. Some of those who are against the gospel of grace argue that if it is of the Lord, it should not be causing any division. Well, let's not forget what happened when the apostle Paul preached in Iconium:

They stayed there a long time, speaking boldly in the Lord, who was bearing witness to the word of His grace, *granting*

signs and wonders to be done by their hands. But the multi-
tude of the city was divided: part sided with the Jews, and
part with the apostles.

—*Acts 14:3–4 (emphasis mine)*

Was Paul preaching the gospel of grace? Did it cause a division in the city?

But it was never Paul's intention to cause any division. He simply wanted to preach the word of the Lord's grace. The test of whether the gospel of grace you are hearing is of the Lord, therefore, is not whether it is causing division or not. The truest test is whether or not the Lord is bearing witness to the word being preached through lives changed, healed, liberated, and transformed (see Acts 14:3)!

The test of whether the gospel of grace you are hearing is
of the Lord, is if He is bearing witness to the word being
preached through lives changed, healed, liberated, and
transformed!

One Father, Two Mothers

We all have the same heavenly Father, but not all of us have the same "mother." Let me explain what I mean. In Galatians 4, the apostle Paul used typology to teach about the difference between the old and new covenants. He tells us that the Word records that Abraham had two sons, Ishmael and Isaac. Ishmael was born of a bondwoman named Hagar, whereas Isaac was born of Sarah, a free woman. Paul then explained that Hagar is a type of the law given at Mount Sinai, which produces bondage. On the other hand, Sarah is a type of grace, which produces freedom and liberty. You can read the details of Paul's explanation for yourself in Galatians 4:21–27.

For now I want to show you something interesting. The apostle Paul said, "Now we, brethren, as Isaac was, are children of promise. But, as he who was born according to the flesh then persecuted him who was born according to the Spirit, even so it is now" (Gal. 4:28–29). Isn't it amazing that the Bible actually tells us that those who are born under the law will persecute those who are born under grace? It was Ishmael who persecuted Isaac, not the other way around. And as foretold by the Word of God, "even so it is now"—it is still going on today.

You see, while we Christians have the same Father, unfortunately, we don't all have the same mother. Some have made Hagar (the law) their mother, instead of Sarah (grace). And the children of Hagar are still persecuting the children of Sarah—those who are under grace. Do you want to know what the Lord says about Hagar and Sarah? "Cast out the bondwoman and her son, for the son of the bondwoman shall not be heir with the son of the freewoman" (Gal. 4:30). God is not for mixing law and grace. Cast out the old covenant of the law and focus on being under grace to inherit all that God has promised in the new covenant!

Focus on being under grace to inherit all that God has promised in the new covenant!

Be Someone Who Receives Much from the Lord

When I was flying to America for the Power of Right Believing USA Tour, the Lord spoke to me about John 3 and John 4. He began to open my eyes to the two accounts that the Holy Spirit recorded side by side for our benefit. John 3 is about Nicodemus, who came to Jesus by night. John 4 is about the Samaritan woman at the well, whom Jesus intentionally met by day. In John 3 you have a scholarly theologian, a Pharisee of Pharisees, a master rabbi whom our Lord called "the teacher of Israel" (John 3:10).

In John 4 you have a woman from the other end of the social spectrum—she had no accomplishments to speak of, she was a broken woman who had had five divorces, and she was living with a man who wasn't her husband. The difference between the two couldn't have been starker—it was literally like night and day. Nicodemus sought the Lord. The Lord sought the woman. Nicodemus came to the Lord in the *stealth of night*. The Lord came to the woman in *broad daylight*. At the end of these two conversations, the woman at the well had received much more from the Lord than the learned Nicodemus had. In fact, this Samaritan woman was the one to whom the Lord revealed Himself as the Messiah. Not to Nicodemus, the great theologian.

Isn't it beautiful to see how, when she said to our Lord, "When He [the Messiah] comes, He will tell us all things," our Lord smiled at her lovingly and said, "I who speak to you am He" (John 4:25–26). If you look at your Bible, you will notice that the word "He" is in italics. This means that it wasn't in the original and was added by translators. In Young's Literal Translation, it reads, "I am [he], who am speaking to thee." In other words, our Lord revealed Himself to her as the great "I AM." That's the name of God. The God of the burning bush (see Exod. 3:14). Hallelujah!

In the natural, you would think that our Lord would reveal Himself as Messiah to the scholar, who would have studied the Scriptures from his youth. But that's not what happened. I love seeing how our Lord was comfortable ministering to a broken woman who was entangled in a life of sin, gently restoring her dignity to her and rebuilding her. To Nicodemus our Lord spoke the language of the Old Testament, but to the woman He used the language of everyday things—He talked to her about the water that was in front of her. With divine skillfulness, He used simple, understandable, and practical illustrations to tell her very tactfully that she had been drinking from all the wrong wells, which were not satisfying her. Let's listen in on what He said to her:

> *"If you knew the gift of God, and who it is who says to you, 'Give Me a drink,' you would have asked Him, and He would have given you living water.... The water that I shall give him will become in him a fountain of water springing up into everlasting life."*
>
> —*John 4:10, 14*

Our Lord didn't use theological language or concepts, and He didn't tell her that she had to be "born again." In contrast, look at what He said to Nicodemus:

> *"Most assuredly, I say to you, unless one is born again, he cannot see the kingdom of God."*
>
> —*John 3:3*

At the end of these two conversations, the theologian Nicodemus, who came at night because he didn't want to be seen with the Lord, left without seeing Him as the Messiah. He had eyes but he could not see, and the last record of what he said was, "How can these things be?" The Lord's reply to him was, "Are you the teacher of Israel, and do not know these things? Most assuredly, I say to you, We speak what We know and testify what We have seen, and you do not receive Our witness" (John 3:9–11). You see, while Nicodemus knew the Bible, he didn't know the Author of the Bible, Who was standing right in front of him.

Beloved, just because you don't know the Bible from cover to cover, don't be intimidated by learned theologians who use very high-sounding theological words to impress or intimidate you. The gospel of grace is so simple that even fishermen like Peter, who were not as highly educated as the Pharisees, could grasp it. And yet it could also confound the most intellectual scholars in Jerusalem then. Now, please understand that I am not in any way against theologians, Bible schools, or the deep study of the Word of Christ. In fact, I believe that one day, our church will have a Bible school for those around the world who desire to study the Word more deeply!

Don't Miss the Forest for the Trees

I believe that in comparing and contrasting the accounts of Nicodemus and the Samaritan woman, the Lord wants to demonstrate to us that it is entirely possible for one to miss the forest for the trees. It is possible for one to completely miss the entire point about the will of the Father, the work of the Son, and the witness of the Holy Spirit in the gospel of grace.

The learned Nicodemuses of today might hear the gospel of grace preached and leave wondering, "How can these things be?" In contrast, look at what happened to the woman who was living in shame, who went to draw water from the well at the hottest time of the day to avoid meeting the condemning stares of others. She ended up completely changed and transformed by the Lord's love and grace. After encountering Him she left her water pot behind (who needs a water pot when you have been filled with living water!) and became an evangelist in the city, going about saying, "Come, see a Man who told me all things that I ever did" (John 4:29). And the Bible records for us as a memorial and an honor to her that "many of the Samaritans of that city believed in Him because of the word of the woman" (John 4:39). What an impact encountering Jesus had on her!

Today the grace revolution is led by precious people just like the woman at the well. The testimonies recorded in this book are just a few examples of how imperfect people, whose lives may have looked very much like that of the woman at the well, have risen up to become evangelists of the gospel of grace. They may not be as qualified as the Nicodemuses of this world, but what they do have is a life transformed and restored after an authentic encounter with our Lord Jesus Christ. Once they have tasted for themselves His abundant grace and gift of righteousness, their lives are never the same again, and they can't help but proclaim, "Come, see a Man!" and point people to the Savior!

A Life Transformed and Restored

Edwina is a case in point. This is her testimony:

> I was raised to memorize the Ten Commandments. Yet, my family was dysfunctional, I grew up with violence and gambling, and I was taught to lie and cheat. When I was sixteen, a college friend got me born again. I felt so much joy and attended a Christian church. But after some time, my joy faded. I learned that I was saved from hell but that I still needed to please God. I was told that I should behave well,

dress conservatively, and keep God's commandments. I felt a heavy demand placed on me.

Every church I attended taught that we should keep God's laws to please Him. I felt that God was just waiting for my next wrongdoing in order to condemn me. As a result, I became rebellious. I started having premarital sex, had an abortion, and ended up attempting suicide more than once.

I got married and had kids at a young age. When I got older, I tried my best to keep my life in order. I attended a church, stayed true to my husband, and worked hard. Yet my life was still a mess because I believed that I was in and out of fellowship with God.

My husband was a womanizer, heavy smoker, gambler, drug addict, and an alcoholic. To keep him away from drugs, I sent him to work in Singapore. I eventually joined him to earn money to clear my debts. In Singapore, I found out that he was in huge debt, still an alcoholic, and had a few girlfriends. I felt that he only wanted me to help pay his debt and it was not worthwhile to remain faithful. I started an online chat relationship that led to an affair. I felt wanted again but it just didn't feel right.

Devastated, I cried out to God. Then, I remembered that my pastor had mentioned New Creation Church. So I attended a service with my husband and I cried throughout the sermon. Pastor Prince shared how Jesus loved the woman caught in adultery unconditionally, giving her the gift of no condemnation to empower her to stop sinning. It was the first time I heard about a God Who doesn't condemn me.

I kept returning to New Creation Church, with or without my husband. I also listened to Pastor Prince's sermons on my way to and from work. Not only did my affair come to an end, but Jesus also turned the water into wine in my marriage. I now love my husband even more than before, and my husband also loves me. He has quit smoking, gambling, and drinking. We believe his debt cancellation is also on the way, in Jesus' name!

I'm now so in love with Jesus and feel comfortable in His presence, whether I've done good or not. And I'm seeing more right living in my life now. I'm more honest and loving. I don't boast in myself, but I boast in what the Lord has done in me. Thank you, Pastor Prince, for being faithful in preaching the truth. And thank You, Lord Jesus, for loving me.

Thank you for sharing your testimony, Edwina! What a powerful testimony it is of the difference our Lord Jesus can make in every broken life that encounters His grace!

Experience Perfect, Unconditional Love

Now, I want you to notice what struck Edwina most when she first heard the gospel and encountered Jesus: "It was the first time I heard about a God Who doesn't condemn me." That's exactly what the woman at the well experienced. She met our Lord, Who knew every detail about the failures of her past and present, and yet did not condemn her.

In fact, His words to her were full of grace. When she tried to hide her present situation (which she wasn't proud of) and said, "I have no husband," the Lord didn't call her out. Instead He complimented her, saying, *"You have well said, 'I have no husband,' for you have had* five husbands, and the one whom you now have is not your husband; in that *you spoke truly*" (John 4:17–18, emphasis mine). Do you see the "divine sandwich"? He complimented her first ("You have well said"), gently mentioned her sins, and then finished off with another compliment ("you spoke truly"). Such is the overflowing graciousness of our Lord.

Now, why did the Lord reveal her sins to this initially unbelieving woman? Because He wanted her to know that He knew everything about her and still loved her. Beloved, the Lord knows everything about you—every failure, every sin, and every shortcoming. But He still loves you with an everlasting love, a love that is completely unconditional, a love that nailed Him to the cross. Only our Lord, Who has perfect knowledge about us, can still love us perfectly. There is nothing we need to hide from Him. We can talk openly and confess our mistakes and failings to Him, knowing that He already knows them all and yet still loves us.

We can talk openly and confess our mistakes and failings to the Lord, knowing that He already knows them all and yet still loves us.

The truth is that you *are*, right now, the righteousness of God through Jesus' precious blood. You can have a true and intimate relationship with the Lord because when you confess your sins, it is not *in order to be forgiven*; you confess your sins knowing that you have *already been forgiven*, and that you are having conversations with THE LORD YOUR RIGHTEOUSNESS. There is a huge difference!

God's Definition of *Basic* and *Mature*

There are some people who dismiss what God is doing in the grace revolution as "basic." They will never come out and say that they are against the gospel of grace, but they see it as something that is too simple, too easy. They question, "Where is man's part?" They think that grace is good for new believers, but believe that they have to mature into more "important" and "advanced" things like holiness and repentance. Well, please allow me to show you what is "basic" and what is "mature" in the eyes of God. Let's look at Galatians 4 together:

> *Now I say that the heir, as long as he is a child, does not differ at all from a slave, though he is master of all, but is under guardians and stewards until the time appointed by the father. Even so we, when we were children, were in bondage under the elements of the world. But when the fullness of the time had come, God sent forth His Son, born of a woman, born under the law, to redeem those who were under the law, that we might receive the adoption as sons. And because you are sons, God has sent forth the Spirit of His Son into your hearts, crying out, "Abba, Father!" Therefore you are no longer a slave but a son, and if a son, then an heir of God through Christ.*
>
> *—Galatians 4:1–7*

In this passage, the Greek word used for "child" is *nepios*, which means "an infant, little child."[3] When Israel as a nation was a *nepios*, it was put under the law. When the fullness of time came, God sent His Son to redeem those who were under the law, so that they might receive "adoption as sons." The Greek word used for "sons" is *huios*, which speaks of "sons grown up to maturity."[4] In other words, when Israel was a baby, God placed it under the law. But when Christ came, God placed all who believed in His Son under mature sonship. This tells us that in God's eyes, the law is basic; grace is maturity.

Look at it this way: when your friends come to visit your home with their young children, you place laws on their young children. You tell them not to play in the kitchen, not to touch the kitchen knives, and not to touch the stove. You inevitably end up issuing lots of "thou shall not"s because the children are young and don't know any better. But I am sure you won't tell your adult friends, "Don't go into the kitchen," "Don't play with the kitchen knives," or "Don't touch the stove." It would be ridiculous to issue such laws to mature adults.

In the same way, the old covenant law is for the immature, whereas grace is for those who are mature sons and daughters of God. The Bible also tells us, "For everyone who partakes only of milk is unskilled in the word of righteousness, for he is a babe" (Heb. 5:13). In other words, such a person is unskilled in the revelation of the grace revolution—THE LORD OUR RIGHTEOUSNESS.

A Restoration of Assurance

In one of Peter's first encounters with the Lord, he saw how the Lord gave him so much fish that his net began to break and his boat began to sink. His response was to fall on his knees and say, "Depart from me, for I am a sinful man, O Lord!" (Luke 5:8). No one had to teach him that he was sinful. Now, in this encounter with the Lord, which aspect of the Lord was he conscious of? His love or His holiness? From

Peter's statement it is clear that he was most conscious of the Lord's holiness, in contrast with his own unworthy state of sinfulness.

Now let's fast-forward to Jesus' last supper with His disciples in the upper room, where the Lord said to Peter, "I tell you, Peter, the rooster shall not crow this day before you will deny three times that you know Me" (Luke 22:34). We know how this all panned out, but I particularly like Luke's account of what happened. Luke describes how our Lord Jesus was arrested and brought inside the high priest's house. Outside in the courtyard, while Peter was still vehemently denying that he knew Jesus, the rooster crowed. Our Lord then turned and looked straight at Peter, and Peter remembered the words of Jesus (see Luke 22:55–62).

There must have been something about that look.

It wasn't a look of judgment and condemnation. It was a look that said, "Peter, I still love you. Don't despair. I knew that this would happen and I have prayed for you, My beloved Peter." It was the Lord's look of love that broke Peter and caused this burly fisherman to go out and weep bitterly.

Following that, about two weeks after our Lord Jesus had been crucified, the Bible tells us that Peter was out fishing with some of the disciples (see John 21:3). A little-known fact is that Peter had already had a private audience with the Lord prior to this scene (see Luke 24:34, 1 Cor. 15:5). The entire meeting was veiled from other eyes, as it was a personal time of restoration for Peter. Now, in John 21, we see the Lord restoring Peter, this time to *ministry*. The risen Lord appeared and stood on the shore, but the disciples did not recognize Him. When Peter realized that it was the Lord, he immediately plunged into the water and swam toward Him.

Now, what do you think caused Peter to swim to our Lord Jesus?

Was it the Lord's holiness, or His grace? What was Peter most conscious of this time? Come on, if it had been the Lord's holiness, Peter would have jumped out of the boat and swum in the opposite direction from Jesus! His shame from denying the Lord three times would have driven him away. But that's not what happened. Peter didn't even wait for the boat to make it to shore—he plunged into the sea and swam toward the Lord.

In Peter's early days with the Lord, he didn't understand Who the Lord was, and it was *the sense of His holiness* that he was most conscious of. But after Peter had walked with the Lord, he knew the Lord. He knew His heart and he knew that the Lord had already forgiven him. It was the Lord's beautiful grace and love that gave Peter the courage to draw near to Him with full assurance of faith. Now, this is *true maturity—a growing revelation of His grace and forgiveness.*

True maturity is a growing revelation of the Lord's grace
and forgiveness.

Come Boldly, Even When You Have Failed

What Peter experienced is what so many people are experiencing around the world in the grace revolution. They are receiving a restoration of the assurance that they can come boldly before their Lord in the throne room of grace, even when they have failed!

The enemy may have stolen the intimacy and closeness between you and the Lord, but I want you to know that God is restoring relationships today. The grace revolution is a revolution of restoration—and the grace revolution is here. As our heavenly Father has promised, He is setting up shepherds all around the world who are preaching THE LORD OUR RIGHTEOUSNESS. And His precious people shall no longer be fearful, no longer be discouraged, and no longer be lacking.

Right now I pray that as you receive the good news of the gospel of grace, you will be set free from every bondage that is weighing you down. In the name of our Lord Jesus, I see you healed from the crown of your head to the soles of your feet. I see you freed from that secret addiction that has held you captive for years. I see you whole in all your relationships. Amen!

CLOSING WORDS

It's been my privilege and honor to take this life-transforming journey with you, one where we've delved deep into understanding what the grace revolution is all about. The grace revolution is not about a movement, teaching, or doctrine. It is all about our Lord Jesus. It is He Who brings about the inside-out transformation of countless lives to the glory of His name. It is He Who brings about God's much-more restoration, putting an end to wasted years, lost health, estranged relationships, and shattered dreams, and bringing in fresh, new beginnings. And what a joy it has been to put the spotlight on our beautiful Savior, the person of grace, to see His love, sacrifice, and finished work!

Many believers lead defeated lives today because they do not know how precious they are to God, and how through the cross His Son has set them free to live above any defeat and entanglement with sin. Through the powerful truths and many inspiring, real-life stories shared in this book, I hope you've been blessed to see how an encounter with Jesus and His grace has set and is still setting people free from the bondages of sin. The truth of the matter is that people begin to live unconsciously holy and victorious lives when they become conscious of our Lord Jesus and everything He accomplished at Calvary.

My dear friend, we've unveiled the gospel that has birthed and fueled the grace revolution. I pray that the powerful truths of God's forgiveness and gift of righteousness will go deep into your heart, establish you in the security of your eternal salvation, and liberate you from every kind of defeat. I believe that God will restore to you all the lost years the locusts have eaten as you allow His grace to renew your mind and change your heart from the inside out.

It is my prayer that all you've read in this book will release you to have the closest, most loving relationship you could ever ask for with your heavenly Father. That even now you are experiencing the sweetness of falling in love with our Lord Jesus as you lean in to His love for you. Beloved, the more you grow toward having bullock-size revelations of Jesus and His grace, the more your life will be infused with the fragrance of His presence, peace, and victory.

To this end I encourage you to get ahold of *Destined To Reign*, *Unmerited Favor*, and *The Power of Right Believing*, and to allow the gospel truths you'll also find in these books to establish your heart and give you a strong foundation for lasting breakthroughs. I also want to encourage you to plant yourself in a local church, as I've emphasized throughout *Grace Revolution*, because that is where and how you can continue to grow in and receive from the Lord in every area of life.

Once again, thank you for taking this journey with me and for giving me the opportunity to unveil more of our glorious Lord Jesus to you. I look forward to hearing about the manifestation of the breakthrough, freedom, and restoration you've been trusting the Lord for. I believe that you are already experiencing the grace revolution in your life and are beginning to live above defeat! Do write to me at www.josephprince.com/testimony and allow me to share your joy.

Till we meet again, know that my love and prayers are with you and your family.

In His loving grace,
Joseph Prince

NOTES

CHAPTER 1: *Let the Revolution Begin*
1. NT: 266, Joseph Henry Thayer, *Thayer's Greek Lexicon*, electronic database. Copyright © 2000, 2003, 2006 by Biblesoft, Inc. All rights reserved.

CHAPTER 2: *Inside-Out Transformation*
1. Retrieved April 27, 2015, from www.hebrew4christians.com/Holidays/Fall_Holidays/Elul/Teshuvah/teshuvah.html.
2. Retrieved April 27, 2015, from www.hebrew4christians.com/Grammar/Unit_One/Pictograms/pictograms.html.
3. Retrieved April 27, 2015, from www.hebrew4christians.com/Grammar/Unit_One/Numeric_Values/numeric_values.html.
4. OT: 7725, William Edwy Vine, *Vine's Expository Dictionary of Biblical Words*. Copyright © 1985, Thomas Nelson Publishers.
5. NT: 3341, Joseph Henry Thayer, *Thayer's Greek Lexicon*, electronic database. Copyright © 2000, 2003, 2006 by Biblesoft, Inc. All rights reserved.

CHAPTER 3: *Hear the Word of His Grace*
1. Retrieved January 27, 2015, from www.preceptaustin.org/ephesians_115-17.htm.

CHAPTER 4: *Receive the Greatest Blessing*
1. Retrieved October 23, 2014, from www.preceptaustin.org/ephesians_17-8.htm.
2. Retrieved February 13, 2015, from www.preceptaustin.org/new_page_40.htm.
3. NT: 3956, William Edwy Vine, *Vine's Expository Dictionary of Biblical Words*. Copyright © 1985, Thomas Nelson Publishers.
4. NT: 3956, James Strong, *Biblesoft's New Exhaustive Strong's Numbers and Concordance with Expanded Greek-Hebrew Dictionary.* Copyright © 1994, 2003, 2006 Biblesoft, Inc. and International Bible Translators, Inc.
5. Retrieved October 23, 2014, from www.merriam-webster.com/dictionary/sanctification.

CHAPTER 5: *Begin Living with Confidence*

1. Lizzie Alldridge, *Florence Nightingale, Frances Ridley Havergal, Catherine Marsh, Mrs. Ranyard (L.N.R.)*, London; Paris; New York & Melbourne: Cassell & Company, Limited, 1890.
2. Jennie Chappell, *Women Who Have Worked and Won: The Life Story of Mrs Spurgeon, Mrs Booth-Tucker, F. R. Havergal, and Ramabai*, London: S.W. Partridge & Co. Ltd., 1904.
3. Retrieved October 23, 2014, from www.preceptaustin.org/1john_17_commentary.htm.
4. J. Gilchrist Lawson, *Deeper Experiences of Famous Christians: Gleaned from Their Biographies, Autobiographies and Writings*, Chicago: Glad Tidings Publishing Company, 1911.
5. Retrieved February 11, 2015 from nethymnal.org/htm/l/i/likriver.htm.
6. Retrieved February 11, 2015 from www.cyberhymnal.org/htm/t/f/tfountfb.htm.
7. NT: 2920, Joseph Henry Thayer, *Thayer's Greek Lexicon*, electronic database. Copyright © 2000, 2003, 2006 by Biblesoft, Inc. All rights reserved.
8. Joseph Prince, *Unmerited Favor*, Florida: Charisma House, 2011.
9. NT: 3670, Joseph Henry Thayer, *Thayer's Greek Lexicon*, electronic database. Copyright © 2000, 2003, 2006 by Biblesoft, Inc. All rights reserved.
10. NT: 264, William Edwy Vine, *Vine's Expository Dictionary of Biblical Words*. Copyright © 1985, Thomas Nelson Publishers.

CHAPTER 6: *Why Preach Grace?*

1. NT: 2098, Joseph Henry Thayer, *Thayer's Greek Lexicon*, electronic database. Copyright © 2000, 2003, 2006 by Biblesoft, Inc. All rights reserved.
2. NT: 2097, Joseph Henry Thayer, *Thayer's Greek Lexicon*, electronic database. Copyright © 2000, 2003, 2006 by Biblesoft, Inc. All rights reserved.
3. NT: 1096, Joseph Henry Thayer, *Thayer's Greek Lexicon*, electronic database. Copyright © 2000, 2003, 2006 by Biblesoft, Inc. All rights reserved.
4. NT: 4991, Joseph Henry Thayer, *Thayer's Greek Lexicon*, electronic database. Copyright © 2000, 2003, 2006 by Biblesoft, Inc. All rights reserved.

CHAPTER 7: *Will the Real Gospel Please Stand Up?*

1. Retrieved October 27, 2014, from www.bibletools.org/index.cfm/fuseaction/topical.show/rtd/cgg/id/2074/epagonizomai-.htm.

CHAPTER 10: *Glorious Grace*

1. NT: 38, James Strong, *Biblesoft's New Exhaustive Strong's Numbers and Concordance with Expanded Greek-Hebrew Dictionary*. Copyright © 1994, 2003, 2006 Biblesoft, Inc. and International Bible Translators, Inc.

CHAPTER 11: *Grow in Grace by Hearing Him*

1. "Whoever Takes the Son Gets It All," Bible Probe, retrieved December 29, 2014, from prorege-forum.com/messages/781.html.
2. OT: 7965, Joseph Henry Thayer, Francis Brown, Samuel Rolles Driver, and Charles Augustus Briggs, *The Online Bible Thayer's Greek Lexicon and Brown Driver & Briggs Hebrew Lexicon.* Copyright © 1993, Woodside Bible Fellowship, Ontario, Canada. Licensed from the Institute for Creation Research.
3. NT: 1453, James Strong, *Biblesoft's New Exhaustive Strong's Numbers and Concordance with Expanded Greek-Hebrew Dictionary.* Copyright © 1994, 2003, 2006 Biblesoft, Inc. and International Bible Translators, Inc.
4. NT: 4074, Joseph Henry Thayer, *Thayer's Greek Lexicon*, electronic database. Copyright © 2000, 2003, 2006 by Biblesoft, Inc. All rights reserved.
5. OT:3290, Joseph Henry Thayer, Francis Brown, Samuel Rolles Driver, and Charles Augustus Briggs, *The Online Bible Thayer's Greek Lexicon and Brown Driver & Briggs Hebrew Lexicon.* Copyright © 1993, Woodside Bible Fellowship, Ontario, Canada. Licensed from the Institute for Creation Research.
6. Retrieved April 14, 2015, from www.abarim-publications.com/Meaning/John .html.

CHAPTER 12: *A Revolution of Relationship*

1. OT: 6726, Joseph Henry Thayer, Francis Brown, Samuel Rolles Driver, and Charles Augustus Briggs, *The Online Bible Thayer's Greek Lexicon and Brown Driver & Briggs Hebrew Lexicon.* Copyright © 1993, Woodside Bible Fellowship, Ontario, Canada. Licensed from the Institute for Creation Research.
2. OT: 1657, Joseph Henry Thayer, Francis Brown, Samuel Rolles Driver, and Charles Augustus Briggs, *The Online Bible Thayer's Greek Lexicon and Brown Driver & Briggs Hebrew Lexicon.* Copyright © 1993, Woodside Bible Fellowship, Ontario, Canada. Licensed from the Institute for Creation Research.

CHAPTER 14: *Fully Possess the Finished Work*

1. NT: 3364, James Strong, *Biblesoft's New Exhaustive Strong's Numbers and Concordance with Expanded Greek-Hebrew Dictionary.* Copyright © 1994, 2003, 2006 Biblesoft, Inc. and International Bible Translators, Inc.
2. Retrieved April 29, 2015, from http://goldengatebridge.org/research/ConstructionPrimeContr.php.
3. Retrieved February 4, 2015, from http://science.kqed.org/quest/audio/life-on-the-gate-working-on-the-golden-gate-bridge-1933-37/.
4. Retrieved February 4, 2015, from www.pbs.org/wgbh/americanexperience/features/general-article/goldengate-safety/.

5. NT: 5487, James Strong, *Biblesoft's New Exhaustive Strong's Numbers and Concordance with Expanded Greek-Hebrew Dictionary.* Copyright © 1994, 2003, 2006 Biblesoft, Inc. and International Bible Translators, Inc.
6. NT: 5487, Joseph Henry Thayer, *Thayer's Greek Lexicon*, electronic database. Copyright © 2000, 2003, 2006 by Biblesoft, Inc. All rights reserved.
7. NT: 2101, Joseph Henry Thayer, *Thayer's Greek Lexicon*, electronic database. Copyright © 2000, 2003, 2006 by Biblesoft, Inc. All rights reserved.

CHAPTER 15: *Love Life and See Good Days*

1. NT: 2127, James Strong, *Biblesoft's New Exhaustive Strong's Numbers and Concordance with Expanded Greek-Hebrew Dictionary.* Copyright © 1994, 2003, 2006 Biblesoft, Inc. and International Bible Translators, Inc.
2. NT: 5056, Joseph Henry Thayer, *Thayer's Greek Lexicon*, PC study Bible–formatted electronic database. Copyright © 2006 by Biblesoft, Inc. All rights reserved.
3. Retrieved May 5, 2015, from http://dictionary.reference.com/browse/l'chaim.

CHAPTER 16: *The Power of Identity*

1. Zig Ziglar, *See You At The Top.* Gretna, Louisiana: Pelican Publishing Company, 1986.

CHAPTER 17: *Release the Power to Reign*

1. Retrieved February 17, 2015, from www.loc.gov/exhibits/americancolony/amcolony-family.html and www.spaffordcenter.org/history.

CHAPTER 18: *Receive God's Much-More Restoration*

1. NT: 1184, Joseph Henry Thayer, *Thayer's Greek Lexicon*, PC study Bible–formatted electronic database. Copyright © 2006 by Biblesoft, Inc. All rights reserved.

CHAPTER 19: *Live with Full Assurance of Faith*

1. NT: 1184, Joseph Henry Thayer, *Thayer's Greek Lexicon*, PC study Bible–formatted electronic database. Copyright © 2006 by Biblesoft, Inc. All rights reserved.

CHAPTER 20: *The Grace Revolution Is Here*

1. NT: 32, James Strong, *Biblesoft's New Exhaustive Strong's Numbers and Concordance with Expanded Greek-Hebrew Dictionary.* Copyright © 1994, 2003, 2006 Biblesoft, Inc. and International Bible Translators, Inc.
2. OT: 3072, James Strong, *Biblesoft's New Exhaustive Strong's Numbers and Concordance with Expanded Greek-Hebrew Dictionary.* Copyright © 1994, 2003, 2006 Biblesoft, Inc. and International Bible Translators, Inc.
3. NT: 3516, Joseph Henry Thayer, *Thayer's Greek Lexicon*, electronic database. Copyright © 2000, 2003, 2006 by Biblesoft, Inc. All rights reserved.
4. Galatians 4:1–7, Matthew Henry, *Matthew Henry's Commentary on the Whole Bible*, PC study Bible–formatted electronic database. Copyright © 2006 by Biblesoft, Inc. All rights reserved.

SPECIAL APPRECIATION

Special thanks and appreciation to all who have sent in their testimonies and praise reports to us. Kindly note that all testimonies are received in good faith and edited only for brevity and fluency. Names have been changed to protect the writers' privacy.

SALVATION PRAYER

If you would like to receive all that Jesus has done for you and make Him your Lord and Savior, please pray this prayer:

Lord Jesus, thank You for loving me and dying for me on the cross. Your precious blood washes me clean of every sin. You are my Lord and my Savior, now and forever. I believe You rose from the dead and that You are alive today. Because of Your finished work, I am now a beloved child of God and heaven is my home. Thank You for giving me eternal life and filling my heart with Your peace and joy. Amen.

WE WOULD LIKE TO HEAR FROM YOU

If you have prayed the salvation prayer or if you have a testimony to share after reading this book, please send it to us via www.josephprince.com/testimony.

STAY CONNECTED WITH JOSEPH

Connect with Joseph through these social media channels and receive daily inspirational teachings:

Facebook.com/Josephprince
Twitter.com/Josephprince
Youtube.com/Josephprinceonline
Instagram: @JosephPrince

Free Daily E-mail Devotional

Sign up for Joseph's FREE daily e-mail devotional at JosephPrince.com/meditate and receive bite-size inspirations to help you grow in grace.